KING EDWARD VII HOSPITAL, MIDHURST

The first three Presidents, King George V, King Edward VII, King Edward VIII.

King Edward VII Hospital Midhurst

1901~1986

The King's Sanatorium

S. E. Large

Phillimore

1986

Published by
PHILLIMORE & CO. LTD.
Shopwyke Hall, Chichester, Sussex

© S. E. Large, 1986

ISBN 0 85033 628 7

Printed and bound in Great Britain at
REDWOOD BURN, LTD.
Trowbridge, Wiltshire

Contents

List of Plates

(between pages 18 and 19)

Frontispiece: The first three Presidents

List of Text Illustrations

Grateful acknowledgement is made to the following for permission to reproduce illustrations: British Architectural Library, fig. 5; *The British Medical Journal*, no. 36 and fig. 1; Michael Chevis, no. 48 and front cover picture; *The Edwardian*, figs. 8-12 (drawn by Philip Shurlock); *The Evening Argus*, Brighton, nos. 40 and 44; the Francis Frith collection, nos. 8 and 10; Victor Hopkins, no. 35; Margaret Knight, no. 3 and fig. 4; Rosalind Maingot, no. 34; *The News*, Portsmouth, nos. 45 and 47; *The Nursing Times*, nos. 11-13; Dennis Pearce, no.4; S & G Press Agency, no. 19; Martin Seagrove, nos. 52 and 53; Mrs. Charles White, nos. 2, 5, 20, 21, 24-28, 41-43, 51; other plates and fig. 2 are from the King Edward VII Hospital collection.

Acknowledgements and Introduction

A few days before my retirement from Midhurst in 1983, I was asked by the Chief Executive if I would write a history of the Hospital. No such work had yet been undertaken and, apart from a few descriptive brochures, there was nothing available to satisfy frequent requests from patients, staff and public for an account of the institution which had played, and was playing, so considerable a part in their lives. As eighty years have passed since King Edward VII opened his Sanatorium at Midhurst in 1906, a record of its development and achievement is timely. So with some trepidation I accepted the challenge and this book is the result. I hope people will derive as much pleasure from reading it as I have had from writing it.

I must first express my thanks to the Council of the Hospital for granting me permission to carry out the work and for allowing me unrestricted access to the records of the Hospital from the time of its inception as a Sanatorium to the present day. On these I have relied for most of the factual information contained in this book. The minutes of the original Executive Committee and, from 1912, of the Council have been especially valuable, and the official letters and reports which still exist, together with a multitude of official letters, have proved to be a mine of useful information. Further valuable sources have been the minutes of meetings of the Consultants, and the reports and memoranda prepared each month by the Consultant on 'visiting duty'. These, often hand written, provide a fascinating glimpse of Midhurst as it must have been before the First World War.

Research into the very early history of the Sanatorium, the period when it was being built, was complicated by the fact that Volume I of the minutes of the original Advisory Committee is missing. Volume II is extant, but this includes minutes of the last few meetings only; the record of the committee's first 74 meetings is, regrettably, lost. For this reason I have had to rely on other sources, chiefly newspaper accounts and letters, for my information about the planning and building of the sanatorium. Another source available to me was the unpublished (and uncompleted) account by a former patient in the Hospital who sent her draft in the 1960s to Sir Geoffrey Todd. Only the first chapter of this work still exists and from it I have drawn some of the information relating to the Advisory Committee's early activities. There is reason to believe that the author was given access to the official records, and it is a distinct possibility that she saw Volume I of the minutes and culled her information from them.

From a much more recent period, the reports and minutes of the 'London' Medical Committee and the 'local' Medical Committee have proved to be invaluable, especially in regard to the diversification of the Hospital and its close relationship with the neighbouring Medical Research Institute.

The veracity of several of the stories I have related cannot be vouched for, but they have been 'going the rounds' at Midhurst for so long that they have become part of the legend. No work about the Hospital would be complete without them, and if copyright has been infringed I can only plead the indulgence of anyone claiming original authorship.

A most important source of information has been Sir Geoffrey Todd himself. In 1978 and 1979 he was prevailed on to record on video-tape his impressions of life at Midhurst. These covered the period from before 1933, when he applied for the post of Medical Superintendent, to 1979, when he had retired from his hospital post and was still actively engaged as Administrator of the Midhurst Medical Research Institute. Sir Geoffrey gave me permission to play these tapes and to include what information I thought might be of general interest. To hear the voice of authority, and to see on the video-screen the figure who exercised it, was unforgettable. Many of the anecdotes and accounts of events at Midhurst are derived from these tapes, and it gives me great pleasure to express my thanks for the opportunity I was given to quote from them.

To Mr. John Boulton, for so many years a leading figure at Midhurst, I owe a very special debt of thanks. His knowledge of events over the last 50 years is unrivalled, and he spent many hours correcting my proofs and expanding my knowledge. Mr. W. H. Mitchell has likewise gone to great lengths to edit my drafts and to confirm and ascertain facts. To him and to Mrs. Marian Bradley, who has given up hours of her own time on typing and re-typing the many drafts of this book, I am particularly grateful.

I have received advice, information and encouragement from many past and present members of the staff and a number of former patients, many of whom I have had the privilege of looking after during my own period in office at Midhurst. My gratitude goes to them all, with apologies in advance to any whose names I have omitted, either through inadvertence or, if they were former patients or members of staff, in a well meant endeavour to spare them embarrassment.

Throughout the book I have quoted liberally from other people's writings and I express my gratitude to the authors, publishers and copyright holders of the books, journals and newspapers mentioned for permission, where necessary, to quote from them. I am grateful, too, to all those who have lent me photographs and given consent for their reproduction. Those who have assisted me in various ways, to all of whom I owe grateful thanks, include: Mrs. Mavis Batey, Mr. Jack Booker, Mr. A. F. Bradley, Mr. P. A. Bullock, Dr. E. H. Burrows, Mr. Michael Chevis, Mr. C. E. Drew, the Rev. D. B. Evans, Mr. W. F. P. Gammie, Mr. Geoffrey Godber, Brigadier Sir Geoffrey Hardy-Roberts, Mr. Norman Harris, Mrs. Hillman, Mrs. Muriel Julius, Miss Margaret Knight, Mr. Peter Kratz, Mrs. Joan Lash, Sir Norman Longley, Mr. Peter Longley, Mr. Chris Mills, Mrs. Sheila Patchett, Mr. Dennis Pearce, Mrs. A. G. Pittar, Mrs. Elaine Pope, Mr. V. T. Powell, Dr. Hugh Ramsay, Mr. and Mrs. T. Ralph, Dr. A. John Robertson, Mr. and Mrs. Ted Rogers, Miss Margaret Schofield, Mr. I. S. Scott, Mrs. Denny Sharp, Mrs. Anne Strudwick, Mrs. Shirley Turton, Mr. Varnes, Mr. F. S. Wills, Mrs. Charles White and Mr. G. P. Woodrow.

Foreword

by The Lady Pamela Hicks

When my great grandfather, Sir Ernest Cassel, was helping King Edward VII to plan and develop the Sanatorium at Midhurst, I am sure that neither he nor His Majesty had any conception of the immense social changes and great advances in medical knowledge which were to occur during the ensuing 80 years. Not least of these was the discovery of antibiotics. This had a dramatic impact on the prevailing treatment of tuberculosis. It no longer remained the dreadful scourge which it had been for centuries.

It cannot be easy to write a readable 'biography' of an institution. The careful research undertaken by General Large, who worked for a number of years in the Hospital following his retirement after a distinguished career in the Royal Army Medical Corps, has proved a great success.

I like to think that this book will be regarded as a tribute to all the people who, in their various capacities, have endeavoured to fulfil the aims of the Founder by providing a valuable service for the community. More recently the Sanatorium has taken on the role of a private general hospital in partnership with the local health authorities of the National Health Services.

In recent years circumstances have prevented me from playing an active part in the management of the Hospital. But I value my long connection with it, which enables me to say that it has been an inspiration to us all that Her Majesty the Queen, on coming to the throne, graciously consented to succeed George VI as President of the Hospital and has never ceased to take an interest in the work that goes on there.

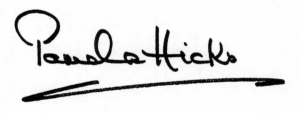

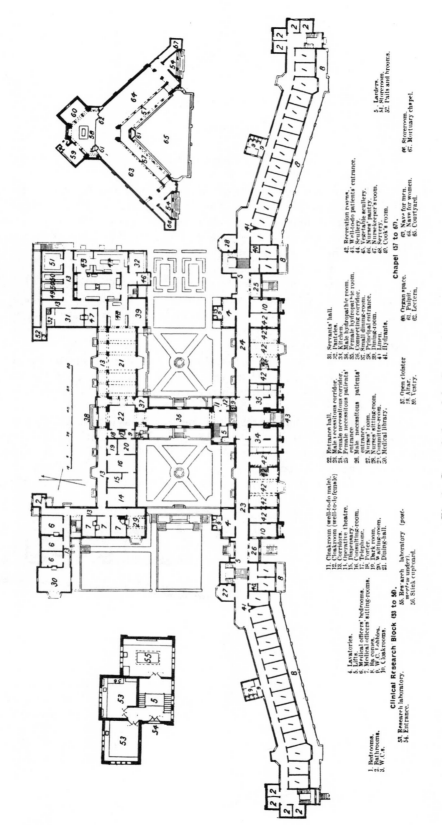

Fig. 1 Ground plan of the Sanatorium.

1. Bedrooms.
2. Bathrooms.
3. W.C.s.
4. Lavatories.
5. Lifts.
6. Medical officers' bedrooms.
7. Medical officers' sitting-rooms.
8. Recesses.
9. W.C. lobbies.
10. Cloakrooms.

11. Cloakroom (well-to-do male).
12. Cloakroom (well-to-do female)
13. Corridors.
14. Operative theatre.
15. Dispensary.
16. Consulting-room.
17. Telephone.
18. Porter.
19. Dark room.
20. Waiting-room.
21. Dining-hall.

22. Entrance hall.
23. Main necessitous corridor.
24. Female necessitous corridor.
25. Female necessitous patients' entrance
26. Male necessitous patients' entrance.
27. Nurses' room.
28. Nurses' sitting-room.
29. Committee-room.
30. Medical library.

31. Servants' hall.
32. Pantries.
33. Kitchen.
34. Male hydropathic room.
35. Female hydropathic room.
36. Connecting corridor.
37. Small dining-room.
38. Principal entrance.
39. Dining-room.
40. Linen.
41. Hydrants.

42. Recreation rooms.
43. Well-to-do patients' entrance.
44. Scullery.
45. Vegetable scullery.
46. Nurses' pantry.
47. Nursekeeper's room.
48. Servery.
49. Cook's room.

5. Larder.
51. Storeroom.
52. Pails and brooms.

Clinical Research Block (53 to 56).
53. Research laboratory.
54. Entrance.
55. Research laboratory (*post-mortem* under).
56. Stink cupboard.

Chapel (57 to 67).
57. Open cloister
58. Altar.
59. Vestry.
60. Organ space.
61. Pulpit.
62. Lectern.
63. Nave for men.
64. Nave for women.
65. Courtyard.
66. Storeroom.
67. Mortuary chapel.

Chapter I

Early Days: 1901-1906

On Wednesday, 13 June 1906, His Majesty King Edward VII declared open the Sanatorium on Lord's Common, Easebourne Hill, Midhurst, which henceforward was to bear his name. Until then the Institution had been known colloquially as the King's Sanatorium, or the King's Hospital for Consumptives, but after the official opening ceremony the King gave assent for the Institution to be called the King Edward VII Sanatorium, Midhurst, and for its letterhead to bear the Tudor Crown. This title and emblem it bore until 1964 when, under Royal Charter, the term 'Hospital' was substituted for 'Sanatorium', the change properly reflecting its altered function and expanding role. But so closely has the Institution become integrated with the West Sussex community, that, even today, more than twenty years after it became a 'General' Hospital, many local people still refer to it in a familiar and affectionate way as the 'Sanny' or simply the 'San'.

Throughout his life, King Edward VII always showed a keen interest in hospitals and when, on his accession, his financial adviser, Sir Ernest Cassel, put at his disposal the sum of £200,000 for charitable or utilitarian purposes his thoughts turned towards some form of benevolence which would benefit the sick, more especially those sick with pulmonary tuberculosis, or consumption as it was then called.

At the turn of the century tuberculosis was widespread in Britain. At least a quarter of a million people suffered from it and 40,000 died every year, many of them in their youth or in the prime of life. The story was all too familiar. The onset was usually insidious. There might be lassitude, some loss of weight, a little coughing, often with blood in the sputum. Then would come the fever, the sweating, the wasting and the inexorable march of events to chronicity, disablement or death. Little was done except to put patients to bed in stuffy, un-ventilated rooms and to starve them. No wonder consumption was regarded with the same dread and suspicion as surrounds cancer today.

Yet abroad, particularly in Germany, a new form of 'open air' sanatorium treatment was being practised which promised great things for the afflicted. The idea had first been thought of in 1840, when an Englishman called Bodington wrote a medical paper advocating the merits of fresh air and sunlight in the treatment of consumption. He opened a small institution at Sutton Coldfield in Warwickshire wherein he practised his ideas on a small scale. Alas, his theories were severely criticised by his professional colleagues and by *The Lancet*, and his little hospital had to be closed down; but in Germany the seed bore fruit. Bodington's ideas were systematised and elaborated by Brehmer and Dettweiler and the first sanatorium was opened in Silesia in 1859, to be followed by others all over Germany; by 1900 there were 250 in existence.

1

King Edward VII had been greatly impressed with the Sanatorium at Falkenstein in the Taunus mountains near Frankfurt which he had visited when staying with his sister, the Empress Frederick, at Kronberg. He decided therefore to use the money made available by Sir Ernest Cassel to found an even better institution in England with the twofold object of looking after sufferers from the disease and of serving as a centre for research and the advancement of scientific knowledge.

It is generally believed that the King himself made the decision to found a sanatorium, but he may well have been influenced by Sir Ernest Cassel whose wife had died of tuberculosis and whose only daughter (mother of Edwina Ashley, later Lady Louis Mountbatten) suffered from the disease and, indeed, died from it in 1911. The Queen may also have had some influence – she was interested in nursing, had given her name to the Army Nursing Service and had become patron of a sanatorium bearing her name in Davos. From whomsoever the initiative came, however, it was certainly the King who sketched the broad lines along which the project should develop.

'What we require' he said to Sir Felix Semon, one of his medical advisers, 'is a sanatorium for the poorer middle classes. Rich people can avail themselves of private sanatoria; the really poor are provided for by municipalities and through public benevolence; but between these there is a stratum of educated yet indigent patients such as teachers, clergymen, clerks, governesses, young officers, etc, who cannot afford the costs of a private sanatorium, whilst they are too proud or too bashful to avail themselves of public charity. My sanatorium is principally meant to take care of them'.*

The new sanatorium was not quite the first to be built in this country. There were a few others, much smaller, already built or being built, at Banchory in Scotland, Ringwood in Hampshire and Pinewood, Berkshire, to mention three, and many special hospitals for consumption already existed. But all were in cities and they were not, on that account, suitable for the practice of 'open air' treatment which required a site in the country and an abundance of pure air. Midhurst was, however, the first institution to provide sanatorium treatment at a cost which people of limited means could afford and it was to be unique in its size, (accommodation for 100 patients), its research facilities, and in providing standards of comfort hitherto available only to the rich and privileged.

Having described what he wanted, the King next formed a committee to look into ways of putting his ideas into practice. As first appointed, the Committee consisted of three Royal Physicians, Sir William Broadbent, Sir Francis Laking and Sir Felix Semon, but as none of these eminent men possessed any expert knowledge of sanatoria they recommended that three authorities on the subject should be added – Sir Richard Douglas Powell, Sir Hermann Weber and Dr. Charles Theodore Williams. Two secretaries were appointed, Dr. John (later Sir John) Broadbent and Dr. Percival Horton-Smith (later Sir Percival Horton-Smith Hartley).* The full committee (henceforward known as the Advisory Committee), met for the first time in Sir Ernest Cassel's rooms in London on 21 December 1901.

On the first occasion they met, the Advisory Committee decided to institute a prize competition for the best essay on sanatorium design and in 1902 details of the competition were published in the world medical press. Essays on the design and function of sanatoria were to be the work of medical men alone or jointly with architects. The King approved that a sum of £800 be awarded in prizes and 173 entries were received from all parts of the world. The first prize of £500 was awarded to Dr. Arthur Latham and Mr. William West, from London, their essay being entitled 'Give him air; he'll straight be well'.

Although much useful information was obtained from the competition, none of the entries was considered entirely suitable, nor had a site yet been chosen, although it was generally agreed that it should be somewhere in the country in the south or west of England and be accessible from London. A leading architect of the day, Mr. Percy Adams, F.R.I.B.A., was therefore appointed and instructed to prepare his own plan.* This he did, but only after he and members of the Advisory Committee had visited several sanatoria in Germany and sought advice from leading authorities at home and abroad.

The next stage was to select a site. The sanatorium had to be built on dry, permeable soil on sunny, south facing, rising ground well protected by trees from the prevailing winds. A supply of pure water must be available, a farm nearby would be an advantage, and there must be ample space for outdoor recreation and exercise. Dr. Horton-Smith was deputed to visit the most likely places and for the next two or three months, often using a bicycle, he inspected them in turn. Eventually 150 acres of land on Lord's Common, Easebourne Hill, the property of the Earl of Egmont, was found and selected as being the most suitable of the dozen or so other sites which had been considered.

While the competition was still in progress and negotiations were under way for purchasing the site, a leading German authority on tuberculosis, Dr. Gustav Besold, senior physician at the Falkenstein Sanatorium, was invited by the Committee to accept the post of Senior Physician and Medical Superintendent for a period of five years. The invitation was couched in peremptory, one might even say imperious, terms. The salary was to be £600 per annum with board and lodging. No private practice was to be undertaken. The Superintendent was himself to be supervised by, and defer to, the opinion of a panel of consultants who were to visit the Sanatorium regularly. A number of other conditions was imposed, each seeming to limit his authority further. Nevertheless, Dr. Besold accepted the appointment, and the Committee invited him to come to England in March 1902 to meet them and to discuss terms.

In March 1902 the proposed site was visited by all the members of the Advisory Committee, accompanied by Dr. Besold. They met Lord Egmont's agent and solicitor and inspected the area and the farm nearby. At the end of the visit it was confidently expected that the contract of sale would be duly drawn-up and quickly approved, but it was not to be. A multitude of unexpected difficulties arose, not the least of these being the delaying tactics employed by Mr.Aman, Lord Egmont's agent, with whom the Committee were negotiating the sale. He produced one difficulty after another and was little moved by letters apprising him of the King's growing impatience over the delay. He agreed to meet the Committee in London to explain a point about the sewers, but on being summoned to the room he was found to have absented himself and gone home. The matter was not resolved until the next year and then only by the adoption of an unusual expedient: Mr. Aman ceased to act as Lord Egmont's agent and became instead an employee of the Advisory Committee!*

A major difficulty concerned the water supply. Despite assurances as to its purity, the water was found to be so full of sand that it clogged the filters. An alternative source had to be found and a pumping station and reservoir constructed, all at considerable extra expense.

At first the King was very enthusiastic and took an active part in the Committee's work, but he became increasingly irritated by what he considered to be needless delays in deciding on a site and proceeding with the work. He expressed his vexation with the Committee for appointing the Chairman's son, Dr. John Broadbent, as joint secretary and for proposing that he be paid an honorarium of £300 for his work. What finally provoked a royal explosion was when news reached him of the failure of the water supply. He rebuked the Committee in the following terms: 'I will tell you something: you doctors are nearly as bad as the lawyers; and God knows that will say a great deal!'* Sir Felix Semon, to whom the remark was addressed, succeeded in calming him down, but as time went on his early enthusiasm waned and his visits to the site became less and less frequent.

The King's dissatisfaction notwithstanding, the Committee continued patiently with their work and, in August 1903, after tenders had been invited, awarded the initial contract for the foundations to Messrs. Longley of Crawley. The specification taxed the company's expertise in several respects because the drainage system was elaborate and excavation was through rock in several places. Work proceeded during the late summer of 1903 and by the time the foundation stone was laid on 3 November the ground had been prepared and the walls were a foot or two high.

The foundation ceremony was a larger and in some ways a more impressive function than the official opening nearly three years later, although the crowds did not turn out in the same numbers as they were to do in June 1906 when the Sanatorium was opened. The King, attended by his suite, arrived at Haslemere Station at 11.55 a.m. where he was received by the Lord Lieutenant of Surrey (Lord Middleton), the Sheriff (Mr. Walpole Greenwell) and Under Sheriff (Mr. Charles Wigan) of Surrey, the General Officer Commanding the District (Major General Sir Leslie Rundle) and Sir William Broadbent. His Majesty then drove to Lord's Common in a four horse open carriage with an escort of Sussex Yeomanry, the site being reached at 12.45 p.m. Mr. Ralph, of Lindford, Bordon, whose father was a labourer on the building site, was then a boy of six at Fernhurst. He remembers the procession with its mounted escort passing through the village, the route at this point being lined by soldiers. The school had been given a holiday so that the children could wave, and every pupil had been given a porcelain mug to mark the occasion. At the parish boundary near Fernhurst a ceremonial arch had been erected bearing on the one side the word 'Welcome' and on the other 'Encore'.

At the site, a decorated pavilion had been erected in which the ceremony was to take place. Hundreds of spectators thronged the high ground to the north of the pavilion (where the flag pole stands today) and others were seated on tiers of seats which surrounded the pavilion on three sides. When the King and his entourage arrived he was received by the Lord Lieutenant of Sussex (the Marquess of Abergavenny) and made his way on a red carpet to the pavilion in which the foundation stone was suspended. In attendance at the ceremony were the Sheriff of the County (Mr. Edwin Henty) and Under Sheriff (Mr. Walter Bartlett), the Chairman of the West Sussex County Council (Earl Winterton) and Members of the Advisory Committee. Sir William Broadbent read an address to which the King replied, and a Service was conducted by the Bishop of Chichester, the Right Reverend Ernest Wilberforce. Mr. Percy Adams, the architect, then handed the King a specially designed enamel trowel with a jewelled handle bearing the Imperial crown in gold. The stone was lowered to its bed and as it

THE DAILY GRAPHIC, NOVEMBER 4, 1903.

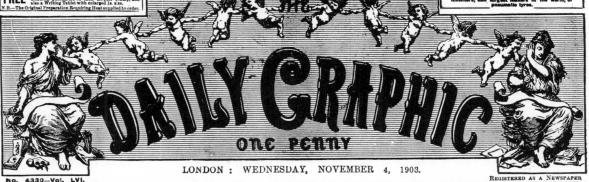

THE DAILY GRAPHIC
ONE PENNY

LONDON : WEDNESDAY, NOVEMBER 4, 1903.

No. 4330—Vol. LVI.   REGISTERED AS A NEWSPAPER

THE WEATHER

"NORTHERLY BREEZES ; FINE GENERALLY."
(See page 6.)

General Rundle.

THE KING'S SANATORIUM.

SPEECH BY HIS MAJESTY.

His Majesty was yesterday engaged in a perfectly
congenial task—that of laying the foundation stone
of the King Edward VII. Sanatorium, at Lord's
Common, near Midhurst, Sussex. Being aware of
the large mortality prevailing in this country from
tubercular disease, the King, with that thoughtful
and sympathetic interest which characterises his
dealings with the people, decided to devote a large
sum of money which had been placed at his disposal
to build and endow a Sanatorium for people suffering from tuberculosis, and to further this benevolent
purpose he appointed an advisory committee, con-
sisting of Sir William Broadbent, Sir R. Douglas
Powell, Sir Francis Laking, Sir Felix Semon, Sir
Herman Weber, and Dr. C. Theodore Williams. To
this list were recently added the names of Lord
Sandhurst, Sir Frederick Treves, and Colonel
Lascelles. Dr. Horton Smith and Dr. John F.
Broadbent were named as secretaries. The important duty of the committee was to search for an
appropriate site, and many districts in England were
visited and reported upon. Of all these the Cowdray
estate, and especially Easebourne Hill, near Midhurst, offered the greatest advantages in shelter,
altitude, soil, and vegetation, and after very careful
investigation the present site was purchased from
the Earl of Egmont. The ground slopes gently to

(Continued on page 3.)

Sir W. Broadbent.
The Bishop of Chichester.
Mr. Percy Adams (architect).

The King.
"I declare this stone well and truly laid, in the name of
God the Father, God the Son, and God the Holy Ghost."

Sir Francis Laking.
Sir F. Treves.

Fig. 2   King Edward VII laying the foundation stone for the Sanatorium, from *The Daily Graphic*,
4 November 1903.

descended the King struck it three times with a ceremonial mallet pronouncing the words 'I declare this stone well and truly laid. In the name of the Father and of the Son and of the Holy Ghost'. Under the stone was placed a copy of *The Times* newspaper, specimens of coinage up to a sovereign and statements by the Advisory Committee and the architect. A marble replica of the stone, bearing the inscription 'This stone was laid by His Majesty, King Edward VII, November the Third 1903', can be seen today under the Royal Coat of Arms in the entrance hall. The ceremonial mason's mallet in ivory and ebony used by the King was provided by James Longley and Co. (It had only been used once before, by the King himself, when as Prince of Wales, he had laid the foundation stone of the new school buildings at Christ's Hospital, Horsham.)

Although work had already started when the stone was laid in November 1903, another two and a half years were to elapse before the opening ceremony on 13 June 1906. This would not seem to have been unduly long judged by the standards of today, but the King became increasingly dissatisfied with the slow progress which he attributed, perhaps a little unfairly, to the unbusinesslike manner with which his Advisory Committee conducted its affairs. Its members were medical men, all of them well known London consultants, and the King determined that they should be strengthened by the addition of a number of influential lay figures who might inject a measure of urgency into the Committee's work. Lord Sandhurst and Lt. Colonel Lascelles therefore joined the Committee just before the foundation ceremony.

Fig. 3   The Engineer's Lodge, from a patient's drawing.

In April 1904 the general contract for building the superstructure and the sub-contract for the joinery and decorative woodwork were awarded to Longleys. Their estimate of cost was £96,000 for the buildings and £9,650 for the Chapel. The completed work cost less than those sums – £83,300 and £9,540. Charles Longley, son of James Longley, who founded the firm, noted that 'the contract was an expensive one to carry out, the Sanatorium being five miles from the nearest station at Midhurst, and all workmen had to get there starting at 6 a.m.'* The Clerk of the Works, William Atkinson, lived in the Lodge within a few hundred yards of the Sanatorium, and his daughter, Mrs. Ethel Knight, confirmed in a letter to the *West Sussex Gazette* that 'the men who worked at the Sanatorium came from all the villages round about and most of them walked all the way . . . a few who came from London used to walk to Haslemere Station at the weekend'.

Work on the building proceeded steadily and Mrs. Knight recalled an unexpected visit by the King when the work had reached an advanced stage. Members of the Advisory Committee were present and extra scaffolding had been erected for the occasion. 'The King climbed to the top', wrote Mrs. Knight, 'in fact he went up more of the scaffolding than his Committee did. Oh, how disappointed they were that they did not know he was coming! He was delighted with the work and told them so'.

'Generally speaking, we did not make a fortune out of this contract', Charles Longley commented later, but the company 'finished the contract by the time agreed on – about 2½ years – and a very pleasant job it was'.*

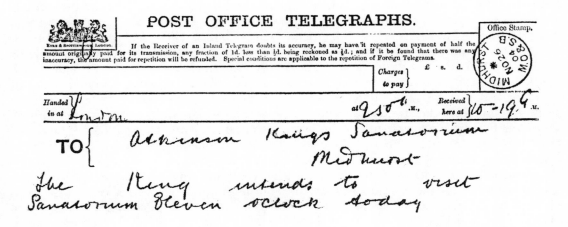

Fig. 4   Telegram announcing the King's visit.

Meanwhile, the Advisory Committee was greatly occupied in dealing with a succession of worrying matters. First was the resignation of Dr. Besold. Having declared himself satisfied with the agreement when he signed it, he later grew temperamental. He wanted a higher salary, a house of his own in the grounds, permission to bring with him a German assistant of his own choosing and the right to engage in private practice. The post had therefore to be advertised again and in 1905 Dr. Noel Bardswell was duly appointed at a salary of £600 per annum. Next, the Committee had to answer a letter in *The Times* alleging that someone else's ideas had been incorporated in the building plans without due acknowledgement, and there were other allegations in the same vein which had to be answered. In addition to this, difficulties arose over the use of Knighton's Well Road and a legal action was settled out of court.*

When work on the building was in progress, the Advisory Committee was strengthened by the appointment of Sir Frederick Treves, a leading London surgeon. Treves had successfully operated on the King for appendicitis in 1902, this necessitating postponement of the coronation for a few months, and he was already a favourite medical adviser to the royal household. Later, Mr. William James, a friend of the King's who lived at West Dean Park, West Sussex, joined the Committee and, on Lord Sandhurst's resignation on departure to South Africa in 1906, their number was further increased by the appointment of Mr. Rowland Bailey and Lord Esher.

The Advisory Committee was kept particularly busy during the last three months of work on the Sanatorium. They met seven times during the months of March, April and May 1906, each time in London, under the chairmanship of Sir William Broadbent or Sir Felix Semon. Numerous and complex were the subjects dealt with. Auditors and solicitors had to be appointed; medical, nursing and domestic staff recruited; contracts negotiated; patients' charges agreed; rules and regulations drawn up; equipment and stores of every kind purchased. The installation of boilers presented special problems. They were towed from Haslemere station by steam engine and were so big that the boiler house had to be built around them. The Sanatorium was to be provided with both horse-drawn and self-propelled vehicles. Mr. William James donated a motor car, for which a liveried chauffeur had to be engaged. For the conveyance of coal and heavy goods from the station a larger vehicle was required, and after consultation with the War Office a Foden steam wagon was purchased. It would carry a load of four tons and was guaranteed capable of climbing an incline of one in four. It remained in good working order until 1932.

Eventually, on 9 May 1906, Sir Frederick Treves informed the Committee that the King would open the Sanatorium 'in the middle of June', the exact day to be fixed later. On 23 May he indicated that the ceremony was to be a semi-private one, the Committee and chief notabilities in the district alone being invited. It was not until 6 June that the Committee was officially notified by Sir Frederick Treves that the King, accompanied by the Queen, would perform the ceremony on 13 June. A programme of the proceedings approved by His Majesty was submitted to the Committee and steps were taken to carry out the arrangements thus sanctioned. These were to be on similar lines to those followed at the ceremony of laying the foundation stone, but on a much smaller scale, the guests (more than half of them local people) being limited to 250, this being all the dining hall could seat. Guests should pay their own travelling expenses and the refreshments offered would be limited to 'tea'.

However serious had been the Committee's intention to 'play down' the opening ceremony, the event itself was the occasion for a demonstration of public loyalty and affection on a scale without precedent in West Sussex. The local press, as well as most national newspapers, devoted columns of typescript to descriptions of the ceremony and praise for the magnificent Sanatorium which was the object of Royal attention that afternoon. (A description in the *Sussex Daily News* of 15 June 1906 is included at Appendix 1.)

The King and Queen arrived by train at Midhurst Station at 4 p.m. and were met by the Lord Lieutenant of Sussex (The Duke of Norfolk); the Sheriff and under Sheriff of the County (Mr. Philip Secretan and Mr. Walter Bartlett); the Chairman of the County Council (Earl Winterton) and the General Officer Commanding the District (General Lord Methuen). A Guard of Honour was provided by a Volunteer Battalion of the Royal Sussex Regiment. Their Majesties then drove to the Sanatorium escorted by a Troop of Sussex Yeomanry. Their route took them through the gaily decorated streets of Midhurst, lined by cheering crowds, through Easebourne and up the long hill to the Sanatorium, where a Guard of Honour was drawn up outside the main entrance.

Mr. Varnes of Fernhurst, who was then only four years old, told the author how he stood at the entrance to the drive as the procession passed and how disappointed he had been that the King was not more gorgeously dressed and not wearing his crown!

The King and Queen were received at the Sanatorium by members of the Advisory Committee and were then conducted to the dining hall where the opening ceremony took place. The hall was full to capacity, there being about 250 persons present. Sir William Broadbent, Chairman of the Advisory Committee, read an address of welcome to which the King replied.

Prayers were then offered by the Bishop of Chichester, the Right Reverend Ernest Wilberforce, a hymn – 'O God our help in ages past' – was sung and the formal declaration of opening followed. Sir William Broadbent then presented to their Majesties the architect, Mr. Percy Adams; the builder, Mr. Charles Longley; the horticulturist, Miss Gertrude Jekyll; the superintendent, Dr. Noel Bardswell and the matron, Miss Blanche Trew. The King and Queen then inspected the building, took tea, and left for London by special train from Midhurst at 5.45 p.m.

At the time the Sanatorium was opened, the main building, looking then very much as it does today,* was divided into an administrative block and a patients' wing, connected by a corridor. The patients' wing, the main part of the hospital building, consisted of a central section of three storeys and two inwardly inclined wings, each of two storeys, with south facing rooms and balconies. Built with alternating dark red and salmon pink bricks, distinguished by its red tiled roof, white facings and green shutters, its appearance at the time was described as 'home-like, yet dignified'. The setting was magnificent, amid pine trees, on an upward rising slope, at an altitude of almost 500 feet, with a superb outlook southward over Midhurst towards the Downs.

The patients' building was arranged for two classes of patients, Class A, who paid the lower rate (of two guineas per week) and Class B, who paid the higher rate (eight

Fig. 5 Architect's impression of the Sanatorium as planned. The clock tower was never completed.

guineas). The rooms reserved for the latter were in the central part of the building and were slightly larger than the Class A rooms, but otherwise there was little to choose between them. Soon afterwards this distinction between the classes was abolished and all patients paid the lower rate. The patients' rooms, connected by corridors on six floors, were so arranged that each class of patient and each sex of each class could gain access to the grounds, or to other parts of the Hospital, without having to pass the rooms of another class or sex. Such were the proprieties of the age! Recreation rooms, writing rooms, sitting rooms and hydropathic bathrooms occupied the groundfloor of the central block.

Partitioned balconies, sun blinds, radiators and electric light were provided for every bedroom, but running hot and cold water was available only in the bathrooms which were situated at the ends of the corridors. The lavatories were (and still are) situated in north facing bays off the main corridors, almost as if they had been added as an afterthought. (A tale used to be told at Midhurst that when the King laid the foundation stone and toured the grounds with the blue print in his hand, he noticed the absence of lavatories and asked the architect for an explanation. Realising that they had indeed been left out, the architect could only mumble an embarrassed confession and the King, so the story went, turned to the architect with that graciousness which endeared him to all his subjects, and remarked in tones of mild reproach 'So *very* necessary, I always feel', and continued his tour.)*

The bedrooms were plastered and covered with washable paper, not hitherto used in this country, which could be washed down with disinfectant. Wood block floors in pitch pine and teak were laid in most rooms. Staircases were made of Moulmein teak, a wood considered to be almost fireproof. The fittings and furniture were simple and so designed as to avoid the collection of dust. The windows opened fully from ceiling to floor with special fastenings intended to prevent rattling.

An electric lift for patients was situated in the central block and hand operated service lifts were provided in each of the wings. The laundry, engine room and boiler house were constructed about 200 yards from the main building, but were linked by a subterranean passageway. Similar passageways, with adjoining basement rooms, were constructed which traversed the whole of the main buildings. The administration block, situated roughly where the accounts department is placed today, had a main central entrance hall where nowadays the voluntary ladies receive visitors and where the foundation stone can still be seen. To the right of the entrance hall was the porter's office, and other rooms leading off were the medical staff room, a dispensary, operating rooms, library (panelled in teak) and records office, billiards room and a staff common room. To the left were (and still are) the dining hall and kitchens. The walls were lined with Doultons Carrara tiles (as they are today) and under floor steam heating was provided. On the first floor of the administration building were the matron's quarters, the nurses' sitting room, the medical superintendent's flat, and nurses' and servants' bedrooms.*

The Chapel, a gift from Sir John Brickwood, a Portsmouth brewer, was built in a V shape with two naves, one for each sex, and a domed octagonal chancel at the apex. The south side of the building was left open to admit as much light and air as possible and within the V was placed a stone pulpit so that in fine weather services could be conducted entirely outdoors. This pulpit still exists, but the open south facing walls were filled in with glass over 50 years later. The altar frontal, the work of Lady Brickwood by whom it was presented, took the form of an emblematic design of the four evangelists with a central figure of the Saviour.

Soon after the opening ceremony, the Sanatorium was described in these terms in the *West Sussex County Times* of 16 June 1906, 'Although its design is picturesquely quaint, the Sanatorium is an up to date and modern institution. A stranger viewing it from any point in the surrounding scenery would imagine it to be an isolated terrace of new suburban residences. The rooms are built to permit of the air rushing freely through the entire building and balconies stand out for the reception of patients who are unable to take the invigorating rambles obtainable.'

Nearly 60 years later, the Sanatorium and Chapel were described by Ian Nairn and Nikolaus Pevsner. 'Immense but not at all crushing; certainly one of the best buildings of its date in the country. The main building faces south on the crest of a ridge and a mixture of gabled free Tudor and artless classical motifs has been used on a fifty-three bay facade so that it always seems friendly and humane. The whole group is a model of how to build very large institutions – something we have not yet learnt. Wings canted slightly to catch the sun: at the west end is the Chapel, a very carefully thought out building. It is L- shaped with the altar diagonally set in the angle of the L (one nave for men, one for women) – in effect two churches with one altar. The inner sides of the L face south-east, are almost completely glazed (open, originally) and have loggias. The style again is a mixture of Tudor and round arches.'*

The Institution's engineering machinery was solid, reliable and built to last, like so much else about the Sanatorium. The steam generating plant consisted of two enormous coal fired Lancashire boilers which remained in use until 1958: they were so vast that they had to be dismantled in situ and removed piecemeal. These boilers provided steam to drive the electricity generating units which consisted of Willans and Robinson's engines and dynamos which generated current for the whole Sanatorium complex. When the Sanatorium went on the grid in the 1930s the Willans and Robinson's units were kept in use for emergencies, and it was not until after the Second War that they were replaced. (Even that was not the end. So well had they been designed and constructed that two of them found their way into museums in Birmingham and America.) Exhaust steam from the Willans engines was not wasted: it was passed through 'calorifiers' which supplied hot water for the radiators and baths.

The Sanatorium was heated by open coal fires in the sitting rooms and recreation rooms and by hot water radiators in the corridors and bedrooms. The heating of the dining hall and chapel was an adaptation of the ancient Roman system of underfloor heating known as the hypocaust, using steam obtained from the main boilers. The kitchen was fitted with coal fired ranges and the sinks had special german-silver linings. Under the kitchen was installed a pasteuriser for processing the milk supplied to the Sanatorium. A cream separator and milk steriliser were also fitted. The laundry had the latest plant and even an electrically heated iron. The electric 'Otis' passenger lift in the main building was of special design so that no attendant was necessary.

The Sanatorium was fitted with an up to date system of internal telephones with an exchange in the porters' lodge, and a complete system of electric bells linked the bedrooms with the ward kitchen and duty room so that sick patients could communicate with the duty nurse.

The water supply, the initial difficulties having by now been overcome, was chlori-
nated and pumped from springs on Henley Common and delivered to a reservoir of
160,000 gallons capacity, situated near to, but 130 feet higher than, the Sanatorium.
The presence of so large a volume of water at such a height was thought to be invaluable
if a fire were to break out. The original oil engines are still in situ in the pump room,
but pumping is now done by electricity.

A number of other items of equipment and machinery was provided which proved
the point made at the time, that the Sanatorium was the most up to date in the country
and probably in the world. A steam disinfector for linen was installed. A vacuum
cleaning apparatus was donated by the manufacturers. Two rooms were fitted with
douches and sprays so that the highly thought of 'hydropathic treatment' could be
applied. All sputum was treated in a destructor before being finally disposed of. Nothing
was forgotten. The Architect, Mr. Dolby the Consulting Engineer, and last, but by no
means least, the Advisory Committee, could properly take their share of praise. The
Sanatorium really was all its founder and supporters had hoped it would be – a model
of its kind.

Chapter II

The Pre-War Years: 1906-1914

Committees, Consultants and Council

Soon after the inauguration of the Sanatorium, a reorganisation of the administrative system was announced. The Advisory Committee was replaced by a new Executive Committee, who were to be responsible for all general administration and financial matters. This Committee met for the first time at St James's Palace on Monday, 18 June 1906. Their first action was to pass a resolution that the Chairman should request permission from the King that all future meetings should be held there. The administration of the Sanatorium, in all its departments, was henceforward to be in the hands of the Executive Committee on whose authority alone orders were to be issued to officials and servants of the Institution.

The new Executive Committee included only two medical men, Sir Francis Laking and Sir Frederick Treves. Lord Esher was Chairman, Sir Frederick Treves was Deputy Chairman, and the members were Sir Ernest Cassel, Mr. William James, Mr. (later Sir) Rowland Bailey, Sir Francis Laking, Colonel Lascelles, and the Hon. Sidney Peel. Dr. P. (later Sir Percival) Horton-Smith Hartley was the Honorary Secretary. The Committee met in London at least once a month at St James's Palace. Apart from a few changes in the membership (Mr. William James became Chairman in December 1908 and Sir Frederick Treves in 1912 on Mr. James's death) this arrangement continued without alteration until 1912 when the Executive Committee became known as the Council, and the Institution became incorporated by Royal Charter. (The Council continued to meet at St James's Palace, in the Armoury or the Tapestry Room, until 1969.)

The Honorary Secretary of the Executive Committee was Dr. Horton-Smith Hartley. He had been joint Honorary Secretary with Dr. (later Sir) John Broadbent of the Advisory Committee until that body was dissolved, and had been personally responsible for reconnoitering and selecting the site on which the Sanatorium was built. When the Council was formed in 1912 Dr. Hartley was asked to continue as Honorary Secretary, but his consulting engagements in London prevented his accepting the appointment unless he could be provided with a secretary. A clerical assistant was found and Dr. Hartley continued as Honorary Secretary to the Council until he relinquished the post in 1920.

On all matters connected with the medical work of the Sanatorium, both as regards the care of patients and the conduct of research, the Executive Committee received advice from the Consultants. The medical men appointed by the King in 1906 as members of the Sanatorium Consulting Staff were Sir William Broadbent, Sir Richard Douglas Powell, Sir Felix Semon, Sir Hermann Weber, Sir Lauder Brunton, Dr.

Theodore Williams, Dr. Kingston Fowler, Dr. Percy Kidd, Professor Clifford Allbutt, Professor William Osler, Dr. J. F. Goodhart and Dr. William Bulloch. They met together in London twice a year and, in turn, one of them visited and inspected the Sanatorium every month and wrote a report or memorandum.

The Consulting Staff met for the first time in London on 11 July 1906 at 84 Brook Street. Sir William Broadbent took the chair and Dr. Theodore Williams was elected Honorary Secretary. Until 1969 their meetings were minuted as 'Meetings of the Consulting Staff'. Thereafter they became known as the Medical Committee.

Their meetings were attended 'on request' by Dr. Horton-Smith Hartley (Honorary Secretary of the Executive Committee) and by Dr. Bardswell (Medical Superintendent), a bond between the medical and executive bodies thus being established, but neither Dr. Hartley nor Dr. Bardswell was appointed to the Consulting Staff until many years later. The link between Consultants and Council was further strengthened by the attendance 'on request' at most Council meetings of Dr. Bardswell together with one of the Consultants, usually the Consultant on 'visiting duty' at the time.

In his biography of King Edward VII, Sir Sidney Lee wrote, somewhat disparagingly, of the Consultants 'that the administrative re-organisation in 1906 had reduced them to the status of an ornamental consultative body'.* Subsequent events suggest otherwise. By acting through a lay executive body on general as well as on medical and scientific matters the Consultants were able to exert a powerful and beneficial influence on Sanatorium affairs to an extent that was beyond them when, as the Advisory Committee, they were in sole executive authority. And this has continued to this day.

During the pre-war years, there were several changes amongst the Consulting Staff. Sir William Broadbent, their Chairman, died in 1907. No one was immediately appointed to fill his place as a member, but as Chairman he was succeeded by Sir Richard Douglas Powell. Sir Lauder Brunton tendered his resignation in 1909 on being appointed to the Committee of the Radium Institution (in his letter of resignation he expressed his belief that the 'chief needs of the Sanatorium had been met and only minor details had yet to be worked out'). Two names were submitted to His Majesty to fill the vacancies thus created; those of Dr. Mitchell Bruce and Dr. Dyke Acland. The King approved the one, that of Bruce, but desired that the other be filled by a Dr. Bertrand Dawson who had recently attended him at Buckingham Palace. In this way began Midhurst's long association with one of the outstanding medical figures of the 20th century. Dr. Acland's turn was not long in coming. In 1910, he and Dr. (later Sir) St Clair Thomson were appointed to fill the vacancies created by the resignations of Sir Richard Douglas Powell (who was later to be appointed to the Council) and Sir Felix Semon. Sir Richard Douglas Powell was succeeded as Chairman of the Board of Consultants by Dr. Theodore Williams, hitherto the Honorary Secretary, and Bertrand Dawson, now Sir Bertrand Dawson, was asked to become Honorary Secretary. After Dr. Williams' death in 1912,* Dr. Mitchell Bruce became Chairman and Sir Bertrand Dawson continued (until 1919) as Honorary Secretary. Sir James Reid in 1913 and Dr. (later Sir) Hector Mackenzie in 1914 were appointed members of the Consulting Staff following Dr. Williams' death and Sir Hermann Weber's resignation.

When the war broke out in August 1914, the Consultants to the Sanatorium were: Dr. Mitchell Bruce (in the Chair), Dr. Dyke Acland, Sir James Fowler, Dr. Percy Kidd, Dr. (later Sir) Hector Mackenzie, Sir James Reid, Sir St Clair Thomson, Sir James

Goodhart, Sir Clifford Allbutt, Dr. William Bulloch, Sir William Osler and Sir Bertrand Dawson.

For advice on legal matters, the Executive Committee relied on the services of Messrs. Lewis and Lewis whose senior partner, Sir George Lewis, had been appointed Honorary Solicitor to the Institution at its inception. Sir George was to remain Honorary Solicitor until his death in 1927. The firm of Lewis and Lewis, now Messrs. Penningtons and Lewis & Lewis, are still legal advisers to the Hospital. Mr. W. B. Peat, later Sir William Peat, of Messrs. W. B. Peat and Company, was appointed Honorary Auditor to the Institution and was always referred to on questions of financial accounting. Today's firm of Messrs. Peat, Marwick, Mitchell and Company are still Auditors to the Hospital. Whenever problems arose over the state of the buildings, the Sanatorium's principal architect, Mr. H. Percy Adams, was consulted. His advice was not often sought in the early days, but there came a moment in 1911 when he advised that the drainage system be entirely reconstructed. His arguments were considered by the Executive Committee to be unconvincing and his opinion was not sought again, the mantle of adviser falling thereafter upon the shoulders of Mr. Edwin Hall, then Vice President of the Royal Institute of British Architects and well known in connection with hospital work. On all engineering matters, the Executive Committee was dependent on the advice of Mr. Arthur P. Patey. His long association with Midhurst, which lasted 53 years, began in 1906 when Mr. Bailey informed the Executive Committee that he was anxious about 'the enormous consumption of coal' at the Sanatorium, and he would like their agreement 'to invite Mr. Arthur Patey, resident engineer to the Houses of Parliament, to visit the Sanatorium and report what the coal consumption should be'. Mr. Patey's advice was so well received by the Committee that he was consulted thereafter on countless other matters relating to the Sanatorium, its equipment, and its machinery. In 1908, he was officially appointed Honorary Consulting Engineer to the Institution, a position he continued to occupy until his retirement in 1959.

Superintendent and Staff

When the Sanatorium opened there were about seventy persons on the staff. The Superintendent was Dr. Noel Dean Bardswell who had been appointed for a period of five years at an annual salary of £600 in 1905 when Dr. Besold withdrew. He was only 33 years of age on appointment, but he had already acquired a considerable reputation as a physician with an expert knowledge of tuberculosis and had published a book which had attracted favourable reviews in the medical and lay press. He was to remain as Superintendent for 12 years, a period exceeded by only one of his successors, Sir Geoffrey Todd.

Bardswell was first and foremost a clinician, but he was burdened with so much administration, especially after the Sanatorium started work, that he had to leave a great deal of the medical practice to his subordinates, by whom he was fortunately very well served.

Fig. 6   Dr. Noel Bardswell.

To begin with, the Superintendent had only one medical assistant, Dr. Basil Adams, whose salary was £150 a year, but after repeated recommendations from the Visiting Consultants, a second assistant, Dr. Burra, was appointed with a salary of £100 a year. The two assistant medical officers usually stayed at the Sanatorium for two years, first as junior and then as senior assistant, but Dr.Bardswell continued to provide supervision and direction from the top. Bardswell's work for the patients and his medical judgement were never criticised, indeed they were widely praised, but as an administrator his efforts did not always receive approbation. In his position as Superintendent he was required to serve, and to defer to, two masters: a body of highly placed Consultants with strongly held opinions on the one hand, an Executive Committee of no less distinguished and influential figures on the other.

Within a year of the Sanatorium opening, the feeling was expressed within the Executive Committee that 'he was unequal to the task of administering so large an Institution' and in July 1907 a letter was sent to him in these terms:

> The Committee are not satisfied yet that your administrative ability is equal to the task imposed upon you, and they think it right to take this opportunity of informing you that a further experience of the working of the Sanatorium might reluctantly force them to make a change in its management. Yours faithfully, [signed] Esher

That he remained in office for as long as he did says much for his character. The Consultants represented his case with vigour. Initially he had only one medical assistant and they felt he was becoming so much involved in administration that he could not devote enough time to the patients. 'It would be very unfortunate', wrote Sir Clifford Allbutt, 'if the Medical Superintendent of this Sanatorium were to drop into the position of too many superintendents of lunatic asylums whose time is wholly taken up with administration. The sooner, to prevent this happening, the scientific spirit is engrafted on the management the better, lest routine should gain too strong a footing'. Pressure from the Consultants induced the Executive Committee to appoint a second assistant medical officer and this relieved Bardswell of some clinical responsibilities, but he continued heavily engaged with administration.

A brush with the Executive Committee occurred in 1907 when he was criticised for displaying an attitude of reserve toward the Committee 'which made confidence between them difficult to maintain, and for inspiring in the Committee some apprehension in the manner in which discipline in the Sanatorium was being maintained'. His next skirmish was with the Consultants, who reproved him in 1908 for not keeping them continuously informed about a minor skin infection amongst the patients. These differences apart, Bardswell's wise judgement and integrity did much to carry the Sanatorium securely through its early formative years. He remained in post at Midhurst until 1915 when he was commissioned in the Royal Army Medical Corps, his Sanatorium duties being taken over temporarily by a long term locum tenens, Dr. Cockill. Soon after Bardswell's final retirement in 1917, he was appointed a member of the Consulting Staff in which capacity he continued to serve the Sanatorium until his death in 1938. He had one characteristic which might have told against him as Superintendent of a Royal Sanatorium: his manner could be casual and his attire informal. The story goes that walking behind King Edward VII and Sir Frederick Treves on one of His Majesty's visits to the Sanatorium, he overheard the King saying 'Who is this burglarious looking tramp following us around, Treves?'.

In July 1906, Miss Ethel McCaul RRC, the first 'Lady Visitor', was authorised by the Executive Committee to organise the domestic arrangements at the Sanatorium. Immediately after carrying out this task, Miss McCaul had to resign owing to ill health. Her place as Lady Visitor was taken by Lady Gifford who was joined later by Mrs. Brinton, and these two ladies continued as Lady Visitors until the First War was well advanced.

The nursing establishment was small. The Matron (Miss Trew), a Head Nurse and two other nurses were appointed before the Sanatorium opened and more were engaged as patients began to come in. Miss Trew was replaced as Matron by her assistant, Miss Jones, in November 1906. Her salary was £60 a year and her duties, in which she was assisted by a housekeeper, were to supervise the nursing staff and female domestic staff. There had been some difficulty initially in obtaining and keeping nurses owing to the monotony of the work, but this was overcome as the number of patients increased. By 1907 the nursing establishment was set at a head sister, two other sisters, five nurses and a number of probationers. The following year the number of staff was increased to eight – two sisters and six nurses – (the probationers were abolished) and at that level the establishment remained until after the First War. In 1908, when Miss Jones resigned, Mrs Hatchell, who was not trained as a nurse, was appointed Matron (the annual salary was now £80) and she remained in post until 1919.

The post of Secretary to the Sanatorium was established in October 1906 and was immediately occupied by Mr. H. C. Price who had previously been Dr. Bardswell's secretary. As Secretary he was given responsibility (under the Superintendent) for all letters dealing with patients' admissions, all commercial correspondence, and for sending out bills and keeping the accounts. He was also required to assume the duties of Steward and be responsible for the stores, equipment and food; the post was therefore designated Secretary/Steward. Mr. Price died in harness in 1912, the post of Secretary/Steward then being held for a short time by Mr. Booth and then by Mr. Clarenbone who was appointed 'Steward' in 1914.

The annual re-election of the principal members of the Sanatorium staff was introduced at the meeting of Council in 1909 when Mrs. Hatchell as Matron, Mr. Price as Secretary/ Steward and the medical officers then in post (Dr. Stirling Lee and Dr. de Gruchy) were re-elected for a year on the same terms as before. (The practice of annual re-election of principal officers, including the Superintendent, was continued until the Second World War.)

The domestic and ancillary staff at Midhurst in 1906 numbered about 50 of whom over half were female. There was a cook, who was paid £40 per annum, a head waitress (£30) and a number of kitchen maids, ward maids, scullery maids, house maids, waitresses and laundry maids whose average wage was about £20 a year. The male staff included a head engineer (from 1908 until 1937 this was Mr. W. H. Oliver who had previously been in service at Windsor Castle and was recommended for Midhurst because he had a weak chest), a hall porter (John Barnes, lately Petty Officer in the Royal Navy and Coxswain of the King's Pinnace. He was followed by Grant Hodder, ex-Rifle Brigade), four general porters, stokers, engine drivers, chauffeurs, labourers, gardeners and a carpenter. The staff were accommodated in the main building or in one of the cottages which had been built in the grounds.

The Midhurst Regime

Dr. Bardswell, the Medical Superintendent, was one of the first doctors in this country to advocate 'Open Air' treatment for tuberculous patients. Soon after the Sanatorium opened he outlined his ideas to the lay press in the following terms: 'We aim to cure our patients and their average stay in the Sanatorium is likely to be about four months . . . We shall endeavour to admit patients who are suffering from the early stages of the disease, as this is not intended to be a home for the dying. Absolute rest will be an important point in treatment. I shall not encourage the patients even to read. Their minds should be like so many cabbages . . . The diet of each patient will be carefully regulated and during rest periods absolute silence will be enforced. I shall encourage each one to do some definite work. Gardening will be the most general occupation and certain marked walks will be recommended. The extent will vary from, say, four to even twenty miles a day. I shall have to prohibit cycling however. Of course, all the patients may not be cured when they leave the Institution. My aim is to teach them how to cure themselves. They can then carry on the treatment even amid the smoke of London itself'. In a nutshell, what Bardswell was saying was: we shall take early cases only and keep them in the Sanatorium for limited periods of time. We shall provide our patients with proper feeding, graduated exercises, controlled rest periods and a regulated open air routine. Finally, we shall prepare them for the world outside by teaching them the principles of treatment which they will have to follow after they have left the Sanatorium. These were the precepts: how far were they actually observed ?

Midhurst had been built as a Sanatorium, that is an Institution intended for the treatment of early consumptive patients. It was never meant for advanced cases who should have been sent in the first place to a hospital for consumptives. Yet time and time again, in the first year of the Sanatorium's existence, the Visiting Consultants on their routine monthly inspections would report that too many advanced cases were being admitted. In spite of measures to tighten up the selection procedure, advanced cases continued to be admitted and eventually it was accepted that the Sanatorium would have to take its share of these if it was to fill its beds. Bardswell's stipulation that patients would not stay long in the Sanatorium proved equally difficult to carry out, even after the statutory period had been raised to six months. Every patient who had been in for longer than six months had to be referred to a member of the Consulting Staff, a rule which was still enforced when Sir Geoffrey Todd was appointed Superintendent in 1934.

The social status of patients was an important factor in deciding whether they should or should not be accepted for admission.* In those days strict egalitarianism in health matters was deemed of less importance than it is today, and the King and his Advisory Committee had indicated quite clearly for whom the Institution was intended: the educated but less well off, middle class, professional people who were neither able to pay full private fees nor were the proper recipients of public charity. The Visiting Consultants frequently remarked on the social standing of the patients, commenting in most cases that it was satisfactory, but sometimes a contrary view was expressed. In 1906 Count Albert Mensdorff's valet was refused admission because he did not belong to the class of patient for which the Sanatorium was intended, and in 1910 one of the Consultants recently appointed, Dr. Bertrand Dawson (later Lord Dawson of Penn), reported that one or two of the women patients were below the social standard which he felt was 'desirable to keep the tone of the Sanatorium good'.

Great emphasis was placed on the therapeutic value of fresh air. The Sanatorium

1. (*above*) Laying the foundation stone, 3 November 1903. The King, wearing a top hat, is to the left of the post bearing the Royal coat of arms.

2. (*below*) The boiler for the King Edward VII Sanatorium arriving by steam engine in 1905.

3. The Sanatorium nearing completion.

4. The Guard of Honour at the King's Sanatorium, 6 June 1906.

5. Midhurst 'en fête', 6 June 1906.

6. The King and Queen on their way to open the Sanatorium, 6 June 1906.

7. Patients at luncheon in the dining hall.

Edwardian Midhurst

8. Patients working in the garden.

9. Off for a drive in the 'motor'.

10. The road from Midhurst to the Sanatorium.

11.   The open-air chapel.

12.   View from the open-air chapel.

13. (*above*) Porters and adminstrative staff in the 1920s. The three moustached figures are Mr. Clarenbone (sitting), Collins and Bill Mills (standing). On the extreme right are Pullinger (standing) and Kent (sitting).

14. (*below*) A group at Midhurst, 1935. From left to right: Miss Quayle, Capt. Arnold (characteristically lighting a cigarette), Dr. Todd's mother, Mrs. Sheen, an unidentified lady, Miss Margot Sheen (later Lady Todd).

15. (*above*) Administrative staff, 1937. Front row, left to right: Rev. J. H. Layton; unidentified; Mr. Clarenbone; Dr. Todd; Jack Williams; JAB; Allen. Second row, left to right: Naldrett's son; unidentified; Danny King; unidentified; 'Bill' Mills; 'Windy' Gale; Prentice; unidentified. Back row, left to right: Naldrett; Dicky Kent; unidentified; Goodall.

16. (*below*) The Sanatorium detachment, Home Guard. Standing in the foreground are, from left to right, Sir Courtauld-Thomson, Lord Wigram, Dr. Todd and Miss Quayle. The detachment is led by Mr. Ashburner. In the ranks are Mr. Hampton, Jack Taylor, Geoff Rumsby, Danny King (wearing Boer War medals) and Collins, the porter. The photograph was taken in 1940.

17. (*above*) Medical and nursing staff, 1935. Front row, left to right: Dr. Hinson; Miss Quayle; Dr. Todd; Dr. Ramsay; Dr. Craig. Second row: Sister Marshall stands behind Dr. Todd, Sister White is on the extreme left and Sister Chapman is first from right. Back row: Nurse Starkey is on the extreme right.

18. (*below*) Medical and nursing staff, 1938. Front row, left to right: Rev. J. H. Layton, Dr. Herington, Dr. West, Miss Quayle, Dr. Todd, Sister Chapman, Dr. Nicholson, Dr. Hinson. Second row: Sister Marshall (with cross belt), Sister Dale on her right and Sister Walters on her left. Jack Williams stands at the back.

19. The Queen, with Dr. Geoffrey Todd and Lord Wigram, greeting patients on the balconies at the Sanatorium, 30 May 1946.

20. (*above*) The Duke of Norfolk, Sir Geoffrey Todd, Lord Courtauld-Thomson and the Duchess of Norfolk at the coronation garden party at Midhurst on 25 July 1953.

21. (*below*) Christmas pantomime, 1954, 'The Desert Wrong'. Sir Geoffrey Todd sits in judgement as Sheik 'O Bey Todd'. John Smyth and Sandy Large are the sisters, with skull-and-cross-bones badges on their aprons. On their right, heavily disguised, are John Boulton, Fred Summers, Douglas Teare, Katie Boyle, Ina Fraser and Liz Adam. The public prosecutor is Bob Elphick.

22. (*above*) An X-ray session, 1956. In the front row is Sir Geoffrey Todd, flanked by Doctors Hume, Teare and Doyle, with Kay Whitmarsh, medical secretary, on Dr. Hume's left. Sister Drane is on the right in the back row.

23. (*below*) Forecourt and pine walk: the Sanatorium has its own flag and all kinds of transport.

24. (*above*) The Queen's visit, 1 August 1956. Staff Nurse Newport presents Her Majesty with a bouquet. From left to right: Miss Schofield, Lady Mountbatten, Dr. Teare, Lord Portal and Sir Geoffrey Todd.

25. (*below*) The Queen talks to Sisters Church, White and Young. The mural is by Adrian Hill.

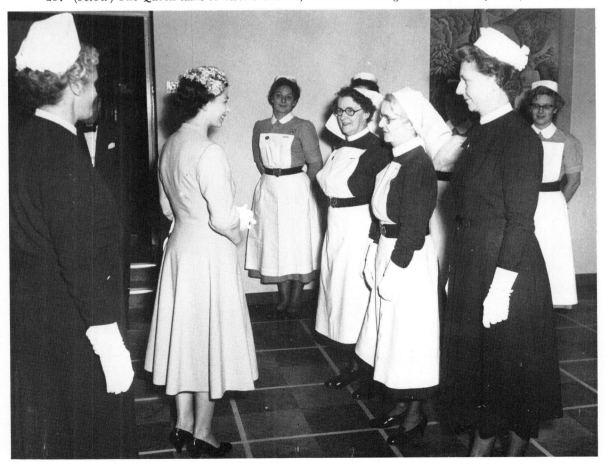

26. Her Majesty acknowledges the cheers of patients after her visit to Midhurst on 1 August 1956.
Mr. Boulton holds the umbrella. Also shown are Lord Portal, Sir Geoffrey Todd, Miss Schofield and
Lady Mountbatten.

27. Princess Tchichibu of Japan at the Sanatorium in the 1960s. From left to right: Lord Cowdray, the Princess, Sir Geoffrey Todd, Dr. Teare, a Japanese lady and Mr. Boulton.

28. Conference on the treatment of pulmonary tuberculosis at the Sanatorium, May 1962. Front row, left to right: Dr. V. H. Springett, Mr. O. S. Tubbs, Dr. J. G. Scadding, Dr. N. V. Oswald, Sir Geoffrey Todd, Sir Geoffrey Marshall, Sir Clement Price Thomas, Dr. N. Lloyd Rusby, Dr. J. L. Livingstone, Dr. A. Brian Taylor, Mr. N. R. Barrett, Dr. J. C. Hoyle, Prof. P. R. Allison. Second row, left to right: Dr. D. A. Mitchison, Mr. Dillwyn Thomas, Mr. F. R. Edwards, Mr. W. P. Cleland, Dr. J. E. Wallace, Mr. V. T. Powell, Lt. Col. S. E. Large, Dr. E. W. Thompson Evans, Dr. N. W. Horne, Dr. K. F. W. Hinson, Dr. E. H. Hudson, Dr. J. R. Bignall. Back row, left to right: Dr. W. I. Gordon, Dr. A. F. Foster-Carter, Dr. F. Max Elliott, Lt. Col. R. MacFarlane, Dr. K. M. Citron, Dr. H. D. Teare, Dr. Kennedy, Dr. K. M. Hume, Dr. H. M. Foreman, Dr. P. J. Doyle, Dr. E. Rhys Jones.

29. (*above*) Aerial view, 1938, showing the main building, the chapel, golf course and the pine walk.

30. (*below*) Aerial view, 1975. The surgical wing, nurses' home, Marshall Hall, X-ray Department, Research Institute and car park have been added. The main building, chapel and pine walk remain, but the golf course has disappeared. The Mountbatten wing has yet to be built.

had been designed to permit the free entry of outside air without the introduction of draughts – 'an unknown word in sanatorium language' – and patients were encouraged to spend rest periods on their balconies and to sleep outside even when the temperature fell to well below freezing point. An arduous experience indeed.

Proper feeding was an important part of treatment at Midhurst. Great store was laid on providing an adequate balanced diet so that not only were the essential nutrients given in the correct proportions, but the total calorie value was regulated according to individual circumstances. Patients in bed were given reduced diets and those below their normal weight increased diets, but great care was taken to prevent them putting on too much weight. In this, Midhurst differed from some overseas institutions, where the practice was to encourage patients to eat, and to go on eating, as much as they could. Alcohol was prescribed only when thought desirable by the Medical Superintendent, and this was very unusual. A Visiting Consultant, Sir Hermann Weber, reported in 1913 after lunching in the patients' dining hall, 'The drink of the patients consisted of milk or water, none had either beer or any other alcoholic beverage. It was interesting to observe the great change which has taken place in this respect during the last 50 years. At Grobersdorf, Dr. Brehmer gave his patients a very fair amount of wine and beer, the same was the case with Dr. Dettweiler at Falkenstein and with Dr. Spengler at Davos where a rather strong wine was in use. These distinguished physicians considered a certain amount of alcoholic stimulants as an important part of the treatment. When I argued with them on this point they maintained that alcohol, especially in the form of wine, improved the digestion and assisted a fibrous change of the local affection [sic].'

This advice notwithstanding, the consumption of alcohol at Midhurst was to remain strictly forbidden for many years, and up to the 1939-45 war patients found to be in possession of alcohol were liable to be dismissed. Any patient entering a public house in Midhurst, and unfortunate enough to be observed, suffered a similar fate. However, leniency might be exercised if a patient's pension rights were at risk: the culprit might then be permitted to resign and to leave the Sanatorium without fail by a given date. Even after the war and up until the 1970s, alcohol was discouraged.

Between 10 a.m. and 12 midday, except on Sundays, 'up' patients (those not confined to bed) were required to undertake light work in the garden or to take exercise, which usually took the form of walking. The walks, all measured and marked, were graded according to the patients' condition. They varied in length from half a mile to three miles and even longer in some cases.

Light work in the gardens and grounds, using specially constructed light tools, was often prescribed instead of walking. It was divided roughly into three grades of severity, the lightest of which consisted of weeding, edging and hoeing; the heaviest, of digging, rolling and mowing. By 1908, 75 per cent of the patients were given some form of work to do in the garden instead of the morning walk, but the Consulting Staff, almost to a man, were critical of the lack of other forms of occupation. They maintained the opinion that patients would become bored with gardening and walking. 'If a piggery, a poultry farm and an apiary were introduced', wrote Sir Felix Semon in 1906, 'this would be a real boon for many patients not particularly fond of gardening and might enable some of them to turn their attention to these occupations when leaving the Sanatorium'. Sir Clifford Allbutt wrote in 1907 that 'in all Sanatoriums the want of occupation becomes tedious and this tends to discontent and to slackening of recovery, besides breaking down the habit of application to work'. All kinds of occupation were suggested – farming, poultry farming, wood cutting, even work in the gravel pit, but Bardswell was entirely opposed, holding the view that there was already plenty for the patients to do in the Sanatorium gardens and grounds without committing them further. Later he relented to the extent of permitting carpentry and games, and he encouraged the patients to form their own Entertainments Committee which did useful work arranging concerts, tournaments and competitions. Indoors, deck quoits, draughts, dominoes, whist, bridge and chess were allowed. Outdoors, patients could play croquet, clock golf and garden games. In 1912 a four-hole 'mashie' golf course (later extended to nine holes) was constructed on the open ground to the south of the gardens where the cricket pitch is situated today. Games were allowed between tea and the evening rest hour, and again after dinner until bedtime, but at no other time. A magazine entitled the *King Edward VII Magazine* was produced by the patients, the first edition appearing in November 1906. Its contents, innocuous though they were, seem to have worried the Executive Committee, for the Medical Superintendent was instructed to act as informal censor for any subsequent editions. (Only the first edition is still extant [*See* Appendix 3]. Whether any subsequent editions appeared at the time is uncertain, but a Sanatorium Magazine called *The Edwardian* was produced in 1947 and production continued for some years.)

A valuable asset was the piano in the main hall. A good pianist was always to be found amongst the Hospital inmates and often competent instrumentalists and singers as well. Concerts were held, often played by the patients themselves, and on 1 January 1908 the first of many dramatic performances was put on by the patients for the benefit of the staff. This set a theatrical precedent which has continued ever since (although nowadays the Hospital shows are more often performed by the staff for the benefit of the patients!).

Sanatorium treatment had an educational as well as a therapeutic purpose. Bardswell had said that he would prepare Sanatorium patients for the hard world outside by teaching them the principles of treatment which they should continue when they left. Patients were taught the advantages of fresh air and open windows, instructed in methods of sputum disposal,* warned of the dangers of spitting and coughing, and trained to lead an orderly, regular life. Bardswell did all this and more: he went to endless pains, unfortunately not always with success, to find gainful occupation for his patients when they were discharged from his care. He considered this to be part of his job as Superintendent and his efforts added greatly to the Sanatorium's reputation.

The patients' day would begin at 7.30 a.m. with the sounding of a gong to signify that it was time to get up. Patients had their own thermometers and took their own temperatures. Most of the 'up' patients then had a bath and massage or attended the Hydrotherapy Department. (There were two hydrotherapy rooms, one for each sex, containing shower baths, hose pipes, sprays and douches. Treatment was ordered for suitable cases in the belief that it encouraged free action of the skin thereby reducing toxaemia.) A second gong would sound at 8.15 and a third at 8.30 to indicate that breakfast was ready. All meals, except for those on Sunday, were attended by the doctors, who sat at their own table in an alcove, and the nurses. Men and women sat at separate tables. Segregation of the sexes was strictly observed, not only at meal times but throughout the day also. Their rooms were on separate floors and they had their own recreation rooms and wash rooms. Even in chapel the rule was observed, with one nave being occupied by ladies, the other by gentlemen. After breakfast, all patients would retire to their own rooms and the doctors would do their rounds. 'Bed' patients were seen by a doctor every day – 'up' patients less frequently, but never less than once a week.

From noon to 1 p.m. was the first 'rest hour', the limits being marked by the sounding of gongs. A second rest hour was observed between 6 p.m. and 7 p.m. These rest periods were imperative: no patient was excused them, however advanced his recovery. They had to be spent in lounge chairs on the balconies, or in their bedrooms. Talking and writing was forbidden: reading permitted, for all but the most serious cases.

At luncheon, taken between 1 and 2 p.m., the same rules were observed but between 2 p.m. and 2.30 p.m. patients could do what they liked. The second exercise period was between 2.30 and 4.30 p.m. and tea, not a compulsory meal, followed at 4.30 p.m. The evening was devoted to recreation, with a rest hour (6 to 7 p.m.) followed by dinner at 7.15 p.m. Bedtime was 9.30 and lights had to be out by 10 p.m. This was signalled by the dimming of lights several times before the generators were finally switched off punctually at 10 p.m. (On one occasion the warning came an hour too soon. Mr. Oliver, the engineer, rushed over from his cottage to find out what was going on. He discovered an inebriated stoker swinging backwards and forwards on the operating lever. Oliver was a teetotaller. The stoker was dismissed instantly.) After the generators went off, night time lighting came from storage batteries. Emergency lighting was provided by six candlesticks – one for each Ward – sited, with matches, in the Assistant Matron's Office. At Midhurst, nothing was overlooked!

On Sunday the routine was varied in certain ways. Patients could eat as much or as little as they chose. They need not take exercise walks, or work in the garden. They could receive visitors and attend the service in chapel at 4.30 p.m.

It was a disciplined and regular life, perhaps even a monotonous one, but life for patients at Midhurst appears to have been happy and there was no lack of fun. Cheerfulness and an optimistic attitude to life were encouraged and most contemporary writers declared that it was impossible to be miserable. One patient wrote: 'I entered the Institution expecting to find a number of fragile spiritless men and women, but was agreeably disappointed to find my fellow sufferers buxom, rosy faced and high spirited'.* This cheerfulness, this sense of belonging to a country club in a well ordered world, was described in this extract from the *Morning Post* of 14 June 1906: 'The cheery red brick building gives no sense of forlornness such as the best of town hospitals must do. It looks homelike, and when the patient reaches the interior, glowing with colour, spotlessly clean and filled with every comfort, he will feel that he has come to a remarkably well kept hotel than to a hospital. In no disease does cheerfulness of mind do more for the recovery of the patient, and cheerfulness everywhere is the keynote at Midhurst'.*

Medical Practice and Research

Bardswell always insisted on records being kept of the patients passing through the Sanatorium and he instituted a system of following them up by sending every discharged patient an annual questionnaire, which they were asked to complete and return. The requests were on the whole well responded to and the results were interesting, if not altogether unexpected. They showed that the more extensive cases fared worse than the less advanced cases and that cavitated disease did particularly badly; but they also showed how successful the Midhurst regime was in curing patients with early and only moderately advanced disease, the great majority of whom were found to have been cured and able to resume their previous employment. Commenting on the results, the *British Medical Journal* remarked on 11 April 1914: 'Enough has been said to convince the most sceptical that the Midhurst Sanatorium has fully justified its existence. At the opening of the Sanatorium, the late King Edward said "It is our earnest hope that the Sanatorium . . . may assist to advance the physiological knowledge of pulmonary diseases and that this institution may . . . be the means of prolonging the lives of those whose career of honourable usefulness has been interrupted by this terrible malady." Both these objects have been amply fulfilled'.

Many of the patients admitted with pulmonary tuberculosis suffered also from tuberculosis of the larynx. These patients were the special concern of Sir Felix Semon and, later, of Sir St Clair Thomson, both of whom were in turn members of the Consulting Staff with a particular interest in diseases of the throat. One of the main planks of treatment was that patients were put on 'Silence' (No talking) or 'Whispers'. Communication was by note pad (in the hands of wags these provoked much mirth). *The British Medical Journal*, referring in 1914 to Sir Felix Semon's results at Midhurst wrote that laryngeal tuberculosis was not invariably fatal, as it was formerly held to be, but that a certain proportion of patients could be cured.

During the years leading up to and including the Great War, the diagnosis of pulmonary tuberculosis depended solely on the clinical findings and the results of sputum examinations. X-rays had already been invented, but for chest work they were of limited value because exposure took longer than the patient was able to hold his breath. Nevertheless, it was felt by some Consultants from 1906 onwards that Midhurst should be provided with 'an apparatus for taking skiagrams', as X-rays were often called, particularly in view of the fact that some other Sanatoria had them, Tor-na-Dee in Scotland for example. But it was not until 1916 that the Consultants formally recommended to Council that an X-ray set should be provided as soon as possible.

It had always been the intention that research should go hand in hand with treatment at the Sanatorium, and a laboratory block was allocated for research purposes in a small building standing a short distance from the main building on a site which now forms the west end of the Surgical Wing. The laboratory block was not equipped when the Sanatorium started work, nor had a pathologist been appointed, but in 1907, after repeated recommendations by the Consultants, equipment was purchased and the post was filled. The first person appointed resigned after only a few months, but his successor, Dr. Radcliffe from Belfast, who arrived in 1908, was an enthusiastic investigator who contributed much to the Sanatorium's reputation. Besides undertaking laboratory work, Radcliffe had clinical responsibility under the Superintendent for a number of the patients, thus setting a pattern of appointing clinically orientated pathologists to the staff, which, though broken between the two wars, was resumed in 1949 when Dr. Gordon was appointed.

In Radcliffe's time, the positive diagnosis of pulmonary tuberculosis depended on finding the organism in the sputum. Much of Radcliffe's early work was directed to the search for other diagnostic methods. Variations in what used to be called the 'Opsonic Index', and the presence or absence in the blood of antibodies, were methods examined but found wanting. He was on surer ground when he embarked on a study of the individual's skin reaction to small injections of tuberculin, an extract from tubercle bacilli. After testing patients at Midhurst for some years he suggested that whilst it was impossible to draw definite conclusions, a negative reaction in a doubtful case probably indicated the absence of disease – an hypothesis which has subsequently proved to be quite correct. Radcliffe worked on several other ideas none of which came to anything, but for his work on tuberculin as an aid to diagnosis he was awarded the Parkes Weber prize in 1912.

It was suggested at the time that tuberculin might be used for treatment as well as for diagnosis, but its value was uncertain and some thought it was dangerous. Bardswell had used it on a few cases at Midhurst since 1908, but, appreciating that its use was controversial and that a properly conducted trial would sooner or later be asked for, he saw to it that reliable statistics were kept. Sir Bertrand Dawson had asked for a joint report in 1909 to throw light on this important and disputed question, but it was not until 1912 that the Consulting Staff as a body finally agreed that a systematic trial was necessary and instructed Bardswell and Radcliffe to conduct it jointly. Radcliffe had already visited various centres on the continent for which he had been granted 50 guineas (from the Research Fund which had recently been set up in 1906 with money donated by Mr. and Mrs. Henry Bishoffsheim). He had written a paper on what he had learned and asked for the Consultants' consent to publish it, but the Consultants at first refused to give their permission. Their grounds were that, as Radcliffe had been paid by the Sanatorium, the report should in the first instance belong to them, but they later relented and reversed their decision. Meanwhile the Bardswell-Radcliffe joint trial was continuing and a detailed report was prepared in 1913. This showed that tuberculin had limited application only in the treatment of pulmonary tuberculosis. Nevertheless, it continued to be used in selected cases until well into the 1930s when the newly appointed Superintendent, Dr. Geoffrey Todd, convinced of its lack of effect, ordered that the practice be terminated.

Edwardian Midhurst

In general, the pattern and tempo of affairs at Midhurst remained remarkably unruffled during the first few years of the Sanatorium's existence. As its reputation grew, so the number of applications for admission increased. The 30 patients originally in residence quickly became 70, and by March 1907 every one of its 100 beds was occupied, and a waiting list had to be started. The patients continued to be treated very much as they had been when Bardswell first expounded his ideas in June 1906. The staff changed but little. Life went on.

There was some difficulty to begin with in finding a chaplain for the Sanatorium, and pending the appointment of a clergyman, Dr. Bardswell was required to read the services. However, in April 1907, the Reverend Douglas Barton, the new vicar of Fernhurst, accepted the chaplaincy at an honorarium of £100 a year. In November of that year, the Executive Committee decided that the Chapel should be dedicated as soon as the vacancy in the See had been filled, and on Sunday, 28 June 1908, the service of dedication took place. At about the same time Dr. Bardswell was instructed by the

Committee that he or the acting Superintendent should attend the Sunday service regularly. (This injunction then became incorporated in the Rules for the Medical Superintendent.) All those patients fit enough to do so were also expected to attend. When the communion service was administered to patients, the Sacrament was received by intinction (the dipping of the bread into the wine). This practice had been initiated at Midhurst on Christmas Day 1906 by the late bishop as a precaution against the spread of infection, and the practice was continued for many years.

The monthly reports by the Visiting Consultants throw light on contemporary life at Midhurst. After Sir Hermann Weber visited in August 1906 he wrote, 'a landau would be much better than a motor for taking patients from Haslemere to Midhurst'. Sir Robert Douglas Powell, however, considered that 'the motor – if quietly driven' was better still. Another Consultant gave his approval to the motor being used for patients as long as it was fitted with a 'wind shield'. Sir Lauder Brunton remarked that he had greatly enjoyed the drive from the station and was impressed with the scenery and the driver's skill. Sir Kingston Fowler, on the other hand, complained bitterly about the car sent to meet him at the station. 'I feel obliged to record a rather decided protest against being required to use such a motor car as was sent to meet me at Haslemere. I think Consulting Staff should be conveyed in a car that is both comfortable and reasonably safe . . .'

Following complaints about noise at night, the Consulting Staff recommended in 1908 that greater attention should be paid by Medical Officers to their night rounds, in the course of which they should wear felt or india rubber slippers and always be accompanied by a nurse. This also became incorporated in the Rules for Medical Staff.

Sir Clifford Allbutt warned against 'letting the Sanatorium slide into complacency' and advocated 'all that science could achieve should be used to benefit the patients. The King's Sanatorium should be a centre or school from which advances in our knowledge and treatment of tuberculosis should continually flow'. The importance of achieving a high scientific output was emphasized by every Visiting Consultant and in 1908 Sir Felix Semon was able to report that, 'The Sanatorium has practically achieved the purposes for which it was founded, not only to restore health to its inmates, but to serve as a model for other Institutions'.

For the staff, medical, nursing and 'ancillary', living and working at the Sanatorium must have been a thoroughly satisfying and rewarding experience. Certainly there was no shortage of applicants to fill the posts. The wages were reasonable, the food plentiful and the accommodation adequate, if not luxurious. The routine was austere, but not harsh. Rules had to be observed, and discipline was strict, but imposed in so just a fashion that there was no bitterness. Rather, a spirit of service and loyalty to the Institution was kindled and fostered which has remained a feature at Midhurst ever since. Of course, as in most walks of life, there were those who rebelled or who would not conform, but these were few and far between and in general the atmosphere was happy and relaxed. One of the Sanatorium perquisites, dating from 1907, was that patients and staff could travel from London to Haslemere or Midhurst at concessionary fares (3s. 9d. on the London and South Western Railway); another that the Sanatorium motor car could be used to convey them to and from the station. Insurance and pension schemes were arranged and all Sanatorium employees (or servants as they were then described) were encouraged to make use of them. A recreation room and hard tennis court were provided for the staff and books were sent down to their reading room by the Chairman and members of the Committee. Once a week the servants could be taken out for drives in the motor if they so desired, and provided a servant stayed more than a month at the Sanatorium his railway fare home was paid one way. Insignificant benefits by today's standards, but they counted for much.

All the time the Sanatorium amenities were being improved. The establishment of a Post Office in the Sanatorium was sanctioned in August 1908 by the Right Hon. Sydney Buxton, the Postmaster General, after approaches by Lord Esher and, so it was always said, personal intervention by the King. Two deliveries and collections of letters on week days, and one on Sundays, were authorised. Telegrams could be sent (and received) from 1908 after a double wire had been laid between the Sanatorium and the Midhurst Post Office, but a telephone, with an extension system for the use of patients, was not installed until 1910. An organ with 'an electrical blowing apparatus' was installed in the Chapel in November 1906 and in 1911 a 24-inch bell, which had been selected by Dr. Hartley and Mr. Bailey after visiting a local foundry, was erected over the vestry.

Buildings, Gardens and Grounds

The structure of the building itself gave rise to concern in 1910 when dry rot was discovered in the eastern staircase. No sooner had this been eradicated than a more serious incident occurred. In 1912 a large part of the ceiling collapsed on to a patient's bed, happily not occupied at the time, and it was found that dry rot had spread to the ceilings of several floors in the patients' wing. The situation called for the summoning of Council to its first 'emergency' meeting, on 30 January 1912 (at H.M. Stationery Office, by permission of the Comptroller, Mr. R. Bailey), to consider what should be done. The floors had to be closed one by one so that the ceiling timbers could be replaced with fire resistant material, and the isolation block had to be taken into use to accommodate patients as they were displaced. In due course, the work was done (at a cost of £2,600, plus £1,200 for repairing the balconies) without it being necessary to send a single patient home.

Whilst the matter of dry rot was being dealt with, complaints were coming in from patients of unpleasant odours from the drains. A drainage expert recommended that the entire drainage system should be reconstructed, but he later agreed that modifications to the existing system would suffice and the work, at an estimated cost of £500, was put in hand accordingly, and completed 18 months later.

In 1909 the Chapel roof was found to be leaking. The Clerk of Works called in to investigate advised that the best method of dealing with the trouble would be to remove entirely the oak turret over the chancel and cover the space with lead. Sir John Brickwood, who had given money for the Chapel, sanctioned the removal of the tower if no alternative course was available, but he felt that to remove it might spoil the architectural effect. The Committee decided to leave the matter in abeyance – the leaks had already been sealed quite effectively with concrete – and the oak turret remains intact over the chancel to this day.

The discovery of dry rot, the defects in the drainage system and the leak in the chapel roof, all occurring so early in the Sanatorium's existence, caused something of a stir. The Executive Committee decided that an objective report on the general state of the buildings was called for and they invited Mr. Edwin Hall, an architect of distinction with experience of hospital building, to advise them. He very soon gained their confidence and in 1911 supplanted Mr. H. Percy Adams (the principal architect of the Sanatorium) as Consulting Architect to the Institution. He was to remain in this position until his death in 1923 when his son, Mr. Stanley Hall, succeeded him.

When the Sanatorium had been built, no provision had been made for the isolation of patients suffering from infectious diseases. In 1907, after a case of measles had occurred, the Consultants recommended that the top floor of the administration block be used to isolate infectious patients. If more than two cases appeared, they were to be isolated in tents erected in the grounds. A cottage in the grounds was next considered, after a case of diphtheria had occurred, but none suitable could be found. The Rural District Council was approached, but said it was not their responsibility to provide accommodation for such patients. The Executive Committee thereupon decided that the sanatorium would have to build its own isolation block and an estimate of £1,300 for the construction was accepted. The block was to consist of two sets of three isolation rooms, each with its own kitchen, bath and lavatory. In January 1910 the work was put in hand and a year later the building had been completed. The building was later used as overflow accommodation for tuberculosis patients when floors in the main building had to be evacuated to enable repair work to be done. It was never utilised fully for infectious cases and in 1934 it was converted for domestic use by Sanatorium staff.

At the time the Sanatorium was opened, the ground immediately around the building was still undeveloped and, beyond the immediate vicinity, trees, heather and scrub invested the area closely. The design of the gardens to the south of the building and between the administration and patients' blocks had been placed in the hands of Miss Gertrude Jekyll of Godalming who had worked in conjunction with Sir Edwin Lutyens. Together they had worked on some 120 houses; he planning the layout, paths and vistas, she the plantings. Here at Midhurst she was responsible both for the layout and the character of the gardens and provided many of the plants and shrubs herself. Under her direction, assisted by a couple of gardeners (one of whom was called Squelch!) and a number of patients, the gardens made steady progress, although two years were to elapse before there was enough grass on the lawns for games.

The gardens were built on terraces on several levels to the south of the main building, with stone walls separating one level from another. On these terraces, lawns and flower beds were laid out and shrubs, flowers and aromatic herbs planted. To the north, the pine trees came down much closer to the building than they do today with the result that the occupants of the north facing rooms complained that they were dark and damp. In 1911 these trees were thinned and cut back and the view northwards through the pine trees was established, but the present lawn (where the flagpole is situated) was not developed until after the Second War.

Fees, Finance, and the Royal Charter

Immediately before the Sanatorium opened, the fees which were to be charged were examined by a sub-committee which recommended that 'well-to-do' patients (of whom 12 were to be admitted) should be charged eight guineas a week and the 'necessitous' (of whom there would be 80) two guineas a week. For six months the two guineas and eight guineas rates were charged, but by November 1906 it was apparent that too few of the higher rate beds were being used and the decision was taken by the newly formed Executive Committee that no further high rate patients should be admitted and that the rooms hitherto reserved for them should be made available to all.

Sir Ernest Cassel had provided the King with the sum of £200,000 for the foundation of the Sanatorium, the building of which had cost something over £100,000, including the Chapel. Even after other expenses had been paid, there was still over £60,000 in reserve and the Advisory Committee were therefore not unduly concerned about the excess of expenditure shown at the end of the first working year. But as time went on the financial position did not improve and in 1912 Mr. Bailey, then a member of the Committee, drew up a statement which revealed a generally unsatisfactory state of affairs. Interest from invested reserves amounted to £2,500 per annum, yet the annual outgoings were never below £2,820. Hence the minimal annual deficit was £320 – and it would be considerably more, Mr. Bailey pointed out, if depreciation were to be taken into account (as the auditors advised) and more still if money were to be put aside, as it must be, for the replacement of boilers, motor cars, machinery and equipment. The matter was referred to Sir Ernest Cassel who stated that he could put the Sanatorium on a sound financial basis provided an extra 30 or 40 beds could be found. A plan was drawn up by the Consulting Architect, Mr. Edwin Hall, to provide accommodation for an extra 40 patients and 17 extra staff at an estimated cost of over £13,000. Sir Ernest Cassel seemed later to have changed his mind because at the first meeting of the new Council on 25 July 1912, the Chairman, Sir Frederick Treves, announced that it was not after all Sir Ernest's intention to supply funds for the work. The plan for extending the building had therefore to be abandoned and other means found to stabilise the financial   position.

The advice of Mr. Isodore Salmon was requested, he being a Director of Lyons and an expert in hotel management. He visited the Sanatorium with Mr. Bailey in November, weighed up the situation, and reported. Following his recommendations, measures were sanctioned in 1913 which were calculated to lead to a saving of £500 per annum. There was to be a reduction in some staff and the re-allocation of duties of others, the number of nursing staff was to be cut by two, the serving of meals was to be re-organised, and the quantity of milk provided for staff and patients to be reduced. Whilst these measures certainly helped, what really restored financial stability was a further endowment by Sir Ernest Cassel to the Sanatorium of £25,000 – a most generous donation which the Council accepted with gratitude at their sixth meeting on 24 April 1913.

The National Insurance Act of 1911 had important implications for the Sanatorium. Under the Act, it was necessary for any Institution desirous of admitting 'Insured' persons to obtain the 'approval' of a local government board. Dr. Bardswell informed Council in 1912 that there were several such insured persons who wished to be admitted. After advice from the Consultants, the decision was taken to approach the Board for the necessary 'approval' provided that assurance could be given that no restriction would be placed on Council's freedom to admit and treat patients as they wished. The Board gave the assurance asked for and the Sanatorium was accordingly 'approved' for a six month period from 15 July 1912 subject to agreement that the Board's Inspectors could visit at any time. The procedure was repeated at six monthly intervals for several years until there was no further necessity for doing so.

When King Edward died in 1910, an address of condolence was sent to the new King expressing sorrow and hoping that His Majesty would be pleased to take the same interest in the Sanatorium as the late King had done. To this King George replied in June 1910 that it would be his constant desire to promote the well being of all Institutions which had for their object the relief of suffering, but that this Sanatorium, so dear to his father's heart, would always have a special interest for him.

This assurance enabled the Executive Committee to take steps to place the position of the Institution on a more permanant basis. In July 1911 they decided that a petition should be made to His Majesty for the granting of a Royal Charter, the business in connection with which to be placed in the hands of a sub-committee headed by Sir Frederick Treves. The Charter was to provide, amongst other matters, for the management of the Sanatorium to be in the hands of a Council, and for a number of influential and well disposed persons to be on a list of 'Members of the Institution'.

The Charter stated that there should be a President and a Vice-President of the Institution who were to be the King himself and Sir Ernest Cassel and it laid down that the Council should consist of not more than ten members, of whom two were to be the President and Vice-President. The Council was to be subject to the paramount authority of the Institution and members of Council were ipso facto to be members of the Institution.

In June 1912, the King approved the names (listed in Appendix 2), and permitted the Executive Committee to call itself the Council, but it was not until January 1913 that the Royal Charter of Incorporation received the consent of the Privy Council.

Chapter III

The Great War and Afterwards: 1914-1924

The War

August 1914 found the Sanatorium totally unprepared for the outbreak of war. At the Council's last meeting in peace time, on 23 July 1914, domestic matters only were considered: the minutes reveal no inkling of impending crisis. Sir Francis Laking had died and a letter from his son was read thanking Council for their message of sympathy. A second assistant medical officer had been appointed. The cost of running the Sunbeam car for the first year amounted to 7.9 pence per mile (total miles run 9,509). Religious Services for Roman Catholic patients were approved. The Hon. Secretary, Dr. Hartley, gave notice that he would be abroad from 5 August to 7 September and Sir Rowland Bailey was appointed to act for him during his absence.

Great Britain declared war on 4 August, and on the afternoon of 6 August an emergency meeting of Council was held at Thatched House Lodge, Richmond Park (the home of the Chairman, Sir Frederick Treves, given to him on his retirement from practice by King Edward VII). Sir Rowland Bailey and Dr. Hartley had just returned from a visit to the Sanatorium where, with Dr. Bardswell, they had considered the situation at Midhurst in the light of the fact that the country was at war.

The position was that several of the staff had left, or were about to leave, to join the forces and that the supply of patients was likely to diminish if not cease altogether. Moreover, the principal contractors to the Sanatorium had written repudiating their contracts and there might be difficulty in maintaining the requisite dietary for the patients. Under the circumstances it was decided to close the Sanatorium temporarily and send home all the patients then in residence. The decision was made easier because most patients expected it, and many were already preparing to leave.

The plan proposed was that once all the patients had gone home, the Sanatorium would be left in the hands of Dr. Bardswell, the Matron, the Heads of Departments and a small caretaker staff, thus enabling the remainder to join up if they so wished. Places would be kept open for them on their return and their army pay would be made up to their previous salaries. Families who occupied cottages in the grounds would be permitted to stay there.

This historic decision, with its far reaching consequences, never had to be put into effect. As Sir Frederick Treves explained to Council when they met again on 29 October, the decision was rendered unnecessary by an act of extreme generosity by Lord Cowdray. In a letter to the Chairman dated 8 August he had written expressing his desire to be responsible for any extra expenses which might be incurred in keeping the Sanatorium open, this to continue until one month after peace had been arranged. Thus was the Sanatorium's future secured. A poignant reminder of the times is that on 29 October, the day the Council expressed their appreciation for Lord Cowdray's generosity, they were obliged also to express their sorrow over the death of his son killed fighting in France.

A second wartime emergency meeting of Council was held on 16 November to consider what response should be made to the War Office who had offered to take over the Sanatorium for the treatment of sick and wounded soldiers, accommodation for whom at the front had been exhausted. The proposal from the Army Medical Department was that the Sanatorium and all its staff might either be transferred lock, stock and barrel to the War Office, or that the building alone should be handed over and the present staff continue to work there as Sanatorium employees. The Council decided, in view of the national emergency, to accede to the War Office request, subject to the King's approval. The terms were that the War Office would take over the entire management of the Institution and all the Staff and be responsible financially for the upkeep and maintenance. The King gave his approval and Sir Frederick Treves wrote to the Director General, Army Medical Services (Sir Alfred Keogh), offering to hand the Sanatorium over to the Army.

On 10 January 1915, Sir Frederick Treves heard again from the War Office asking if the Army could now take up to 50 beds in the Sanatorium for cases of tuberculosis of the lung at a charge of £2 2s. 0d. a week for each patient. This was more acceptable to the Sanatorium than handing over the beds for the care of the wounded, because the special purpose for which the Sanatorium had been founded could be carried on without interruption, so Sir Frederick immediately responded in the affirmative without even calling a meeting of Council. He made the point also that the patients must wear khaki, not hospital blue. By the time the matter was reported to Council on 25 February 1915, the 50 army beds were already occupied under the aegis of the National Health Insurance Commissioners. The remaining 50 beds were retained for use by civilian patients, but owing to the administrative difficulty of segregating them by sex it was decided that lady patients could not in future be admitted. A month later, in March 1915, a further 20 beds were offered to the War Office for use by soldiers as it was proving impossible to fill the 50 civilian beds with male patients. The War Office accepted the offer and the 20 extra beds for soldiers were quickly occupied.

In May 1915, the National Health Insurance Commissioners informed the Sanatorium that in future soldiers discharged from the Army with tuberculosis could elect to be sent to hospitals near their homes. The consequence of this was that fewer soldiers would in future be sent to the Sanatorium and those soldiers already being treated at Midhurst would be transferred elsewhere. The Commissioners offered to send a few NCOs and men to the Sanatorium, but it was to be for short periods only and it was considered unlikely that as many as seventy beds would be required.

The Council thereupon decided to ask the War Office if their offer of the previous November, to take over the whole Sanatorium for wounded soldiers, still held. The Director General, Army Medical Services, now took the view that it would be impolitic to use Midhurst as a military hospital because the public might be concerned that wounded soldiers would contract tuberculosis, so the answer was 'No'. As soon as the Council heard this they decided that the Sanatorium should now revert to its original function of treating civilian patients of limited means, also those holding commissions in the Services, and the Honorary Secretary informed the Health Insurance Commissioners that the Sanatorium would be unable to admit NCOs and men as the Commissioners had proposed. At the same time, in May 1915, the Council decided that an advertisement should be sent to *The Times*, the *Morning Post*, the medical journals and to selected doctors announcing that the Sanatorium was reverting to its original function of admitting civilian patients. The War Office was again approached on the matter of admitting Officers discharged from the Army and the Navy with pulmonary tuberculosis and it was agreed that they could be admitted on a special form of medical certificate without examination in London by the Medical Superintendent and that the Local Authority would be responsible for the payment of the usual charges. In these ways the Sanatorium continued for the duration of the war to attract a sufficient number of patients to occupy all the beds, a waiting list had to be maintained, and a delay of several weeks was incurred before applicants could be admitted.

During the four years of war the Council continued to meet regularly at St James's Palace, their meetings usually being preceded by meetings of the House Committee composed of Sir Rowland Bailey, Mr. Murray and Dr. Hartley. The records demonstrate the comparative normality of life at Midhurst once the Sanatorium had reverted in 1915 to its pre-war role. Domestic and financial matters comprised most of the business. Only an occasional reference to this or that former employee having fallen in action draws attention to the grim reality of events in France.

In January 1915 there occurred an incident in which prompt action by the Chairman of the Council quickly put a stop to a story about the Sanatorium which might otherwise have been damaging. At a meeting of the West Sussex Insurance Committee a member criticised the Sanatorium, and her remarks were printed in the *Sussex Daily News* of 9 January. The paragraph was brought to the attention of Sir Frederick Treves who wrote to the newspaper saying:

> Sir, In your issue of 9th January there occurs the following paragraph:
> Lady Beaumont thought it might help a little if members knew that there was a gigantic white elephant of a Sanatorium at Midhurst, which was never quite full, and was not properly run for want of adequate funds. This enormous hospital was built by Sir Ernest Cassel at a cost of a quarter of a million. Most of the money was wasted on the building, and the upkeep was very expensive.
>
> In reply to this remarkable statement, may I say that the Sanatorium has only 100 beds, and is therefore not gigantic. It has done splendid work, and has been the greatest boon to a vast number of tuberculosis patients, as the Annual Reports amply demonstrate. It has been quite full since it opened, and is full now. Patients have to wait their turn for admission. It is very handsomely endowed, and has adequate funds. It did not cost a quarter of a million to build, and its upkeep is remarkably economic. - Yours, &c.

The Sanatorium finances during the war years were under constant review. In 1918, the Council was told by Sir William Peat, the Honorary Auditor to the Sanatorium, that the annual excess of expenditure over fees received amounted to over £2,000. In view of the fact that repairs to the building had been postponed as much as possible, and would have to be put in hand when the war ended, it was decided in July 1918 to raise the weekly charge per patient to £3 3s. 0d.

The composition of the Council changed little until 1918 when Sir Frederick Treves resigned, but the frequency with which members attended varied according to their war time engagements. It was because he had accepted an appointment at the War Office that Sir Frederick Treves felt obliged to seek the King's permission to resign his seat, and with it his position as Chairman of the Council. He was presented with an inscribed parchment in a silver cylinder recording his many notable services to the Sanatorium as a member of the Advisory Committee and later of the Council. His place as Chairman was taken by Sir Walter Lawrence, who had been a member since the Council had been first established under the Royal Charter in 1912.

Sir Walter was to remain Chairman until 1922 when he succeeded Sir Ernest Cassel as Vice President of the Sanatorium and the Institution, a position he was to occupy until his death in 1940. His place as Chairman of the Council was taken by Sir Courtauld Thomson who later became Lord Courtauld-Thomson and who continued as Chairman for no fewer than 32 years, the longest period that any person has ever occupied the position.

The Consulting Staff met formally on only three occasions during the war, in November 1914, October 1916 and February 1918. Whether the infrequency of their meetings was by design or accident is uncertain, but the records suggest that, at this time, the Consultants played a less influential part in Sanatorium affairs than they had in the past and were to do again in the future. Changes in the medical staff were made without reference to them. They were not consulted (at least there is no record of their having been consulted) when a temporary Superintendent was appointed to cover Dr. Bardswell's absence abroad on military service. When one of their number, Sir James Goodhart, died in 1916 it was the Council not the Consultants who decided that Dr. Samuel West and Sir John Broadbent should be appointed.

The Chairman of Council, Sir Frederick Treves, was, after all, a medical man of immense standing himself, and the Consultants appear to have been content to leave Council to proceed with the business of running the Sanatorium and to offer advice only on the rare occasions when they felt it necessary to do so. One of these was at their meeting in 1916 when they formally carried a motion that an X-ray apparatus should be provided as soon as possible. Council accepted the recommendation, but decided not to act upon it for the time being because war-time prices were so high. However, by February 1918, after further prodding by the Consultants, they decided to proceed with the purchase and install the set in the men's hydropathic room, but difficulties then arose over a permit to adapt the room and it was not until 1920 that the set was brought into use.

A second occasion was in February 1918 when they recommended that the 'operation' of artificial pneumothorax be adopted at the Sanatorium in carefully selected cases; and a third was when they advised the Council to submit the diet in use at the Sanatorium in 1918 to Professor Leonard Hill, F.R.S., (an expert in nutrition) in order to be satisfied that it was adequate. (His report showed that for the staff it was satisfactory, but that for the patients it needed revision.)

A matter in which the Consultants played a part was in persuading the Medical Research Council to grant funds for the furtherance of research at the Sanatorium. The sum of £100 was granted for Dr. Radcliffe to continue work on the detection of tubercle bacilli in the blood, and a similar sum to assist Dr. Bardswell in his research on the 'after histories' of patients who had passed through the Sanatorium since it opened in 1906. These grants were awarded annually and were subsequently raised to £200 a year on each project.

It can be assumed that the Consultants continued to visit the Sanatorium at monthly intervals, as they had before the war, but their reports must have been verbally expressed because only one, by Sir St Clair Thomson in July 1916, is still in existence. It reads:

> On July 1st I made my monthly visit to the Sanatorium and, as Sir J. Kingston Fowler [another member of the Midhurst Consulting Staff] is abroad with the Army at present, I send a few notes of my inspection of the Institution. Curiously enough, I accidentally met Sir J. Kingston Fowler last week in a Military Hospital in Rouen!
>
> The Sanatorium is going on as satisfactorily as usual. All the beds are full and, judging from the diminished number of 'bedders' and of laryngeal complications, the present set of patients are more promising cases than usual.
>
> The quality and quantity of food still maintains the high pre-war standard. Possibly the Council do not wish to depart from this, but it has occurred to me that there would be no harm done to the patients' physical welfare, and considerable benefit might accrue to their morale, if, in common with the rest of the kingdom, they were gradually accustomed to a simpler but equally nutritious dietary. They doubtless come from houses where the pinch of war is being felt and where some cheaper foods have been substituted for the usually extravagant and wasteful British cuisine. It is a pity that they should return to these homes with their expensive appetites untuned to the increased price of foods. A recent three weeks' tour in France has impressed me with the appetizing variety of the dietary in the French Hospitals compared with the solid monotony of the extravagant English camps. The keep of a patient in a French Military Hospital averages 2 fr 50 cs. per day: in the most luxurious it is 3fr 50cs. I do not know what the cost per head is in the British camp.
>
> At this time of year at Midhurst one is again struck with the absence of fruit and vegetables in the grounds. Such trees as gooseberries, plums and apples are not difficult to grow and tend: and rhubarb, onions, beetroot and lettuce will grow almost anywhere, even if neglected. The Sanatorium now supplies itself with fresh parsley, and even this must save the institution a few pounds every year. Surely, some economy could be effected by starting the growing of fruit and vegetables and the cultivation of them would be a source of great interest, an educational factor, and a healthy value to the patients.

The Council considered his report and decided that as there would be no loss in nutritive value, foreign and colonial meat of the best quality should be tried in place of the English and Scotch meat hitherto supplied. It was also decided that the kitchen garden should be extended in order that more vegetables could be grown.

While the composition of Council and Consulting Staff remained virtually unchanged throughout the war, the same could not be said for the resident medical staff. The Superintendent, Dr. Bardswell (who in 1914 had been awarded the Parkes-Weber prize for his essay on the therapeutic value of tuberculin), was granted a commission in the Royal Army Medical Corps in 1915 in order to take charge of a military hospital in Malta. Dr. Cockill, one of the assistant medical officers, was appointed Acting Superintendent in his place. Dr. Bardswell returned to the Sanatorium in December 1916 and Cockill reverted to his previous position; but in October 1917, Bardswell resigned to take up a new post as medical adviser to a London Insurance Committee and Cockill resumed duty as Acting Superintendent. Bardswell's departure was keenly felt, although Cockill proved to be a most successful substitute. Bardswell had been in office since before the Sanatorium had opened its doors to patients. His contributions to the advancement of medical knowledge had been considerable, his authority unquestioned. After his retirement, he received glowing testimonials from many of his patients and from the Consultants. The Sanatorium's debt to him was recognised by Council a few years later when he was appointed at their behest to the panel of Consultants in 1920. Apart from these changes at the top, there was a constant coming and going of junior medical staff: Dr. Radcliffe joined the Army in 1915 but his place as pathologist was not taken up until after the war.

There were changes also amongst the remainder of the Sanatorium staff. In December 1915 it appeared that, of the 21 members of the male staff, 12 were ineligible for service with the armed forces, including four who had been refused on medical grounds and two who were deemed essential for maintenance of Sanatorium services (the 2nd engineer and the Foden steam wagon driver). Three men were given permission to join the colours – Messrs. Newell, Moseley and Thayer. The Steward, Mr. Clarenbone, joined the Army as a private soldier in 1916, by which time conscription had been introduced. He returned safely from the war in 1919 and continued in the post of Steward until 1936 when he became responsible for the accounts only. During his absence, his duties at Midhurst were assumed by two ladies: first Miss Blanche Tucker and then Miss Marjorie Jacomb. Soon after being called up, Private Clarenbone wrote to ask whether Council would make up the difference between his army pay and his previous salary. The answer came back that since the introduction of compulsory service the Council were not allowed to make good any loss of income, but they would allow his wife and child to stay on in his flat in the Sanatorium. The Honorary Secretary was requested to point out to him that whilst in the Army he would be clothed and fed at Government expense and to that extent his personal expenses would be reduced!

The Chaplain, The Rev C. E. Hoyle, Vicar of Easebourne (who had succeeded Mr. Barton in 1913), resigned in 1917 and an ex-patient, the Rev. Alban Hope, was asked to accept the position temporarily until a permanent Chaplain could be found. He stayed for two years and was offered and accepted Dr. Bardswell's house to live in.

Matron of the Sanatorium at the start of the war was Mrs. Mary Hatchell. She was the last of the old style matrons who were not trained nurses. In May 1915 ill health forced her to send in her resignation, but Council would not accept it, giving her a further two month's sick leave instead. Heartened by this mark of confidence, she withdrew her resignation and returned as Matron in which capacity she remained in charge until 1919. She experienced considerable difficulty in finding and keeping nurses and maids, and even after nurses' wages had been raised in 1917 (to £30 per annum rising annually to a maximum of £36) there was still a shortage. In the end recourse was had to the expedient of engaging a number of uncertificated nurses, but for the duration of the war only.

Key members of the staff to continue working at Midhurst throughout the war included Mr. Oliver, the resident engineer, and Miss Ward, the head cook. Grant Hodder, the hall porter who had taken over from Barnes, the first to occupy the post, combined his portering duties with acting as sub-postmaster at the Sanatorium. He was replaced early in the war by a Mr. Caplin who came to grief in 1915 when he absconded with about £14 of Post Office funds and was imprisoned for three months! He was replaced by Mr. Tubb who was followed in 1915 by Mr. F. J. (always known as Bill) Mills, whose service was interrupted by periods of indifferent health, but who remained in post until after the end of the Second War. He retired in 1947 at the age of 71, a very well remembered and much loved figure who liked to play the part of unofficial 'host' from his position in the main hall. He greeted all new arrivals at the Sanatorium and was particularly solicitous of any who appeared to be shy or nervous.

The porters played an important part in the lives of patients and staff at Midhurst. Staff rules provided for doors to be locked at 10 p.m. and permits were required to return after that time. The night porter had a roving commission and would be at the main entrance to admit authorised late arrivals at the agreed time. Those who arrived more than a few minutes late could often find the porter had left, leaving them the problem of access. Movement between female and male sections of staff quarters was checked by three iron gates at strategic points in the basement and these were locked at 10 p.m.

Changing Times

There is nothing in the records to show how the Sanatorium celebrated the Armistice in November 1918. No doubt the occasion was marked by an outburst of rejoicing as spontaneous and enthusiastic as occurred elsewhere throughout the country, but the minutes merely record the facts that the Council and House Committee met on 22 November at St James's Palace as usual, and that ordinary financial and domestic matters were considered.

Apart from the appointment of Sir Walter Lawrence as Chairman in March 1918 when Sir Frederick Treves retired, the composition of Council had remained unchanged throughout the War until November 1918 when Mrs. Brinton, who had been Lady Visitor until then, was appointed a member. In November 1920, Sir Courtauld Thomson was appointed a member, but the next change did not occur until after the death of the Vice President, Sir Ernest Cassel, in October 1921. Although as Vice President he had played little part in Sanatorium affairs since 1912, he had been associated with the Institution since its inception. Indeed the Sanatorium owed its very existence to his generosity in having made funds available in the first place. On his death, Sir Walter Lawrence was appointed Vice President and Sir Courtauld Thomson became Chairman of the Council, a position he was to occupy for no fewer than 32 years. Other changes in the composition of the Council at this time were the resignation of Sir Evelyn Murray and the appointments of Sir John Brickwood as a member in 1921 and of Miss Edith Parry as full-time Secretary to the Council in 1922. She had previously been assistant secretary, but assumed the duties of full-time secretary when Sir Courtauld Thomson became Chairman.

Much of the Council's work in these early peace time years was concerned with making good the fabric of the buildings. No sooner had the war ended than it was decided to begin work on repainting all the patients' bedrooms in the Sanatorium, a much needed task which had been repeatedly put off until now. Reports from the Consulting Architect, Mr. Edwin Hall, on the state of the building and from the Consulting Engineer, Mr. Patey, on the engineering plant, showed that some work was needed there too, but on the whole the reports were reassuring. Building and plant had stood up remarkably well to the exigencies of war. Dry rot had been contained, but stonework had perished here and there, and water pipes had occasionally burst and now needed lagging. But the boilers and generating plant were sound, the central heating system was in good order, the lift and telephones were working, and wiring throughout was intact. The van bought for light loads had performed admirably and the 'motor' was running well, but the Foden steam wagon had to have its engine repaired during the war. Only one item of machinery needed urgent attention, the engines working the pumps in the pumping station, and the necessary repairs were put in hand right away.

With the return to normal conditions it was proposed that work be started on converting the men's hydropathic room into accommodation for the new X-ray set and by 1920 the work was finished and the X-ray department declared operational. In 1920, two staff cottages were built in the grounds. (The original proposal had been to construct six cottages and a working men's 'bothy' or hostel, but funds would not run to it and the plan had to be changed to something less ambitious.)

While the material alterations consequent upon the war were comparatively slight, changes amongst the staff were considerable. Not the least important of these was the appointment of a new Superintendent. In May 1919 Dr. Cockill* (who had been acting superintendent since Bardswell's departure) informed the Council that for reasons of health he was anxious to resign as soon as he could be replaced. The post of a permanent Medical Superintendent was advertised at a salary of £800 a year with annual increases to a maximum of £900. Applications poured in and the Council decided they should first be submitted to the Consultants so that a short list could be drawn up. In regard to this, the Council wished to emphasize to the Consultants their feeling that, while the new Superintendent should be a good physician, he must above all else be a capable administrator. In July 1919 a joint panel of Council and Consultants interviewed the short listed candidates and decided unanimously that Dr. H. O. Blanford, formerly a temporary Surgeon Lieutenant in the Royal Navy, should be recommended to Council as the most eligible candidate for the post. Amongst the other candidates, two in particular stood out: Dr. F. G. Chandler, who was later appointed to the Sanatorium Consulting Staff, and Dr. O. L. V. S. de Wesselow, who was in due course to become Professor of Medicine at St Thomas's Hospital. To have achieved selection in the face of such competition, Dr. Blanford must have impressed the selection panel very favourably. He was duly appointed and took up the post later in 1919.

The post of pathologist had still to be filled. After Dr. Radcliffe had joined the Army in 1915 his position as pathologist was left vacant until 1919. The post was then advertised in the usual way, but the first three applicants to be interviewed proved to be unsuitable, and it was not until later in the year (1919) that Dr. Baker was appointed. He remained in post until 1922 when he moved to another appointment and his place was taken by Dr. Miller.

After the war, the rest of the Sanatorium staff changed little, once those who had been serving in the armed forces had returned to their posts. In 1920, the Reverend F. R. Evans took over the chaplaincy from the Rev. Alban Hope, who had occupied the position since 1917. Mrs. Hatchell, who had been Matron since 1908, resigned in 1919 and her replacement, Miss Hilda Banbury, was Matron for only 15 months before she too submitted her resignation, her daily routine at Midhurst having been the subject of some criticism. She herself considered she had had too many duties to perform and when her resignation was received a small committee was appointed by the Council to examine her complaints and to consider the question of appointing an assistant matron. They found that her duties had indeed been exacting but that they should have been within the powers of one person. A new Matron, Miss Minnie Ethel Ruby Barr, was accordingly appointed in December 1920, but not, for the time being, anyone to assist her.

During the war, the Consulting Staff met as a body on only three occasions, but as soon as they had been released from their war-time commitments they became increasingly engaged in Sanatorium activities. Their first post-war meeting was in July 1919, when they short-listed the candidates for the posts of Medical Superintendent and Pathologist, and they met again three times in that year alone. Their main concerns were the selection of medical staff, the development of the X-Ray department and the organisation of research. On Sir William Osler's death in 1920, Dr. Mitchell Bruce, Chairman of the Consulting Staff, put forward four names for the vacancy thus created. Dr. Horton-Smith Hartley's was the first of these, but after he had signified that he did not wish to accept the post, Council offered it to Dr. Bardswell, who accepted. The other two, Sir Humphrey Rolleston and Dr. Perkins, joined the Consulting Staff in 1923 after the resignation of Dr. Acland and the death of Sir James Reid.

The position regarding X-rays in the Sanatorium was that in 1916 the Council had agreed that a set should be bought, but had decided to defer the issue until after the war when prices were likely to be lower. In 1918, however, they were persuaded by the Consultants to go ahead with the purchase of a set (at a cost of over £500), but it could not immediately be installed in the men's hydropathic room as planned because a war-time permit for the conversion could not be obtained.* By April 1919, however, building restrictions were lifted, work on converting the room was put in hand, and the set was eventually brought into use in May 1920. Meanwhile, the Consultants recommended that Dr. Ironside Bruce, a London specialist, be invited to supervise the work of installing the set and a year later, in 1919, he was appointed 'Honorary Radiographer' to the Sanatorium. (Only later was the term 'radiologist' used to denote medically qualified individuals.)

As soon as the X-ray set was in working order, it was decided by the House Committee that X-ray pictures should only be taken in special cases, and it was left to the Medical Superintendent to decide which these should be. Dr. Ironside Bruce died in 1921 and was replaced by Dr. Hugh Walsham who made several changes in the department including the introduction of new safety measures and provision for a trained engineer to take X-ray films under medical direction.

In February 1918, at their third and last war-time meeting, the Consulting Staff had recommended that 'the operation of artificial pneumothorax be adopted at the Sanatorium in carefully selected cases'. This was a decision of the greatest significance because the procedure represented the most important single advance in the treatment of tuberculosis since the concept of Sanatorium treatment in the early part of the century. The acting superintendent, Dr. Cockill, had written a paper on the subject and to him was accorded the privilege of carrying out the procedure at Midhurst. He was empowered by the Council on 22 February 1918 to perform the operation and to do the subsequent refills, but no patient was to be operated on, except in cases of extreme urgency, without previous reference to a member of the Consulting Staff. As it was appreciated that X-rays would be a great help in connection with the operation, the Council resolved at the same time to install an X-ray set (thus reversing their previous decision to postpone purchase until the conclusion of the war).

On the subject of medical research, the Chairman of the Consulting Staff Committee, Dr. Mitchell Bruce, represented medical opinion in a report to Sir Walter Lawrence in 1920 outlining the ways in which the Sanatorium might remain in the forefront of medical thinking. Apart from research into X-ray appearances and their correlation with the physical signs, a proposal which Council had perforce to reject on the grounds of expense, the report suggested that further investigation might be undertaken into the relationship of diseases of the throat and nose with pulmonary tuberculosis. This project was dear to Sir St Clair Thomson's heart – he had been working on the idea for 10 years – and Council were able to approve that £50 be granted for him to complete the study. A statistical enquiry into the hereditary factors in the transmission of pulmonary tuberculosis was another aspect of research advocated in the report and a grant in aid was obtained from the Medical Research Council. The report went on to suggest that in the development of tuberculosis the 'medical officers should note the presence or absence of glandular tuberculosis and pay particular attention to the question of antecedent pleurisy'. Finally, the report recommended that as Dr. Blanford had amply proved his competence he be authorised to induce artificial pneumothorax whenever he considered it was necessary, without first having to seek agreement from a member of the Consulting Staff.

The Council agreed with the recommendations of the Consulting Staff and the course was thus set for the advances in treatment and furtherance of medical research which were to mark the inter-war years at Midhurst.

Blanford's departure

Dr. Blanford's term of office as Medical Superintendent lasted nearly five years, from July 1919 to May 1924. It was a period marked by considerable medical progress and the inauguration of a number of medical research schemes, but otherwise it was an uneventful if not a particularly happy chapter in the Sanatorium's history. A visit by King George V in July 1920 provided everyone at the Sanatorium with a welcome break from routine affairs and His Majesty expressed himself as much pleased with all he saw. In May 1920, arrangements were made for the Ministry of Pensions to refer patients to the Sanatorium, and 30 beds were reserved for them. Preference was to be given to officers and nurses referred in this way, and the Ministry was told bluntly that the arrangements gave 'their officials no right of entry, control or interference'. New patients from the Ministry of Pensions notwithstanding, too few patients of the kind for which the Sanatorium had been designed were being admitted, namely 'educated persons of limited means suffering from pulmonary tuberculosis at an early stage'. The Council sought to rectify this by mounting what today would be described as a publicity exercise. On the basis of a memorandum from Dr. Blanford, a leaflet was prepared pointing out the aims of the Sanatorium and the advantages of Midhurst. This was enclosed in the Annual Report and a further 2,000 copies were sent to selected medical practitioners in England and Wales. A few months later the fees paid by patients, which had been raised to four and half guineas a week in 1921, were reduced to four guineas a week at which level they were to remain until May 1939.

Meanwhile life at the Sanatorium went on in its normal quiet way and the administration concerned itself with mainly domestic issues. To prevent dust, a new method of room cleaning was introduced using damp dusters and sawdust. The patients' diet was revised, the milk ration reduced and butter substituted for margarine. Experiments with a 'listening in' apparatus in the lounge were carried out and a four-valve Siemens wireless set with loud speakers was procured at a cost of £140. A proposal to change from coal to oil fuel boilers was not sanctioned: coal continued to be used to fuel the boilers until 1958. The question was raised at a meeting of Council whether to allow maids to go to dances at Midhurst lasting until 1.00 a.m. Council decided not to allow it because it would create a dangerous precedent.

The original Foden steam wagon, which had needed extensive repairs during the war, finally broke down in 1923 and had to be replaced. The Consulting Engineer, Mr. Patey, was of the opinion that another Foden steam wagon capable of eight m.p.h., faster than the original, would be most suitable for Sanatorium work and a five-ton model was purchased accordingly.

As Medical Superintendent, Dr. Blanford was undoubtedly saddled with a great many duties of a kind which would these days be undertaken by non-medical men or secretaries. He was asked to report on the condition of the entrance drive, and he read the meteorological instruments. He inspected the meat, he looked into the filing system. He supervised the cooking and serving of meals. In effect, he was responsible to the Council for everything that went on at the Sanatorium, medical as well as domestic. He was a firm disciplinarian and his manner was brusque and dictatorial. He was the first Medical Superintendent to insist on being present at Council meetings, his predecessor having had to sit in an outside room until summoned. But he got his way only by being blunt to the point of rudeness with the Chairman, Sir Walter Lawrence, and this more than robust attitude was to cost him dear because he lost friends in high places who might have helped him when things began to go wrong.

He had brushes with authority on several occasions, the first being in May 1921 when two patients complained to Sir Walter Lawrence about the Superintendent's rude and overbearing manner. On being shown their letter, Dr. Blanford denied the charges of rudeness and claimed that other patients had found his manner admirable in every way. Nevertheless, the Council found some grounds for the allegations made and the Chairman wrote to Blanford to point out that his attitude and manner left something to be desired. Sir Walter went further. He said the Council would like to see more 'brightness, happiness and sympathy' introduced to the Sanatorium and he urged the Superintendent to consider these points in his attitude towards the patients.

After this, Blanford's relations with the Council improved, but in 1923 further misunderstandings arose, this time with the Consulting Staff. The row was over Professor Dreyer's new vaccine which was to be tried out at Midhurst. The Medical Research Council would not release the vaccine for trial until they had approved the scheme. The Consulting Staff had drawn up the plan for the trial and left it with Blanford to send on to the MRC. Unfortunately, he forgot to do this, and months of inaction passed before the error was discovered. Blanford accepted responsibility for the delay and took the blame, but there were other aspects of his administration which concerned the

the blame, but there were other aspects of his administration which concerned the Consultants. It was alleged that he took no interest in research, that he had lost the confidence of his juniors and the respect of his patients, and that his discipline was too severe. The Consultants therefore wrote to the Council to say that they were not altogether satisfied with his management as Superintendent and recommended that he be informed of their concern before being re-appointed at the next annual selection. On receiving this information, Blanford demanded to know in what way his administration had failed. An exchange of correspondence followed, all in the politest terms, and Blanford was told that while it was recognised that he had devoted himself wholeheartedly to his duties it was felt that a change of Superintendent was desirable. So Blanford was asked to go, but at least he was given time to apply for another post before he left. His letter of resignation was dated 24 March 1924, but that was not quite the end of the matter. Blanford wrote again to the Chairman (Sir Courtauld Thomson) on 30 March stating that one of the assistant medical officers (Dr. Vesselovsky) had apparently known about the Council's intentions before he had been informed himself. Nevertheless, Blanford's letter of resignation was accepted, and with it letters from the Matron and the Senior Sister who both resigned in sympathy with the Superintendent.

A report to Council in August 1924 written by a former Superintendent, Dr. Noel Bardswell, reveals the tension underlying recent events at Midhurst and shows the sort of difficulties the new Superintendent was going to have to contend with.

> I went down to the Sanatorium on Saturday August 9th returning on the following Sunday afternoon. The Sanatorium and grounds, as usual, gave a most favourable impression. So far as I could judge, the patients are being treated skilfully. The atmosphere at the Sanatorium is bad. Recent events have left much ill feeling: Sanatorium patients are self-centred, and Sanatorium life tends to aggravate any cause for unrest, gossip and intrigue. Such causes are present, and that they are producing the wonted result is obvious. My impressions are that there is a considerable amount of sympathy for Dr. Blanford, as a man of good intentions who has come to grief. This sympathy is associated with a strong antipathy to Dr. Vesselovsky, who is credited with consistent and brazen disloyalty to his former chief, Dr. Blanford. I have no doubt that there are among the patients active partisans of both Medical Officers. This factional strife is most unwholesome. Admirers of Dr. Blanford among the patients and staff fear and suspect victimisation at the hands of Dr. Vesselovsky. My impressions of Dr. Vesselovsky in his present frame of mind are unfavourable. Dr. Vesselovsky was appointed Acting Superintendent when Blanford left the Sanatorium in May. He had applied for the permanent post when it was advertised in May, but Dr. Trail was selected. He has suffered a bitter disappointment, and perhaps it is too much to expect of him any cordial sentiments towards the Sanatorium governing body. Of one thing I am confident, namely, that Dr. Vesselovsky is a bad influence in the Sanatorium, and that the loyal and friendly co-operation of all members of the staff, which is essential for smooth administration, will not be attained so long as he is in residence. To turn to pleasanter matters. The newly appointed Matron struck me as having the qualifications, tact and character, necessary for her important post. I shall be surprised if she is not a success. Her also I liked.

Thus ended an unhappy episode in Midhurst's history.

Chapter IV

From Twenties to Thirties: 1924-1934

A Fresh Start

Dr. Bardswell's letter to the Council, reproduced at the end of the last chapter, reveals only too clearly the unsettled atmosphere prevailing at Midhurst at the time of Blanford's resignation in March 1924. Things were not much better in the months which followed. Although Dr. Cockill, who had acted as Superintendent during the war, offered to stand in until a new man could be appointed, the job of acting superintendent went to the first assistant, Dr. Vesselovsky. He obviously had hopes of succeeding eventually to the permanent post, but these were to be dashed when the selection panel turned him down in favour of an outside man – Dr. R. R. Trail. In his disappointment, Vesselovsky complained openly of the treatment he had received from the Council and the Consulting Staff and exerted such a disruptive influence that the Council determined that he should go before Trail arrived.

Dr. Trail, a graduate of Aberdeen University, was 30 years of age when he was selected for the position of Medical Superintendent. He had served as a gunner officer in the war and had been awarded the Military Cross. He had been Resident Medical Officer and Registrar at the Brompton Hospital before coming to Midhurst and was one of 24 applicants for the appointment when it was advertised in May 1924. With three other short-listed applicants (of whom Vesselovsky was one) he was interviewed on 20 June and selected for the appointment which carried a salary of £1,000 a year, rising to £1,200. As he had no previous experience of sanatorium methods, he was given two months training on full pay before taking up the appointment in order to visit other sanatoria and study their methods. He visited Aberdeen, Banchory, Mundesley and Copenhagen, amongst others, before arriving at Midhurst in September 1924. He found an almost entirely new staff to meet him. Both assistant medical officers (Vesselovsky and MacCabe) had departed and been replaced by new men – Dr. Jupe and Dr. Yell. Of the doctors, only Miller the pathologist remained, and as things turned out he was not to remain in post much longer.

The Matron and the Assistant Matron were also new. The former, Miss Hope Stewart, had already been appointed, but had not yet arrived. The latter, Miss Maude Butler, had been at Midhurst only three months. She had been appointed senior sister after her predecessor had resigned in sympathy with Blanford. Now her position as Assistant Matron had been confirmed, but she was new to Midhurst and its ways. The other senior sisters, most of whom had been sympathetic to Blanford in his misfortune, remained on duty at the Sanatorium.

Trail's first task on taking up his new post was to restore morale. He did this by establishing his authority on the staff, medical and 'lay,' and by identifying himself closely with all that was best in the Midhurst tradition. First, with the full authority and the assistance of the Consulting Staff, he re-defined the Midhurst 'Routine'. This routine, similar to the Standing Orders which regulate life in the Army, had been allowed to lapse and patients were complaining about their treatment or that they had not been visited by the Superintendent. All this was to change. The 'routine' itself was not much altered, but Trail saw to it that the rules were observed, particularly those relating to doctors' visits. He made a point of seeing every patient himself once a week and bed patients every day. As to his relations with the non-medical staff, these were improved by his insistence on seeing Heads of Departments at a set hour every day, visiting the kitchen and other departments, as well as the wards, regularly and inspecting the meat and stores daily.

Next, again with the authority of the Consulting Staff, he examined and amended the system of 'grading' which had been an issue of contention when Blanford had been in charge. Once again it was not the system which was changed so much as the manner in which it was applied. The heavier grades of work in the garden could still be given to patients at the discretion of the Superintendent, but they were not to be imposed, and patients who preferred walking were to be permitted to take their exercise in that way.

Trail then set before the Consulting Staff some of his ideas on medical practice generally and the management of tuberculosis in particular. He drew up new medical history sheets and charts; he sought and obtained authority to X-ray every patient in the Sanatorium at least once; he was authorised by the Consulting Staff to prepare a full report on the new vaccine (the trial of which had been conducted at Midhurst under Blanford), he reported to the Consulting Staff on the visits he had made to various other sanatoria and commented perceptively on the good results he had seen following the operation of thoracoplasty as carried out at Copenhagen. (This was the first mention made of this operation at the Sanatorium.)

Trail undoubtedly made an excellent impression at the Sanatorium. Writing at the end of December 1924, Professor Bulloch reported: 'I formed the opinion during my visit that the Sanatorium is in a more satisfactory state as regards general working than it has been for a long time'. But there were still difficulties to be overcome, particularly over certain members of staff. The pathologist, Dr. Miller, although he had been most favourably reported on when he was first appointed in December 1922, soon ran foul of Trail, who quickly formed the impression that he suffered from 'an aversion to hard work', a defect for which he had no sympathy. The two never saw eye to eye. The Chairman of the Consulting Staff warned Miller in February 1925, but he never changed his ways and in October 1925 the Consulting Staff decided he must go. He was replaced in January 1926 by Dr. Yell who had been second assistant to Trail since he had first arrived at Midhurst. Yell was succeeded as pathologist by Dr. Doris Stone and she by Dr. Sybil Robinson. In 1931 Dr. Godfrey Garde was appointed.

Trail was always fully supportive of the nursing services at Midhurst, although critical of some of the older sisters. In January 1925 he proposed a reorganisation of the establishment so that, in addition to the Matron, who was henceforward always to be fully nurse trained, there should be an Assistant Matron, who was to be a trained housekeeper and dietitian (but not necessarily nurse trained), three ward sisters, three staff nurses and six uncertificated nurses, preferably V.A.D.s (Voluntary Aid Detachment). The adoption of this scheme was to involve the replacement of most of the old staff of 11 ward and relief nurses by a smaller number of higher paid but 'certificated' sisters and staff nurses, supplemented by a body of V.A.D.s. There was an outcry from the nurses when the proposals were made known. Most of them had been employed since 1908 so their opposition to the scheme was understandable, but Trail was adamant: there must be changes. 'A change is necessary for the efficient working of the Institution', he said in a letter to the Council. 'The majority of the nurses have been resident for some years. They have become too settled and seem to have forgotten that the Sanatorium is for patients and not for staff. They refuse to take responsibility under the plea that they are Staff Nurses: one might forgive this, but not their lack of interest in their patients: for example, on a day of heavy rain they require to be ordered to see that the rain is not blowing in onto patients' beds.'

The Council approved the new scheme in January 1925 and authorised Trail gradually to dismiss the present staff and to recruit the new staff as required. He had difficulty in finding a sufficient number of new staff at the rate of pay offered and eventually he had to retain the services of three of the old staff nurses whose work had improved. By February 1926, he had succeeded in obtaining all the nurses and sisters authorised a year previously, and two more. But this was not all. In 1932 he declared that the Sanatorium needed an additional four nurses who should be properly instructed in the management of tuberculosis and who should take the examination for the certificate of competence offered by the British Tuberculosis Association. Council gave their approval and the extra four nurses were found and trained. Nor was their welfare overlooked. No suitable superannuation scheme had previously been available for nurses. Trail suggested that one be introduced at Midhurst and in 1933 his proposal was accepted and acted upon.

Council, Consulting Staff and Superintendent

In October 1928, four years after Trail had assumed the duties of Superintendent, the Council recognised his services to the Institution by deciding to make him a grant of £300 for a motor car and £50 a year towards its upkeep, this to be regarded as 'personal to Dr. Trail'. Three years later the Chairman stated at a meeting of the Council in February 1931 that he had inspected the Sanatorium and 'could not find the slightest defect in any department, that the discipline was excellent, that the patients were happy and that he wished to place on record his high opinion of Dr. Trail's efficiency . . . and the favourable influence of his personality'.

The Council itself, under the Chairmanship of Sir Courtauld Thomson, underwent several changes during the 'twenties and early 'thirties. Sir Rowland Bailey resigned in October 1924 and Sir Richard Douglas Powell a year later. Lt. General Sir John Goodwin, formerly Director General of the Army Medical Services, served on the Council for two years from June 1925 until his appointment as Governor of Queensland. (He was invited to serve again in 1932 but had to decline.) When Sir Richard Douglas Powell resigned in 1925, his son Colonel Douglas Powell joined the Council and in December 1925 the recently appointed Chairman of the Consulting Staff, Sir Hector Mackenzie, was invited to serve. Sir George Truscott and the Hon. Mrs. Macdonald-

Buchanan joined the Council in 1928. In 1929, after the death of Sir Hector Mackenzie, Sir John Broadbent, as the new Chairman of the Consulting Staff, was invited to serve on the Council. (This was the same Broadbent who, as Secretary to the original Advisory Committee, had visited many of the prospective sites for building the Sanatorium.) Lord Cowdray, who had for many years been a member of Council and who had generously offered at the beginning of the war to defray the costs of the Sanatorium, died in 1927, and his son, the second Lord Cowdray, accepted an invitation to join in 1929. In the same year Lady March resigned as Lady Visitor. In 1931 the Council consisted of Sir Courtauld Thomson (Chairman), Sir Walter Lawrence, Sir John Brickwood, Sir John Broadbent, Lord Cowdray, The Hon. Mrs. Macdonald-Buchanan, Colonel Sir Douglas Powell and Sir George Truscott.

There was a period in the mid 'twenties when Council meetings were very sparsely attended and sometimes only three members were present besides the Chairman; but, after the House Committee had been discontinued (in October 1925), meetings were better attended. With the demise of the House Committee, Council members found themselves having to deal with a mass of finicky detail on domestic issues, but they dealt with them effectively and the Sanatorium continued to develop and thrive. Staff accommodation was improved, the entrance drive was widened, the forecourt reconstituted, a new lounge created by enlarging the corridor connecting the administrative with the patients' blocks. The amenities were improved by installing a cinema apparatus in the dining hall in 1927 – a 'talking apparatus' was added later in 1931 – and an automatic telephone was put in in 1931. Electric bells and wireless earphones for the patients were installed in 1928. Char-a-banc trips for patients and staff were made available in 1927. The gardens, the croquet lawns, the 'mashie' golf course and the hard tennis court all had to be kept in good order. The kitchen garden flourished. The pig and poultry farms continued to function, although on occasion they came in for a measure of criticism from the Chairman on grounds of being 'insanitary, untidy, inefficiently run, and brought no credit on the Sanatorium'. However, they kept the Sanatorium supplied with plenty of fresh eggs and pork, and all at a fraction of the market cost. The buildings themselves had to be maintained, and the old problem of dry rot, thought to have been eradicated totally after the war, reasserted itself from time to time – a roof timber here, a window frame there – but happily never to any serious extent. In 1928 great difficulty was encountered in finding a sufficient number of female domestic servants owing, it was believed, to the isolated position of the Sanatorium, although fear of contracting tuberculosis must also have been a deterrent. Recourse was had to the novel expedient of substituting male servants for female, and providing the new staff with re-built accommodation. The scheme had been adopted at Cheltenham College junior school where, said a member of Council, it had proved to be successful, and so it seems to have been at Midhurst although the arrangement was not continued for long.

In 1933, the Consulting Engineer, Mr. Patey, reported to the Council that the Foden steam wagon which had been in use for 10 years was in need of repairs which might cost anything between £100 and £150. At the same time he drew Council's attention to the high transport costs incurred by the Sanatorium and suggested that £300 might be saved annually if the Foden were sold and the heavy transport details put out to private contractors. The Council agreed. Tenders from various contractors for moving coal, manure, etc, were accepted; the Foden was sold (for £10!) and one of the two men employed on the Foden, Moseley, being 'a good servant to the Sanatorium' was found other work on the premises. (The other man, Boswell, was found a job elsewhere.)

But not all the Council's work was humdrum. They made the arrangements for a visit to the Sanatorium by the King in May 1929; they were always in charge of the financial situation; they appointed trustees to the Thornton's Will Trust, later to become the Florence Josée Fund, which was used for the benefit of needy ladies in the Sanatorium; they managed the Benevolent Fund, which had lain dormant since the war (until the Medical Superintendent induced them to resuscitate it), for the benefit of patients who could not afford to remain at the Sanatorium. It was the Council who in 1927 enquired of Sir George Lewis, their legal advisor, if it might be possible to modify the bye-law governing the use of the Corporate Seal. And it was they who had to accept the advice Sir George gave that the 'Privy Council would not be inclined to facilitate use of the Seal in too easy and informal a way'.

In February 1932, after the death of Sir John Brickwood who had been a member of Council since 1921, it was thought desirable to increase the number of members of Council from ten (including the President) to fifteen. This would have necessitated amendment of the Charter and the legal advisors (Messrs. Lewis and Sons) were asked to obtain approval of the Lords of the Privy Council to the changes. Council were advised that the approximate cost of increasing their numbers would be £130 and as there were two vacancies already on the Council it was decided to make no alterations for the time being. The vacancies on the Council were filled by Sir Felix Cassel, a nephew of Sir Ernest Cassel, and, three years later in 1935, by Mr. B. A. Salmon.

Meanwhile, the Consulting Staff had become increasingly active in Sanatorium affairs, and not only in purely medical matters. In 1925 and 1926, they complained time and time again to the Council about the unsatisfactory domestic and housing arrangements made for the medical and nursing staff, but it was in medical matters that their influence was paramount. At that time, the Consulting Staff included in their number some of the most distinguished figures in the medical profession. During the successive chairmanships of Dr. Mitchell Bruce, Sir Hector Mackenzie and Sir John Broadbent, Sir Humphrey Rolleston joined the staff and he was followed by Dr. (later Sir) Robert Young and, in November 1928, by Mr. A. Tudor Edwards, a pioneer of chest surgery. In 1931 the list of Consultants on the Staff read like a page from medical history: Sir John Broadbent, Dr. Noel Bardswell, Professor William Bulloch, Dr. Frederick Chandler, Professor Lyle Cummins, the Rt. Hon. Lord Dawson of Penn, A. Tudor Edwards Esq., Dr. Stanley Melville, Sir Humphrey Rolleston, Sir St Clair Thomson, Dr. R. A. Young and Dr. Lancelot Burrell. Their names resound like a clarion.

Several changes of staff occurred. In 1931 the Bishop of Chichester wrote to the Chairman of Council to say that he thought he could find a more suitable man than the incumbent (the Rev. F. R. Evans) for the post of Chaplain. In this way the name of the Rector of Tillington, the Rev. F. H. Campion, came to the notice of Council, and in 1932 he was officially appointed Chaplain to the Sanatorium, a post he held until 1938. Miss Parry, Secretary to the Council, left in 1932 and in her place was appointed Captain A. H. Arnold, Secretary to the Chairman (Sir Courtauld Thomson). He was appointed for one year, stayed in post for 18 and saw the Council through the 1939-45 war, and beyond.

With Dr. Trail as Medical Superintendent, both Council and Consultants found their work became immeasurably easier. Trail generally accepted their advice and carried out their instructions without fuss or argument. Yet he had a mind of his own and maintained discipline within the Sanatorium with a softer yet more certain touch than had his predecessor. Eminently practical in his approach to everyday problems, he never lacked for new ideas. One is constantly struck by the references in the Sanatorium records to plans or proposals put forward in the first instance by the Medical Superintendent. Once he had established himself at Midhurst, and the wrangling and unhappiness of the Blanford era had abated, the Sanatorium quickly regained the hopeful and cheerful atmosphere which had previously characterised it.

Very soon after Trail had arrived one of the ward maids died from tuberculosis, apparently contracted from a patient. One of his first tasks therefore was to revise the methods for preventing cross infection and to ensure that they were correctly applied. Then he had to rectify faults in the system of measuring and recording the rainfall and sunshine, details of which had to be sent regularly to the Meteorological Office. He made one of the assistant medical officers responsible for this, but soon decided it was a task which could more appropriately be carried out by the head gardener!

Of course his duties were not all so mundane. He was an active clinician and interested himself in the research programmes which were being conducted at Midhurst at the time. He was an ambassador too. The Council and Consultants encouraged him to attend as many meetings as possible of the Tuberculosis section of the British Medical Association and to act as delegate for the Sanatorium at all gatherings of the National Association for the Prevention of Tuberculosis.

In the winter of 1926, Trail visited various sanatoria in Switzerland and his subsequent report to the Council showed the poor impression he gained. 'I tried to view treatment in Switzerland with an open mind', he wrote, 'but on the whole I am very disappointed. In my opinion, the buildings generally are unsuitable, the nursing wholly inadequate, and the disciplinary side of treatment hopelessly bad ... I could not avoid the conclusion that Tuberculosis is a trade ... I saw very little provision for nursing; one Sanatorium with fifty patients has one day nurse and no night nurse ... as things are at present, the only case that will do well in Switzerland is the case that is already cured.' Clearly, Switzerland had nothing to offer.

Soon after being appointed, Trail sought Council's advice regarding his position when asked to visit ex-patients in their own homes. The Council authorised him to visit them if necessary and to carry out their pneumothorax refills, but no fee was to be charged for his services. In 1926 he was empowered to dismiss patients when he considered it necessary, an authority not granted his predecessors but one which Trail considered essential for the preservation of good discipline. He did not often exert these powers, but in 1930 four patients were dismissed on one day for breaking the rules. Later he was given authority to refuse admission to any patient he considered to be ineligible or unsuitable, even if admission had been recommended by a member of the Consulting Staff.

Trail was naturally anxious to advance himself in his profession and he asked for (and was granted) a day off every week to visit one of the London Hospitals – often the Brompton. In 1930 he succeeded in passing the examination for membership of the Royal College of Physicians.

In February 1927, he informed the Council that he had been offered a post at another sanatorium at a higher salary. This gentle pressure was rewarded by an increased salary (£1,200 from £1,100 a year) on condition he remained at Midhurst for a further three years. He repeated this tactic in 1932 and his salary was again raised (by a further £250) and he was permitted to undertake local consultant work as long as it did not interfere with his work at the Sanatorium.

Trail's last contributions to the Sanatorium before moving on to another appointment in London in 1934 were to press for yet more nurses on the staff and to play a large part with Mr. Tudor Edwards in drawing up plans for the new surgical wing, which was to be built after he had left.

In the autumn of 1933 he tendered his resignation which the Council accepted in October. He had done a great deal for the Sanatorium during his nine and a half years in office and, rightly, received the thanks of the Council, the Consulting Staff, the Sanatorium Staff and, perhaps even more importantly, of the many patients who had passed through his hands; but he had built up a considerable private practice of his own, locally and in London, and discipline at the Sanatorium was beginning to suffer. It was felt, therefore, that the time had come for a change at the top.

Medicine and Research

In the 1920s, Midhurst still regarded itself as primarily a centre for the 'open air' treatment of tuberculosis, and in this it was pre-eminent, but the Consulting Staff were determined that the Sanatorium should not lose ground by failing to take advantage of any therapeutic advances that might be made elsewhere. When the potential value of gold as a possible cure was announced, the Consultants advised that it be taken into use at Midhurst forthwith; but they were less ready to adopt unproven remedies. When a well known expert on tropical diseases, Sir Leonard Rogers, suggested that the Sanatorium might try out chaulmoogra oil, the idea was politely (but firmly) rejected. A measure much in vogue at the time as a supplement to open air and bed rest was the use of artificial sunlight. The Consulting Staff advised Council to send the Medical Superintendent to other sanatoria in this country and abroad to study their methods and evaluate their results. They were impressed by Trail's reports and particularly with his report of Sir Henry Gauvain's work with the Finsen lamp at Alton, and in 1926 artificial sunlight was introduced at Midhurst for patients with laryngeal tuberculosis and selected cases of pulmonary tuberculosis. A Danish nurse even came over from Denmark to instruct the Midhurst Staff how to use the Finsen lamp! Artificial sunlight was used at the Sanatorium for some years, but the results never came up to expectation and after 1931 the method was discontinued except for occasional cases of surgical tuberculosis.

Meanwhile, research in other fields had not been neglected. A long term follow up of all the patients who had been at the Sanatorium was continued, regrettably without the financial aid from the Medical Research Council which had been hoped for.* A report was published on the experience of patients at Midhurst with particular reference to their mortality after treatment. Trials were carried out on animals of injecting bovine tubercle bacilli (to discover if they would infect the lungs) and a trial on the effects of Hydnocarpic Acid by inunction (rubbing through the skin) was conducted. Although neither trial revealed anything of significance, they did show that research still played an important part in medical life at Midhurst. The investigation by Professor Karl Pearson into the hereditary factors involved in the cause of tuberculosis was continued, and the schedules of over 400 patients treated at Midhurst were tabulated.

Lung collapse therapy by artificial pneumothorax had been used since 1918 at Midhurst by Cockill and Blanford and was a well established form of treatment by the time Trail came on the scene. The results were excellent and Trail published the results of 25 cases he had treated at Midhurst, this work further enhancing the Sanatorium's growing reputation, and his own.

In March 1930 the Consulting Staff recommended that a new X-ray set and couch should be obtained and that the Medical Superintendent should attend the Brompton Hospital once a week to learn how to use it. The new apparatus was installed later that year at Midhurst, but Dr. Stanley Melville, the Consultant Radiologist, considered the results were unsatisfactory and complained bitterly that his instructions were not being followed by Dr. Jupe (who had been appointed resident radiologist). It took a good two years before the matter was satisfactorily resolved and the X-ray results came up to Dr. Melville's exacting standards.

Surgery comes to Midhurst

Artificial pneumothorax, the introduction of air between the lung and the chest wall, was one way of ensuring rest for the diseased lung: another more effective and permanent method was by removing a number of ribs and allowing the underlying diseased lung to collapse – an operation known as thoracoplasty. In the mid-'twenties, patients at Midhurst deemed to be in need of this operation were sent to the pay beds at the Brompton Hospital to have it done. There were very few such patients to begin with, only one or two a year at the most, but their numbers increased as the efficacy of the operation became more widely known. It was not only for thoracoplasty that Midhurst patients were transferred to the Brompton: phrenic avulsion, a small operation on the nerve to the diaphragm, was another reason for sending patients there.

In 1928 a vacancy occurred on the Consulting Staff (caused by the death of Dr. Perkins) and, in view of the increasing importance of surgery in the treatment of tuberculosis, the Consultants recommended to Council that it should be filled by Mr. Tudor Edwards, who was already recognised, although still only 38 years of age, as one of the leading thoracic surgeons in the country. There were no surgical facilities at all at Midhurst at the time of his appointment, but, as the number of patients requiring operations increased, he became convinced of the need to provide them at Midhurst if the Sanatorium was to retain its place as the leading institution of its kind in the country. Both he and Dr Trail were concerned at the increasing drift of patients from Midhurst to the Brompton and they pointed out to the Council that not only had the patients to pay for their transport to London, but also for the reservation of their beds at Midhurst while they were away. There was a general feeling that something ought to be done about surgery at Midhurst and eventually a special joint meeting of the Council and the Consulting Staff (the first 'joint' meeting ever to be held) took place in March 1933 to consider the matter. Plans were put forward for building an operating theatre and adapting bedrooms for surgical patients. The Consulting Staff were all in favour of proceeding as soon as possible. 'This was the only way for Midhurst to retain its place as the leading Sanatorium in the Empire' as one Consultant put it. The members of Council were more cautious: they were in general agreement, but the financial position was not easy. What saved the day, and in the end enabled work to proceed, was that Lord Woolavington generously defrayed the cost which amounted to £1,500. Added to this considerable amount was a smaller sum subscribed by patients and ex-patients in appreciation of 'Dr. Trail's interest and patience on their behalf'.

Work to convert the dental room into an operating theatre started in the autumn of 1933. The equipment was then purchased, and a sterilising room, an anaesthetic room and a changing room were prepared. The fees to be paid by surgical patients (six guineas a week, plus the surgeon's and anaesthethist's fees, by arrangement) were fixed. The new operating theatre was ready for work on 3 February 1934. In September 1934, the new Superintendent, Dr. G. S. Todd, announced that three two-stage thoracoplasties and 18 phrenic avulsions had already been completed. It was the beginning of a new era at Midhurst.

Chapter V

A Change in Direction: 1934-1939

A New Superintendent

Fig. 7. Dr. Todd, from *The Edwardian*, 1947.

Dr. Trail's successor as Medical Superintendent was a 33-year-old Australian, Dr. Geoffrey S. Todd. He had graduated Bachelor of Medicine and Master of Surgery in Sydney, Australia, in 1925 and subsequently became Medical Superintendent of the Wagga Hospital before coming to England in 1929 with a view to pursuing a career as a surgeon. An early visit to the Brompton Hospital to play tennis with some Australian friends led to his taking up medicine instead. He soon passed the testing examination to become a member of the Royal College of Physicians of London and assumed the post of Resident Medical Officer at the Brompton Hospital in London. In 1932 he heard that Trail was leaving Midhurst to take up an appointment at the London Chest Hospital. He had by this time made up his mind to build a career in Britain and he was therefore looking for a permanent post as a Consultant or Superintendent.

When the appointment at Midhurst was advertised he asked Dr. R. A. (later Sir Robert) Young, who was on the Consulting Staff at the Sanatorium, whether he should apply. Dr. Young, who had become something of a father figure to Todd at the Brompton, told him that it was indeed a 'career' job and that he must certainly put in for it. There were many other applicants, and Todd was one of three who were short listed. The Consulting Staff agreed unanimously that Dr. G. S. Todd be recommended for the post; and on Friday 17 November 1933 the Council decided to appoint him for one year, with eligibility for re-appointment. He was to remain as Superintendent for no fewer than 37 years. Only once was he ever tempted to leave; during the war he was offered a post at the London Chest Hospital, but he turned it down. He never regretted his decision to stay.

His arrival at Midhurst at the very end of 1933 was not propitious. It was 6 p.m. on New Year's Eve. The night was foggy and cold, the Sanatorium deserted. He rang the front door bell. Silence. He rang again. A figure with a cigarette in his mouth shuffled to the door. 'Who are you?' 'I am the new Superintendent'. 'OK, that door over there'. And that was that. Next morning, things were more welcoming. The Sanatorium had come alive. People were working and patients were up and about. Every bed was occupied and there were 99 patients in residence, most of them early cases and up for most of the day. His first action was to screen each and every one of them.

The assistant medical officers were Dr. E. M. Turner and Dr. Hugh Ramsay. Turner had been at Midhurst for 12 months already, but Ramsay had only joined the staff that day, in place of Jupe. The Pathologist was Dr. G. W. Garde who had replaced Dr. Sybil Robinson in 1931. The Matron, Miss N. C. Quayle, had been appointed in July 1932 to fill the vacancy left after Miss Stewart's retirement due to ill health, Miss Chapman was the Deputy Matron and Sister Priest, the Night Sister. There were 15 nurses working at Midhurst when Todd came, many of them 'uncertificated'. (These unqualified nurses were a feature of the times. Most of them had had tuberculosis themselves, and on that account had been unable to complete their formal training, but they constituted the back bone of the work force on the wards at Midhurst.)

The Rev. F. H. Campion was Chaplain, Capt. Arnold was still the Secretary and Mr. Clarenbone, the Steward. Mr. Clarenbone's duties encompassed everything from keeping the accounts to controlling the supplies. Captain Arnold, as the Chairman's Secretary, lived and worked in London. Todd and he agreed that Todd would do all that was necessary at Midhurst. Arnold, who was chiefly concerned with Sir Courtauld's extensive business interests, would take care of the London side of things which included all the Council business. This scheme worked well. Arnold used to come down to see Todd on Sundays to talk things over and take information back to the Chairman, Sir Courtauld Thomson. A quaint arrangement perhaps, but Midhurst at that time was still very much 'London based', as it always had been since its inception. The Council met regularly at St James's Palace, the Consulting Staff all lived and practised in London, and the Sanatorium still maintained its own consulting rooms in Hallam Street, whither Todd would repair twice a week to examine patients before their admission.

Todd was not a member of the Council, but he had to report to the Chairman in writing every week and, following the pattern set by Blanford, he was in attendance at all Council meetings. He and the Chairman would go through the agenda beforehand. Sometimes there would be twenty or thirty headings. Sir Courtauld had his own unique way of handling these meetings. As each matter came up he would say 'Well, the Superintendent and I have discussed this, and this is what we think; and with your permission I will now move on to the next item'. By disarming his colleagues in this way he was able to complete most meetings in under the hour. He made a fetish of this. Each meeting would commence with the synchronisation of watches at 4 p.m. Members could safely book other appointments for 5 p.m.– and they did.

Todd was required to maintain a 'six-month book' in which were recorded the names of those patients who had been under treatment for six months or longer. This was to enable the Visiting Consultant to authorise their continued stay. Monthly visits by members of the Consulting Staff were still being made when Todd arrived. After each visit the Consultant would report in confidence to the Council, a procedure which irked Todd because remarks were sometimes made which he could have explained if he had been asked. One of the Consulting Staff, Dr. Frederick Chandler, brought matters to a head by refusing to report without first informing him. Thereafter, the reporting continued, but Todd was always told beforehand.

In certain matters he was given a free hand to act as he thought fit: he was empowered to refuse patients for admission if he thought them undesirable and he could recommend that patients be transferred elsewhere if he considered it was in their best interests.

In contrast with his predecessors, Todd never undertook private work; his contract, in fact, specifically excluded it. He was therefore able to devote more of his time to domestic Sanatorium matters than had previous Superintendents. Not only was he responsible medically for all that was done for the patients, but he had to supervise, and indeed be ultimately responsible for, many other Sanatorium activities. He kept an eye on the pigs and poultry, the garden and the grounds. He reported on the weather and the water supply, the milk, the food, and the health of the staff. He was concerned with the cooking and the feeding arrangements, the accommodation, heating and lighting, the activities of the General Purposes Committee and the entertainment and welfare of the staff. Everything and everybody came under his aegis. No wonder he had to 'see everything, know everybody; be omnipresent, omniscient and omnipercipient', as one ex-patient said of him. Some idea of the range of his duties is revealed in the 'Rules for the Superintendent' which covered three pages of foolscap paper (Appendix 5). The Superintendent's office in those days was in what used to be called 'The Board Room', situated on the ground floor in a room which is nowadays used as a rest room for the theatre staff. The Matron and Assistant Matron had tiny offices in a ground floor room which is today used as a store room for the Shop.

There were six wards or 'floors' at Midhurst in the years before the war, three for male patients (with Sister Winnie Marshall in charge) and three for female (Sister Robina White). The two assistant medical officers looked after three wards each. In 1934 the treatment of pulmonary tuberculosis still consisted essentially of rest, fresh air, good food and a graduated return to normal activity. Rest for the lung was often encouraged by the induction of an artificial pneumothorax as had been done at Midhurst since 1918. Surgical methods of collapsing the lung (by thoracoplasty) were being increasingly used elsewhere, but they were not to be employed at Midhurst until soon after Todd arrived. Drugs there were, but they did very little good, and effective anti-tuberculosis drugs were not to appear on the scene for another 15 years or so. The regime for patients had changed but little since the Sanatorium had first opened in 1906. Bed rest, with plenty of fresh air and good food until the disease process had been arrested, was the standard treatment. This was followed by a regulated organised life with strictly controlled rest periods and graduated exercise according to progress. Bed patients were wheeled out on their balconies and windows were kept wide open whatever the weather. (The abiding memory of one patient – an army officer's wife – who had been sent home from India was how cold it was.*) Todd found little to criticise when he took over, but there was one change he insisted on: the compulsory hosing down of patients 'to harden them up' had to cease! He revised the rules for patients, modified the time honoured practice of nursing patients out of doors and of subjecting convalescents to vigorous exercise. He decided also that tuberculin as a therapeutic measure was useless and dangerous, so he stopped the practice. He gave up nursing patients in the open sunlight and artificial sunlight lamps were also discontinued. As far as life at the Sanatorium was concerned, he felt that things had all been a little too free and easy under his predecessor, so discipline was tightened up. The medical officers were to see their patients every day, without fail. 'Up' patients – those who took meals in the main dining hall – would attend at 9 a.m. for a ceremony called 'charting', when the doctor would inspect the temperature chart and issue instructions for the day, including the amount of exercise that could be taken. Only patients confined to bed were seen by the medical staff on their rounds.

Absolute rest in bed was insisted on for all patients showing evidence of disease activity. This stage of treatment, 'Bed 1', was continued until the patients' condition had stabilised and the pulse rate and temperature been brought under control. This might take weeks or months in serious cases, but many patients arriving at Midhurst had already reached a state of comparative stability and were put on one of the more advanced grades of activity. The first of these, '1 L.O.', meant that he was allowed up once a day to go to the lavatory. The next stage, '2 L.O.', denoted visits to the lavatory as aften as necessary. 'Bed 2' meant visits to the lavatory *and* a daily bath. Then came 'Tea', which meant what it said, and then 'L.T.D' which stood for 'Up for Lunch, Tea and Dinner' (but returning to bed between times). If a patient got as far as this without clinical deterioration, he was subjected to a simple exercise test which had to be passed before he was permitted to embark on the graded walks. These began with a walk of half a mile (to the top of the Pine Walk and back) and progressed to walks of one and then two miles (to the Haslemere-Midhurst road and back). A circular tour of the grounds measured three miles – 'Haemorrhage Hill' was the title bestowed, a little unfairly, by the patients on one particular stretch of this walk. Even longer walks, and visits to Midhurst, were permitted for patients nearing the end of their convalescence. Plans were provided of all the walks available and patients had to report on their return what exercise they had taken. One attraction of being put on 'walks' was that a patient was also allowed to take part in outdoor games such as putting or croquet: another was that he might be enabled to meet and pass the time of day with members of the opposite sex. Strictly speaking this was not permitted at Midhurst before the war, but many breaches of the rule were connived at, and small groups of walkers of both sexes would often gather for coffee at West Heath House, then run as a guest house by Mr. Oliver, the son of the resident engineer.

Breaches of the rules notwithstanding, the sexes were still kept apart. Men and women were housed on separate floors, they used their own lounges, they ate at separate tables, and in the chapel there was one nave for men and another for women. They could meet in the public rooms and, at Christmas time, 'mixed visiting' was permitted, but, generally speaking, the segregation rules were less strictly observed than at many other sanatoria. One morning in the 1930s a nurse left Midhurst to take up a new appointment at Frimley Sanatorium. She went on duty at Frimley that afternoon and was asked by a male patient to take a letter to a female patient on the same floor. She was caught, hauled up in front of the Frimley Superintendent, accused of aiding and abetting, and summarily dismissed. She reappeared at Midhurst the same evening, asking if she could continue her engagement there!

There were two rest hours, from 12 noon to 1 p.m. and from 5 p.m. to 6 p.m. (some years later the morning rest hour was brought forward half an hour – to 11.30 a.m.). Rest hours were now marked by the ringing of bells instead of the sounding of gongs. As always, patients had to retire to their rooms where they were allowed to read and smoke, in moderation. Alcohol was, of course, still strictly forbidden. Suspicious looking parcels and luggage were screened and any bottles found were kept 'in bond' until the patient's discharge. A girl admitted in 1934 at the age of 18 remembers today how she was left a bottle of sherry, by her mother, to keep her spirits up. The bottle was discovered; 'Well, my dear', Dr Todd scolded, 'what *would* your mother say if she knew you were drinking sherry at your age?' 'Well actually my mother gave it to me!', she replied. But the bottle was confiscated just the same.

Patients up for meals took them in the dining hall, with the medical staff occupying a table in the window bay. When first built, this dining hall (today used by the nursing staff and 'white coats') possessed a fine decorated ceiling, but this had to be taken down before the First War because it was suspected of harbouring germs. For the same reason the tiled walls of the dining room used to be hosed down and even in Todd's time they were washed down regularly to rid them of bacilli. (It was not until after the Second War, when swabs taken from the walls by Dr. Ian Gordon were cultured and found to be negative, that the practice was modified.)

To prevent their becoming infected, the nursing staff and domestic staff had their meals apart from the patients – the male staff in a dark and poorly ventilated basement room – and their own identifiable crockery and cutlery was separately washed up and sterilised. Another feature was that domestic staff wishing to move about within the building had to make the least possible use of the corridors used by patients. They were required by the rules to make for the nearest access to the basement and to emerge at the nearest point to their target.

In the afternoons, up-patients, who were the great majority, would go to the lounges for tea at 3.30 p.m. followed by bridge, whist, billiards or a chat. The great enemy was boredom. Considerable efforts were made, as they always had been, to keep patients occupied and interested. Wireless programmes were available, of course, and in 1938 a generous donor gave the Sanatorium what must have been one of the first-ever television sets.

Concert parties were staged every fortnight in the winter months. The performances were given in the patients' dining hall. Patients had their evening meal early; the hall was then converted into an entertainment centre, the tables being assembled at one end to form a stage and the chairs arranged in auditorium fashion. A front curtain and back drop was set up during the day. Headlights and footlights were positioned during the hurried conversion from dining room to concert hall. All of this was reversed at the end of the evening to have the dining room ready for breakfast the next day, the work being carried out by voluntary staff labour.

Cinema shows were given each week. Initially they were projected on a single projector so that at the end of each of eight to 12 reels the lights were raised while the old reel was removed and the new one threaded through the machine. In the 1940s two suitcase models were acquired which allowed reel to follow reel with almost imperceptible hesitation – and with no hall lights switched on.

For concert parties and cinema entertainment the patients were separated into groups with the gentlemen on the left and the ladies on the right. The Medical Superintendent, his mother (who kept house for him in those days), the duty doctor and any other person of comparable rank or status occupied a specified row or five seats at the rear of the hall where all activities could be viewed by the Medical Superintendent and his 'retinue'.

The patients formed their own General Purposes Committee which arranged bridge and whist tournaments and numerous outdoor competitions during the summer. This Committee functioned under the guidance of the Medical Superintendent. For some time, patients had been charged for the upkeep of the library, the billiard table, the golf course and other amenities, but soon after he arrived Dr. Todd advised the Council that it would be desirable for the Sanatorium to bear these costs and in June 1934 they agreed to do so. Henceforward, the General Purposes Committee collected subscriptions from the patients and used the money for the purchase of prizes for whist drives, competitions and games.

It was Todd who instituted the regular 'viewing sessions' at Midhurst. X-Rays were shown and treatment discussed with the other doctors and sisters who were all required to attend. He supervised these sessions personally and examined every X-Ray himself. He became so familiar with them that he said he could recognise every patient from his X-Ray picture. He saw every patient at least once a week and was most particular always to see them at their final interview when he would exhort them not to overdo things when they left. His favourite axiom was 'Never run when you can walk. Never walk when you can stand. Never stand when you can sit and never sit when you can lie'. And another : 'Stop before you're tired'.

Weekly screening and refill clinics for pneumothorax patients were also held. Artificial pneumothorax was still the principal weapon in the therapeutic armoury and twenty or thirty patients might present themselves regularly at each clinic. Although surgery began at Midhurst in 1934, artificial pneumothorax as a proven procedure continued to be used until the introduction of anti-tuberculosis drugs in the late 1940s, and even later in some cases.

Mr. Tudor Edwards started to operate at Midhurst in 1934. He used to come down once a week from London in a chauffeur-driven Rolls Royce and was often accompanied by his wife. His reception at the front door was impressive. The Medical Superintendent and his entire medical staff would be on the steps to greet him. Mrs. Edwards would be whisked upstairs to be entertained by the Matron whilst the great surgeon was at work and when all was done, they would be seen off together by the whole staff. No one could accuse Midhurst of not doing things properly.

The President, Council and Consultants

After the death of King George V on 20 January 1936, messages of sympathy and sorrow were sent to Her Majesty, Queen Mary, and to His Majesty King Edward VIII. The Council then decided to approach King Edward at the appropriate moment for his gracious acceptance of the Presidency. In June the Chairman reported to Council that although advice had been received that His Majesty would become Patron, there appeared to be difficulties in regard to his becoming President. A submission from Council dated 13 July was accordingly sent to the Palace explaining how the Sanatorium differed from other hospitals in that it was King Edward VII himself who had founded the Sanatorium, not Sir Ernest Cassel who had only provided the King with the funds. It went on to say how King Edward VII had directed that the funds be handed over not to ordinary trustees but to his Private Secretary, Viscount Knollys; the Keeper of the Privy Purse, General Sir Dighton Probyn V.C.; and Viscount Esher. The submission went on to say how much the King had always considered it his own Sanatorium and that in all documents the official description was 'King Edward VII Sanatorium,

Midhurst (founded by His Majesty, King Edward VII in 1903 with funds provided by the the late Sir Ernest Cassel)'. It finished by affirming that the financial position was strong, that there had never been the slightest trouble or friction, and that the possibility of any unsuitable person ever being appointed to the Sanatorium was safeguarded by the fact that all appointments had to be submitted to the President, as they still are today.

This submission was laid before the King who, after careful consideration, was graciously pleased to make an exception to his general rule regarding Patronage, and, following in the steps of his father and grandfather, became President of the King Edward VII Sanatorium and of the Institution. Lord Wigram's letter conveying this welcome information added that it was not to be taken as an unchangeable precedent, nor would the King be able to take part in any executive work.

After the abdication, and the Duke of York's accession to the throne in December 1936, the following notice appeared in the Court Circular of *The Times* newspaper of 22 December 1936: 'The King has been pleased to become President of the King Edward VII Sanatorium, Midhurst. His Majesty is the fourth successive sovereign to be President of the Sanatorium'.

The Vice President was Sir Walter Lawrence, and the members of the Council in 1936 were: Sir Courtauld Thomson (Chairman), Sir Percival Horton-Smith Hartley, Sir John Broadbent, Sir George Truscott, Sir Felix Cassel, Mr. B. A. Salmon (who had joined in 1935), and the Hon. Mrs. Macdonald-Buchanan, who was Lady Visitor. In the years that followed, Captain H. W. N. Lawrence (son of the Vice President) and General Sir John du Cane were invited to become members.

The Consulting Staff in 1936 were Sir John Broadbent (Chairman), Dr. Noel Bardswell, Professor Bulloch, Dr. Frederick Chandler, Professor Lyle Cummins, Lord Dawson of Penn, Mr. Tudor Edwards, Sir St Clair Thomson, Dr. R. A. Young, Dr. Lancelot Burrell, Dr. Geoffrey Marshall (who had been appointed in 1935 when Sir Humphrey Rolleston retired) and Dr. J. V. Sparks (who became Honorary Radiologist in 1934 after the death of Dr. Stanley Melville). The Honorary Surgeon was Mr. Arthur Bostock of Chichester (who had been appointed on the death of Mr. Ewart) and the Dental Surgeon was Mr. G. D. Fleetwood. There were very few changes in the years leading up to the war. Dr. Burrell died in 1938 and his place was taken by Dr. Hope Gosse. Dr. Bardswell, associated with Midhurst since 1905 and its first Medical Superintendent, died in 1939 and Sir Maurice Cassidy, a distinguished cardiologist, was invited to join in his stead.

The Honorary Auditor to the Sanatorium since its foundation, Sir William Peat, died in 1936 and the Council invited his son, Sir Harry Peat, to undertake the duties. The position of Honorary Solicitor to the Sanatorium continued to be held by Sir Reginald Poole, senior partner of the firm Lewis and Lewis, an appointment he had held since 1927. He was to continue in post until his death in 1941.

Progress and Change

One of the consequences of surgery at Midhurst was that patients were kept in the Sanatorium for longer than they had been. The waiting list grew and there was an increasing demand for more beds. The Consulting Staff recognised this in 1936, and Sir St Clair Thomson prepared a report for the Chairman of Council in which he proposed that if Midhurst's high standards were to be maintained a new 25-bed patient block should be built specifically for the grouping together of all patients who were being prepared for or had undergone surgery – 'Satisfactory work can no longer be carried out in the building as it stands (even when use is made of the additional corridor rooms recently provided) and an extra and separate wing of 25 beds, with the latest modern conveniences, is necessary'. A joint meeting of the Council and Consulting Staff was held in January 1937 to consider this matter. Sir Courtauld Thomson was in the chair. Other members of Council present were Sir Walter Lawrence, Sir George Truscott and Mr. Salmon. There were eight members of the Consulting Staff present, including Mr. Tudor Edwards. Each Consultant spoke. All supported the proposal to build a new wing and pointed out that, although excellent work was currently being done, it was essential to provide extra accommodation if the Sanatorium was to maintain its high reputation.

The Chairman's reply was bleak. He thanked the Consultants for their interest. He said he believed the Founder would have wished the Sanatorium to remain undisturbed as a complete unit in itself and that the Council was not in favour of a drastic reconstruction. Accommodation within the main building to a maximum of 120 beds was all that the kitchens, bathrooms etc. could sustain, and this was all that could be afforded out of the present endowment fund. The new building would necessitate finding £50,000 to £100,000 of new money and the Council were not prepared to appeal for such funds. If that sum was offered, Council would consider again the suggestion of the Consulting Staff. With that the Consultants had to be content for the time being, but the need for specialised rooms for the surgical patients remained. In February the following year, 1938, a memorandum on building a new wing over the doctors' quarters was considered and two further plans were prepared. One, which involved building a three-storey house, was rejected on grounds of expense. The other plan, slightly less ambitious, was accepted, but unfortunately its acceptance led to the resignation of the Consulting Architect, Mr. Stanley Hall,* on the grounds that he did not approve of a building not conforming to existing architectural standards. However, all existing ideas were subsumed in February 1939 by a far more ambitious plan to build a new nurses' home. This was the Chairman's idea and the Minutes record merely that 'the Chairman had thoroughly examined the proposed surgical wing over the doctors' quarters and had come to the conclusion, after consulting with Mr. Tudor Edwards and Dr. Todd, that the additional surgical accommodation could best be provided, and at probably lower cost, by building a nurses' home in the woods to the west of the main forecourt'. The money was to come in part from raising patients' fees to four and a half guineas a week.

Plans for the new building, prepared by Mr. Briant Poulter, F.R.I.B.A. (later to be appointed Consulting Architect), were approved by the Council in June 1939 and the tender submitted by Chapman, Lowry and Puttick was accepted in July. Work was started in August and completed to damp course level, but, after the outbreak of war on 3 September, all work had to be suspended for a few weeks until permits had been obtained and difficulties with the contract overcome. However, by November 1939 work was resumed and before the war was a year old the new nurses' home had been completed.

There were changes too in the medical field before the outbreak of war. The X-ray department was greatly improved, thanks to the efforts of Dr. Todd and the new Consultant Radiologist, Dr. J. V. Sparks, and the willing support of the Council. A new X-ray set was installed in 1935 together with a modern table, new protective aprons and new viewing boxes. A mobile X-ray set and a screening apparatus were purchased later, and a tomography unit was made and erected by the staff themselves. By the time war came, the X-ray department was as well equipped as any in the land. In the operating theatre, diathermy was made available and the operation of extra-pleural pneumothorax was brought into use. Meanwhile, the number of operations carried out at the Sanatorium increased from 95 in 1936/7 to 120 in 1938/9 and the total number of beds was also increased from 99 to 121 by the erection of corridor rooms and the conversion of staff accommodation into rooms for surgical patients.

Although the theatre and X-ray equipment was new, much of the other Sanatorium equipment was beginning to wear out and was in need of repair or replacement – hardly surprising since it had been in constant use for more than 30 years. The patients' beds were fitted with new bases and mattresses in 1938 and new chairs were put into the dining hall. In 1937 there was a change over to the 'grid' for the main supply of electricity, but the original steam-driven Willan's engines which drove the generators were not finally given up until after the war. A complete modernisation of the kitchen and the laundry was undertaken with the co-operation of experts sent down by Mr. Salmon, a Director of Lyons who had recently been appointed to the Council. Central heating was extended, re-wiring of the entire Sanatorium was completed, general maintenance work proceeded and a high standard of decoration was kept up. New cottages were built, the garden and grounds kept in good order, the pig and poultry farms continued in operation, the Gaumont talking pictures apparatus provided weekly entertainment, a Marconi wireless receiver was installed and was connected to head-phones in the patients' bedrooms and to six loudspeakers in various parts of the building. A modern milk pasteurizer was purchased.

There were changes also in the methods and techniques used at the Sanatorium. A story often told by Sir Geoffrey Todd of his early days at Midhurst was about how he, Captain Arnold and Mr Clarenbone (later aided and abetted by Mr. J. L. Williams and Mr. J. A. Boulton) between them managed to double the quantity and quality of the food at the Sanatorium and at the same time halve the running costs. How was it done? By bulk buying from central markets! Mr. Clarenbone had been in the habit of driving to Midhurst and buying the food for the Sanatorium over the counter. When Mr. Salmon came on the Council all that changed. He arranged for his chief buyer, Mr. Deer, to purchase in bulk from the London markets – Smithfield, Billingsgate and Covent Garden – and the Sanatorium would collect from them. The new method was not appreciated by the local retailers, but it was good for the Sanatorium and, in Todd's opinion, the end justified the means. Mr. Salmon helped in other ways too. Ice cream was supplied at 8s. 6d a gallon. Methods of cooking and serving meals at the Sanatorium were examined and revised. (Todd once got into hot water for not warming the coffee cups!) An experienced cook from the private wing at the Brompton Hospital (Miss Ina Fraser) came down to join the staff as Food Supervisor. Waste was reduced. Store-keeping was revised and a 'bin system' introduced. Linen and carpets were bought at advantageous prices on informed advice from Mr. Salmon. These changes were said to have reduced expenditure by something like £900 in the first six months, a lot of money in those days.

Amongst the medical staff, Dr. R. Y. Keers and Dr. Brian Taylor took the places of Turner and Ramsay. Dr. Craig acted as locum assistant medical officer and Dr. Hinson replaced Garde as pathologist. A third assistant medical officer to cover the surgical work was approved in 1938; Dr. Howard Nicholson was appointed, but left on the outbreak of war. In 1939, the three assistant medical officers were Dr. Len West, Dr. Stanley Herington and Dr. Philip Morse.

The nursing staff had grown to a total of 26 by 1939, the increase being due partly to the introduction of surgery and partly to take account of the new regulations limiting their hours of work to 96 per fortnight. A change occurred in the chaplaincy. The Rev. F. H. Campion relinquished the position in 1938 and his place was taken by the Rev. J. H. Layton, an ex-patient living on a small pension.

The resident engineer, Mr. Oliver, who had joined the staff from Windsor in 1908, had to retire on grounds of age in 1937. He was replaced by Mr. Woodrow, a qualified engineer, who left after only a year. Mr. Ashburner, also a qualified engineer, then took over. In 1936 it became apparent that Mr. Clarenbone, who had been appointed in 1914 as Steward, had too many duties to perform.* It was decided that in future his work should be shared with Mr. J. L.Williams. Mr. Clarenbone would be the Accountant responsible for the cash, wages, books, accounts and records, and the pigs and poultry: Mr. Williams would be Steward and be responsible for the stores, shop, equipment and the male staff and their duties.

Clarenbone and Williams had one assistant between them and when this assistant left to get married in 1936 the vacancy was filled by a 20-year-old clerk, who had been working for the previous two years at the British Medical Association in the statistics department, a job he hated. In this unobtrusive way John Boulton, soon to be generally known as 'JAB', started an association with Midhurst which has lasted to the present day. Commencing as clerk to Clarenbone and Jack Williams on an annual salary of £65.00 (all found), and sharing an office with them, he worked his way up through the administrative ranks to become Secretary to the Council, Secretary to the Sanatorium and finally Director of Administrative Services at King Edward VII Hospital. When he retired in 1983 after 47 years' service, a record unequalled before or since, his association with Midhurst did not cease: he still carries on as Chairman of the Association of Friends of King Edward VII Hospital.

Todd made a point of seeing his Heads of Department every day so that he knew exactly what was going on in the Sanatorium, and why. He had working with him in the days before the war a wonderfully loyal and conscientious staff, all of whom were known to him personally and whose names he remembered always. Apart from Clarenbone, Williams and Boulton, there was Mr. Hampton, an engineer, and Jack Taylor, formerly a merchant marine engineer, who took over as senior resident engineer when Mr. Ashburner retired in 1949. There was Miss Ina Fraser a dietitian from the Brompton who had been appointed 'Food Supervisor' a few weeks after Todd's arrival at Midhurst. There was Mr. P. J. Allen, who followed Mr. Melville as head gardener in 1935 and remained there until 1980. There was Mr. Gale, the chauffeur, known as 'Windy' Gale, whose brother set up Gales Coaches of Haslemere. There were the hall porters; Fred (Bill) Mills, tall, moustached, avuncular, who had become head porter in 1915 and whose reign lasted until 1947; Bert Pullinger and Dickie Kent. And there was a body of less widely known figures without whose loyalty and devotion the

Sanatorium could never have flourished: Caleb (Cay) Moseley, stoker and jack of all trades, who had carried bricks to the Sanatorium when it was being built and who had been a soldier in the First War (one of his many jobs at Midhurst was to drive the Foden steam wagon);* Fred Tunks, pantryman, brother of Jack who had been killed in the war; Mould, who saw to the water supply; Newell, in the stores; Danny King, who looked after the pigs; Oliver, the dairy man, ex-R.N.; Goodall, a painter, whose ability to paint scenery and decorations for concerts and shows was always in demand. Many of these splendid characters were later to be gathered together to meet the Queen when she visited the Sanatorium in 1956, its golden jubilee year.

Dr. Geoffrey Todd was encouraged by the Council to visit other sanatoria as often as possible and to attend medical meetings whenever he could afford time away, with the intention of broadening his own experience and at the same time of 'flying the Midhurst flag'. In 1939 he visited sanatoria in Switzerland and attended important conferences in London, Edinburgh, Hastings and elsewhere. In August he was given a month's leave which he spent visiting hospitals in Canada and America. He arrived back in this country on 1 September 1939, the day German troops marched into Poland and only two days before Britain declared war on Germany.

Chapter VI

World War II: 1939-1945

In contrast with the events of 1914, the Sanatorium was not entirely unprepared when Britain declared war on Germany on 3 September 1939. At the time of the Munich crisis 11 months previously, various preparations had been made. These included the organisation of A.R.P. (air raid precautionary) measures, the building of trenches in the woods (dug by staff of all grades, including doctors) and the purchase of extra supplies of food and stores as a safeguard against the possibility of future war shortages.
  In November 1938, after the crisis had passed and war averted, temporarily at least, the Council learned that it had been the government's intention, if war *had* broken out, to use the Sanatorium for accommodating chronic general cases from Southampton. The Council felt this would have been a gross misuse of Sanatorium resources and they asked the Medical Superintendent to take unofficial steps through Sir Arthur MacNalty (the Senior Medical Officer at the Ministry of Health) to have future policy changed so that Midhurst might be used for thoracic surgery. The upshot was that in June 1939 the Council was able to announce that, should war come, the Sanatorium would come under the Civil Defence Scheme (later called the Emergency Medical Service [E.M.S]) and be used as a Hospital for chest surgical cases and the Government would be responsible for the cost. This was just what the Sanatorium wanted, but events did not turn out exactly as planned.
  In July 1939 Dr. Geoffrey Todd had been given six weeks study leave in America and Canada. Sensing that events in Europe were becoming critical, he cabled the Chairman from America to ask if he should return. He received this reply: 'war unlikely; finish your tour'. So he stayed a few weeks longer and only got back to Britain a day or two before war started. When he reached Midhurst, he was met by the Matron, Miss Quayle, with the news that the Sanatorium was being turned into a maternity unit and that 60 patients were about to be sent home to make way for them. Todd had to act, and act quickly, without help from Mr. Tudor Edwards who was ill and who had been replaced as sector administrator by someone less supportive of Midhurst's interests. He immediately got in touch with the Area Medical Officer of Health and between them they had the order rescinded and the maternity unit moved elsewhere. The 60 patients were discharged, nevertheless, but this was in conformity with the agreement reached before the war that the beds thus vacated should be at the disposal of the Ministry for surgical chest patients. The Sanatorium's 60 remaining beds continued to be used as before for patients with tuberculosis.
  Meanwhile, the Sanatorium was preparing itself for war. The trenches in the woods were renovated, sand bags were filled and placed in position and the Sanatorium was

blacked out, not by obscuring the windows with black paint – fortunately this well-meant but entirely inappropriate Government advice was rejected – but by buying enough material (at inflated prices) to make up their own black-out curtains. (Todd always said that if the Council had accepted his advice to buy black-out material the year previously, during the Munich crisis, they could have saved themselves a fortune!) The staff formed their own section of the Home Guard and their own Air Raid Patrol squads whose members were trained in fire fighting, demolition and stretcher drill. An air raid shelter for patients was prepared in the basement. It would have been unnecessary to remove patients there every time the warning sounded, so a system of 'spotters' was inaugurated (the medical officers did this duty in turns) and patients were ordered below only when danger threatened. This manoeuvre, which included the removal to the basement of stretcher cases, was often practised and could be completed very quickly.

In October 1939, at the first war-time meeting of the Council, the Chairman confirmed the agreement which had been reached with the Ministry that the Sanatorium was to be incorporated in the Emergency Medical Service as a base hospital for surgical chest cases. The Council was to continue to be responsible for the administration, but the Ministry of Health would pay for the beds allocated to them, whether they were occupied or not. This was welcome news, because there had previously been a rumour that the Government might take over the entire Institution, lock, stock and barrel.

The early months of 1940 were as bleak and cold as any within living memory. Work on building the nurses' home had to be delayed, production of eggs from the poultry farm was reduced, water supplies froze. With very little encouraging war news from France, and with hardly enough work to do at the Sanatorium (only 60 beds were occupied), life at Midhurst in this period of cold war was sombre indeed. Besides the bitterly cold weather, there was rationing to worry about – of petrol, fuel and food – and other irksome war-time austerities of black-out and restriction of movement to contend with. But if the staff had to put up with some inconvenience, the patients by contrast had little to complain of. The quality and quantity of their food remained unimpaired, their rooms were kept warm by means of a new heating system installed before the war, their morale remained high. Dances, cinema shows, whist drives and concert parties continued as before and Service patients were invited by Lord Cowdray to play golf at Cowdray Park free of charge.

The quiet days of the 'phoney' war came to an end in August 1940 when the Battle of Britain was fought and R.A.F. airfields were attacked from the air. Tangmere was bombed and the raid could be seen clearly from the Sanatorium balconies. Casualties then began to arrive. Not many to begin with, but later, after Southampton and Portsmouth had been bombed, in ever increasing numbers and, by July 1941, 50 had been admitted. (Towards the end of the war the annual intake was almost 300.) Most of the casualties were chest injuries due to bomb fragments, crushing, or the effects of blast, but there were some bizarre injuries also, such as those sustained by a fitter at Tangmere whose pliers had been blown into his chest cavity. The pliers were removed and he survived.

The threat of invasion was such that plans were made for the evacuation of hospitals if the enemy were to land on the south coast. As part of these plans, Midhurst had agreed to accept the transfer of 15 patients from Aldingbourne, which was then a tuberculosis hospital. The patients were to arrive as a unit, together with their beds, bedding, food and nursing staff! Fortunately, no invasion occurred and the plans never had to be carried out. But attacks from the air continued, the number of casualties rose, and admissions to Midhurst increased.

With the arrival at Midhurst of some of these casualties, surgery played an increasingly important rôle at the Sanatorium. Only 100 operations of all kinds were performed in the first 12 months of the war: over 500 in the last, most of them major operations. It was not only the wounded who needed surgery. As a definitive form of treatment for certain types of pulmonary tuberculosis, thoracoplasty was becoming widely used and Midhurst was not slow to follow suit. Forty-four thoracoplasty operations (on 22 patients) were carried out in the first year of the war: 116 (on 58 patients) in the last year. Operations for the removal of a whole lung (pneumonectomy), or part of a lung (lobectomy), were also performed. During the whole course of the war, surgeons at Midhurst carried out 2,340 operations, 1,320 on Service patients and 1,020 on civilians.

Mr. Tudor Edwards had had to give up operating for a time after his illness in 1939, but he returned to work in 1941. During his absence his place was taken by Mr. Clement Price Thomas who was to become the Consulting Thoracic Surgeon in his own right and later was to achieve eminence by operating on King George VI at Buckingham Palace in 1951. The anaesthetist at Midhurst in the early war years was Dr. John Hunter who was also a consultant at East Grinstead where he worked with Sir Archibald McIndoe, the well known plastic surgeon. Even after he returned to work, Mr. Tudor Edwards had to limit his operating hours, and in May 1944 Mr. Price Thomas was appointed as an additional Consultant Thoracic Surgeon, together with Mr. N. R. Barrett, to cope with the work. Dr. Robert Machray was at the same time appointed Consultant   Anaesthetist.

In the early days of the war the operating theatre team consisted of three trained nurses and one or two assistant nurses, but the numbers doubled as the work increased. A full- time masseuse (Mrs. Wanless), trained in respiratory exercises, was taken on to assist in post-operative recovery, and the scope of the X-ray department was increased by appointing a full-time radiographer (Miss D. M. Moore) and installing new equipment. An entirely new branch of treatment was introduced at Midhurst during the war. It began with the artist, Mr. Adrian Hill, who, while still himself a patient at Midhurst, started to give patients individual tuition in sketching and painting in the belief that they would benefit from becoming immersed in a creative pastime. His classes proved to be immensely popular. Art Therapy, as it came to be called, was given the official blessing of the Superintendent and the Consultants and was continued at Midhurst for many years. Art Therapy was but one aspect of Occupational Therapy, a branch of treatment which flourished and grew after its inception in the early days of the war. Full time occupational therapists were appointed (Miss Terry King and Miss Elisabeth Adams were amongst the first) and under their supervision patients were encouraged to develop a hobby and to learn a skill which would fill their time and be of some use to them after leaving the Sanatorium.

Besides being a regional chest centre in its own right, the Sanatorium became a headquarters from which Mr. Tudor Edwards and other consultants would visit neighbouring hospitals, their purpose being to operate or, more often, to advise which chest patients should be transferred for operation to Midhurst and which sent to other chest centres further afield. Teams would go out from Midhurst to hospitals at Chichester, Southampton, Portsmouth or to Goodwood House, which was then being used as a Service hospital. To begin with these visits seem to have been met with some professional jealousy from the surgeons on the spot, but this did not last long. Dr. Todd was usually the team's medical member, Mr. Boulton was often the driver (after his return to Midhurst from service in the R.A.F), and the surgeon would be Mr. Tudor Edwards, Mr. Price Thomas or, on occasion, an R.A.F surgeon who had recently been seconded to Midhurst – Squadron Leader V. T. Powell.

Those patients recommended for transfer to Midhurst were usually admitted to the E.M.S. reserved beds when they arrived. There had been 60 of these when the war started, but, in 1940, 20 had been given back to the Sanatorium for tuberculous patients, leaving 40 for the E.M.S. They were accommodated in a self contained unit of their own on Floors 3 and 4 (now Norfolk and Cowdray Wards) where they were at least risk of infection from the 'Sanatorium' patients with tuberculosis who occupied the remaining four floors.

Most of the E.M.S. beds were occupied by chest casualties, but a considerable number of civilian patients with non-tuberculous medical conditions such as cancer and pneumonia also found their way there, particularly in the first half of the war. Those were the days of M and B 693, the first of the anti-bacterial drugs, and it is not surprising that many pneumonias developed empyema and many wounds became infected. When penicillin became available towards the end of the war, it was in very short supply to begin with and could only be used for selected cases. Midhurst was allocated a small quantity and Todd can still remember vividly the well-nigh miraculous effects of the new antibiotic when used in cases of septicaemia, empyema and fulminating lung abscess.

In 1941, 30 of the 40 E.M.S. beds were allocated for R.A.F. patients, and consultants and nursing staff from the R.A.F. were sent to assist. One of the first doctors to arrive in 1942 was an E.N.T. specialist, Squadron Leader Powell, who had been sent by the R.A.F. 'to learn something about chests'. He did so to such good effect that he stayed on at Midhurst for the duration of the war (despite repeated attempts by the R.A.F. to post him elsewhere). After demobilisation he was appointed Civilian Consultant Thoracic Surgeon to the Sanatorium, a post he occupied until 1971, but even after his official retirement he remained at Midhurst as civilian consultant to the R.A.F. Unit until 1979.

As the war progressed, more and more tuberculosis beds were needed at Midhurst to accommodate officers from the Services, and from the Merchant Navy, who were being sent there for treatment. In 1944 the War Office agreed to build two Nissen huts in the grounds, each of 15 beds, which would be connected with the main building by a corridor. A feature of the agreement was that the beds should be of Hospital pattern not Service pattern! The War Office paid for the equipment and for the cost of patients treated there, and the agreement required them

Fig. 8   Squadron Leader Powell, from *The Edwardian*, 1947.

to provide Army sisters and V.A.D.s (Voluntary Aid Detachment), and to arrange for the local labour exchange to direct to the Sanatorium 'such additional domestic staff as might be required'. The original agreement stipulated that the huts should be removed within nine months of the termination of the war, but when that time came the demand for officers' tuberculosis beds remained so acute that it was agreed that the Officers' Annexe (as the huts came to be called) should remain in situ until alternative arrangements within the Sanatorium could be made. The annexe was not finally vacated until 1949, by which time the new Surgical Wing had been built, but the Nissen huts remained in use as staff accommodation and a lecture hall until long after the end of the war.

Research of two kinds, clinical and documentary, was continued during the war, but the value of what was done was rather overshadowed by the expansion of the medical and surgical work which occurred. All the doctors on the staff took part in clinical research, but a particularly important part was played by Dr. Geoffrey Todd who worked with the R.A.F. to study the effects of altitude on pneumothoraces and other chest conditions. It was important work which made it possible to specify altitude limits for chest patients who were being transported by air.

Documentary research consisted in the careful follow up of every patient with tuberculosis who had been treated at the Sanatorium. This had been started with the very first patients to arrive in 1906 and it was continued through both wars and for many years afterwards. Questionnaires were answered by patients about their state of health and ability to work and, from these, assessments were made of the value of different forms of treatment.

Much that happened at Midhurst during the war never struck the headlines. Work on the partially completed nurses' home, which had had to be postponed during the 1940 winter, was started again as soon as the warmer weather arrived. The building was finally completed in September 1940 and was formally opened in October, thus releasing more rooms in the main building for use by surgical patients. The ceremony was performed by Lord Wigram who had been appointed Vice President following the death of Sir Walter Lawrence earlier that year. (The story is still told of how Sir Courtauld Thomson at the opening ceremony began by saying how disappointed His Majesty had been at not being able to open the nurses' home himself, particularly in view of the close personal interest he had always taken in 'his own Sanatorium'. Lord Wigram, then a little hard of hearing, missed these opening remarks and began his speech by saying he had told the King only that morning at Windsor that he was coming down to open the nurses' home at 'his Sanatorium at Midhurst'. 'Good God', replied the King, 'do I own the Sanatorium too?') On the outbreak of war it had been decided to turn over to vegetable production as much of the garden and grounds as could be spared without interfering too seriously with their ornamental value. Pigs continued to be raised, but rather fewer of them than before the war, owing to shortage of waste food, and the poultry farm produced nearly 50,000 eggs despite the severe winters. Early in the war, a water cart was purchased in case the water pumping station were to be rendered inoperable by enemy action (it never was) and, as part of its contribution to the war effort, the Sanatorium sold the iron railings round the old isolation hospital for scrap, and felled many trees in the woods in response to a Ministry of Supply request for home grown timber.

Although no major structural change was made to the Sanatorium, the main services were maintained extremely efficiently throughout the war and no serious breakdowns of any sort occurred, saying much for the zeal and dedication of the Midhurst staff. The heating, electrical and water services operated effectively, the steam generators were used to provide electric power when the grid became overloaded, the boiler house performed efficiently and economically. Various engineering improvements were however put in hand: a thermostatically operated steam valve calorifier fitted to the heating and hot water systems brought economic savings; electric heating points and electric fires were installed in many bedrooms; the steam mains were extended to the ward kitchens, and sterilisation units were added so that every item of tableware used by bed patients could be sterilised. Even an ice cream making machine was installed!

Many are the stories which circulated, and circulate still, about life at the Sanatorium during the war. Not all are printable, but some can be told. One day, early in the war, two large Admiralty cars, both flying flags, drew up at the front entrance. Out stepped two high ranking Naval Officers, gold braid and all, and with them a civil servant. 'We are taking this place over as a signal station', they said. 'We're a Sanatorium: you can't do that to us' replied Todd. 'Oh yes we can,' said the Navy. 'Oh no, you can't' said Todd. And so it went on until, intimidated, they withdrew, murmuring that perhaps the Sanatorium was not *quite* the place they were looking for. But what finally brought the affair to a close was when Todd telephoned the Chairman of the Council who was (of course) a friend of the First Sea Lord, and, in Todds's words, 'he put a stop to all that'. On another occasion, a General tried to tell Todd how to dig air raid trenches (only officers of very exalted rank featured in the best Midhurst stories!). Todd had to save face by doing as he was told, so a specimen trench was dug in the woods. In it were found the remains of a pig long since perished of swine fever. 'Good God', said the General, 'was he a patient?' 'But you must remember', added Todd, 'they were not all like that: there were any number of quite nice people about!'

Todd had his own way of deflating the self important. Once an R.A.F. Medical Officer, a very senior officer indeed, tried to argue with him about a pilot who was being medically boarded. 'So you say his chest is better now?', said the pompous doctor. 'Better?', replied Todd in his broadest Australian twang, glancing from the pilot's bared torso to the doctor's broad, but unbemedalled chest, 'Its a damn sight better than yours'.*

In May 1940, the Institution lost its Vice President, Sir Walter Lawrence, who for more than a quarter of a century had served the Sanatorium, first as Chairman and later as Vice President, and who had been instrumental in building up the high reputation which the Sanatorium held. Lord Wigram, who had been appointed a member of Council on the resignation of Sir John du Cane, was appointed Vice President. When the war came to an end in May 1945, Lord Wigram was still Vice President and Lord Courtauld-Thomson, who had been recently created a Peer, was Chairman of the Council of which the other members were Sir Percival Horton-Smith Hartley, Sir John Broadbent, Sir Felix Cassel, Mr. B. A. Salmon, Captain Lawrence, Lord Cowdray (who had been appointed a member in 1941, after the death of Sir George Truscott) and Lady Louis Mountbatten* who had been appointed in 1944. Lady Cowdray was Lady Visitor.

Sir Reginald Poole, Honorary Solicitor to the Sanatorium since 1927, died in 1941 and Mr. Roderick Dew, who was next appointed , resigned in 1943. Messrs. Lewis and Lewis and Gisborne were then appointed Honorary Legal Advisers. Mr. Briant Poulter was appointed Architect in 1941 following the resignation of Mr. Stanley Hall. The Honorary Auditor was still Sir Henry Peat, who had succeeded his father, Sir William Peat, in 1936 and the Secretary to the Council was Captain Arnold, but there were several changes amongst the medical Consulting Staff. Professor William Bulloch resigned his place as Consulting Pathologist and Dr. Roodhouse Gloyne was appointed in his stead. Sir St Clair Thomson, who had been the Consulting Laryngologist to the Sanatorium for over 30 years, had to resign in 1942 owing to ill health and Mr. Frank Ormerod was appointed in his place. Dr. Chandler died in 1943, and the final year of the war brought the death of Lord Dawson of Penn, whose name had added lustre to the Sanatorium for many years. The new Consultants appointed were Professor Lyle Cummins and Dr. Maurice (later Sir Maurice) Cassidy.

Dr. Geoffrey Todd, having been elected a Fellow of the Royal College of Physicians in 1940, continued to occupy the post of Superintendent throughout the war, and indeed for many years after it. Dr. Herington, who was medically unfit for military service, stayed at Midhurst for much of the war, holding the position of deputy to Dr. Todd until 1944 when he was succeeded by Dr. Philip Morse, a Canadian, who had been an assistant medical officer since 1938. After Doctors West, Nicholson and Hinson had left to join the Forces, Dr. George Little joined the staff for some years (from 1941 until 1946) and Dr. Noelle Wallace became resident pathologist, being followed after a year by Dr. Paton and then by Dr. C. E. P. Downes. Doctors Lloyd, Osborne and Ansell came and went in rapid succession.

Miss Quayle was Matron for the duration of the war and others on the nursing staff whose names are still remembered were Miss Chapman (Assistant Matron), Sister Marshall, Sister White and Nurse Sharkey. In charge of the Officers' Annex were, first, Sister Cornwell and, later, Sister Bilsborough, known to everyone as Annie B. (Some dismay was felt in Army circles when the two Q.A. Army Sisters sent to run the annex found themselves under the direction of a mere civilian!) Other members of the staff who served at Midhurst during the war were: Mr. A. P. Patey, who had been resident engineer since 1908 (and who was to continue as Consulting Engineer until 1959); the Rev. J. H. Layton, Chaplain; the Reverend Father J. M. O'Connell, Roman Catholic Priest; Mr. Clarenbone, Accountant; Mr. Jack Williams, Steward, and Captain Arnold, Secretary to the Council. Mr. J. A. Boulton, at that time designated Steward's Assistant, joined the R.A.F. on 8 October 1940 but was invalided from the Service in 1943 and immediately returned to work at the Sanatorium.

For his outstanding work as Superintendent during the war years and for his special work in connection with Civil Defence, Dr. Geoffrey Todd was appointed an Officer of the Order of the British Empire and a Commander of the Royal Victorian Order. Very typically, when he addressed the staff on V.E. Day to thank them for their loyalty and co-operation, he gave all the credit to them. He told them, 'It's the ordinary man in the street who wins wars, not the high ups'. And very true this was of Midhurst.

Chapter VII

From War to Peace: 1945-1950

The war came to an end in Europe in May 1945. The occasion was celebrated at Midhurst by a dinner and dance for the patients and staff at which the Superintendent thanked those attending for their help and co-operation during the difficult years of war. The Council decided to grant a peace 'bonus' to all members of the staff as a mark of appreciation for their services and the Medical Superintendent was asked to include with the bonus a written expression of the Council's thanks for their good work. Monetary allowances to members of staff still on active service were to be continued for a further six months.

On the surface, life and work at the Sanatorium went on very much as it had during the war, but a feeling of uncertainty prevailed, caused as much by the continuance of war time restrictions as by the changing circumstances of peace. The Sanatorium was affected too by the deaths of three of its most distinguished Consultants. Lord Dawson of Penn died just before the end of the war and Sir John Broadbent in January 1946. Sir John had been associated with the Sanatorium since its foundation when he had been one of the Joint Secretaries of the first Advisory Committee which had been appointed by King Edward VII. He had been one of the original members of Council and Chairman of the Consulting Staff for 15 years. His death and Lord Dawson's came as grievous blows, but they were followed in August 1946 by one yet more hardly felt – the death of Mr. Tudor Edwards, one of the world's pioneers of thoracic surgery, whose devoted work for Midhurst had led to his untimely death at the age of only fifty-six. It was sad that he did not live to see the ultimate fulfilment of his work at Midhurst, the opening of the new Surgical Wing in 1949.

The immediate post-war years at Midhurst were dominated by three events: the opening of the new Surgical Wing, the inauguration of the National Health Service and the introduction of effective new anti-tuberculosis drugs. The idea that a Surgical Wing might be built had been put forward by the Ministry of Pensions whilst the War was still in progress. The wing was to be for about thirty patients and it would release beds in the main Sanatorium building for occupation by Service patients who had previously been accommodated in the Nissen huts which been put up during the war. Much of the cost was to be met by the Treasury and in return the Ministry of Pensions was to have the right to use up to 60 beds in the Sanatorium. The Council approved of the idea in principle, but limited their financial contribution to half the total cost, or £18,000, whichever was the smaller amount. The Treasury agreed and the scheme appeared to be proceeding smoothly, but, at the last moment, the Ministy of Works announced that they would not sanction the work unless it was completed to war-time utility standards.

This the Council could not contemplate – any extension had to conform with existing Sanatorium architectural patterns – and the scheme had to be postponed for the time being. In June 1945, the war in Europe having come to an end, the Ministry of Works relented, and the work was begun. Messrs. Crosby of Farnham were awarded the contract, and Mr. Briant Poulter, soon to be appointed Honorary Consultant, was the architect. Work began in January 1947 and on 21 July 1949 the new wing was opened. The building consisted of 32 patients' rooms for major surgery, 28 rooms for staff accommodation and a pathological laboratory. With the opening of the Surgical Wing, the patients in the Nissen huts (the Officers' Annex) were transferred to the main Sanatorium where a floor was allocated for them and the huts were used for other purposes.

In November 1946, the National Health Service Act was passed by Parliament. Of the Act's many provisions, that which particularly affected the Sanatorium was the power it gave the Minister to take under his control most of the country's hospitals and sanatoria. Could Midhurst remain an independent institution outside the State system? Informal discussions took place between the Ministry of Health and a deputation from the Council which led to the Minister himself, the Rt. Hon. Aneurin Bevan, visiting the Sanatorium on 27 June 1947. Before he came down, he was sent a memorandum which set out the main points relating to the Sanatorium's origins, its function and organisation, and its special relationship with the Monarchy. The memorandum described how the Sanatorium had been founded in 1903 by King Edward VII with funds provided by Sir Ernest Cassel; how its primary object was for the treatment of educated persons of limited means suffering from pulmonary tuberculosis in its early stages; and how in 1913 the Sanatorium had been granted a Royal Charter under which the right to be President was reserved to the Monarch and the Sanatorium was to be administered by a Council of 10, of which His Majesty was President and a Member. Meetings of the Council had always been held at St James's Palace, by Royal Command the Tudor Crown had to be used in connection with all correspondence, and the appointment of all Members of the Council and of the Consulting Staff had to be approved by His Majesty. The memorandum continued with an account of the Sanatorium's war-time rôle as a Thoracic Surgical Unit under the Emergency Medical Service and of the part it played in treating Officers of the three Services and of the Merchant Navy. The memorandum concluded by describing the new Surgical Wing which was then being built by agreement with the Ministry of Pensions.

Thus well briefed, the Minister's visit turned out to be an unqualified success. He was received by Sir Felix Cassel, Lord Cowdray, Sir Maurice Cassidy, Sir Robert Young, Mr. B. A. Salmon, Dr. Todd and Captain Arnold. Sir Wilson Jameson, Chief Medical Officer to the Ministry of Health, was present and Lord Courtauld-Thomson met the Minister over a cup of tea, and perhaps something stronger, before returning to London. The Minister was benign. Sir Felix Cassel was prepared to outline the case for 'independence', but Bevan was in no mood for legal niceties. From the very outset he was disposed to be friendly. There was a crying need for tuberculosis beds; Midhurst was doing a good job; they must be allowed to continue doing so.

The outcome was that the Minister agreed to the Sanatorium continuing its work under the Charter and remaining outside the National Health Service. By reason of its special type of work the Sanatorium was to be treated by the Ministry of Health on a national basis, but would be freed from control or supervision by the regional Hospital Boards which had been set up for administering those hospitals which had been 'nationalised'. This was welcome news indeed.

The National Health Service came into force in July 1948 and at the same time the Emergency Medical Service Scheme which had operated so successfully during the war was terminated. Although the Sanatorium was not part of the National Health Service, the Regional Hospital Boards accepted financial responsibility for a number of National Health Service patients at Midhurst who would conform to the type for which the Sanatorium had been founded. The Ministry of Pensions would continue to make use of 60 beds for Service patients, and private patients could still be received from any part of the United Kingdom and from overseas. In this manner the waiting list for admission became so long that patients had to wait up to 12 months before a bed at Midhurst became available. The course was thus set fair for full bed occupancy for many years to come.

The introduction of the new anti-tuberculosis drug Streptomycin in the mid-1940s brought about a profound change in the attitudes both of doctors and of patients to pulmonary tuberculosis; of doctors, because it put in their hands a therapeutic weapon of unparalleled efficacy; of patients, because their perception was that cure was at last at hand, perhaps even without their having to undergo surgery.

When it was first introduced to Britain, Streptomycin was used in cases of tuberculous meningitis, miliary tuberculosis, and acute pneumonic phthisis, or galloping consumption. The drug could arrest, even cure, these hitherto inevitably fatal diseases. But success was not yet total because tubercle bacilli emerged which were resistant to the drug when given alone. Midhurst was quick to realise this, and the Sanatorium was one of the centres selected by the Medical Research Council to undertake trials of Streptomycin in combination with other drugs in an endeavour to find regimes which might prevent the appearance of resistant strains.

In May 1946, the Sanatorium was visited by Her Majesty Queen Elizabeth. Her visit so soon after the dark days of war was popular with everyone, and her appearance did much to raise spirits at that time of uncertainty when the Staff were changing and the newly joined members had not yet moulded as a team.

At the end of the War, the Vice President of the Council was Lord Wigram; the Chairman, Lord Courtauld-Thomson. Council members were Sir Percival Horton-Smith Hartley, Sir Felix Cassel, Mr. B. A. Salmon, Captain Neville Lawrence, Lord Cowdray and Lady Louis Mountbatten. As a body they had served together, with very few changes, throughout the whole of the war. The Chairman of the Consulting Staff, Dr. Robert Young, was appointed a Council member after the death of Sir John Broadbent in January 1946 and Sir Maurice Cassidy, another distinguished physician, was appointed in succession to Captain Lawrence who resigned in the same year. Sir Maurice Cassidy died in 1949 and was succeeded on the Council by Dr. Geoffrey Marshall, a member of the Consulting Staff. In 1950 the Duchess of Norfolk was invited to be Lady Visitor and Lord Portal of Hungerford was appointed a member of Council.

In 1947 occurred the resignation through ill health of Sir Percival Horton-Smith Hartley who, with Sir John Broadbent, had been joint Secretary of the original Advisory Committee, which had been set up in 1901 to advise King Edward VII on the form the new Sanatorium should take. Since those early days, Sir Percival had not only attended all meetings of the Council and of the House Committee (when it was in existence), but had been an ex-officio member of the Midhurst Consulting Staff and had attended all their meetings. At the same time he had carried on a busy London consulting practice and had for many years been Senior Physician at the Brompton Hospital and St Bartholomew's Hospital. He had been knighted in 1921 and at the time of his retirement had served the Sanatorium in one capacity or another for 45 years.

After the war, there were several changes amongst the Consulting Staff. Dr. R. A. (later Sir Robert) Young succeeded the late Sir John Broadbent as Chairman, and new members appointed were Mr. Norman Barrett, Dr. Robert Coope, Dr. E. H. Hudson, Mr. Williamson-Noble (an Ophthalmic Surgeon) and Mr. Frank Cook (a Gynaecologist). The full Consulting Staff in 1947 consisted of Sir Robert Young (Chairman), Mr. Barrett, Sir Maurice Cassidy, Professor Lyle Cummins, Dr. Coope, Mr. Cook, Dr. Roodhouse Gloyne, Dr. Hope Gosse, Dr. Clifford Hoyle, Dr. Hudson, Dr. Marshall, Mr. Ormerod, Mr. Price Thomas, Dr. Sparks and Mr. Williamson-Noble.

Dr. Sparks, the Consulting Radiologist, resigned in 1947. He had accepted a resident appointment in Bristol and the Council felt that it would be in the Sanatorium's best interests if a Consultant more immediately available to the Midhurst Staff were to be appointed. Dr. P. J. (later Sir Peter) Kerley, already a well established Consultant at the Westminster Hospital, was accordingly invited. He was an ideal choice for Midhurst. He was a leading authority on the radiology of chest disorders and he and Todd sat together on the X-ray panel of the first trial of Streptomycin organised by the Medical Research Council. Later he was to be the radiologist in the team led by Mr. (as he then was) Price Thomas who attended King George VI at Buckingham Palace in 1951. Other changes which occurred on the Consulting Staff were the deaths in the late 1940s of Sir Maurice Cassidy and Professor Lyle Cummins and, in 1950, of Dr. Roodhouse Gloyne. Sir Horace Evans, later Lord Evans, was appointed to the Consulting Staff in 1950 and, in the same year, Dr. Hinson, who had previously been resident pathologist at Midhurst, joined the Midhurst staff as Consultant Pathologist.

Miss Charlotte Quayle, who had been Matron since July 1932 and who had stayed at Midhurst throughout the war, retired in May 1946, a few days after the Queen's visit to the Sanatorium. She was succeeded as Matron by Miss Margaret Schofield who had been in charge of the private wing at University College Hospital during the war and who was to occupy the post of Matron at Midhurst until 1970, a period of nearly 24 years. Miss Schofield's assistant was Miss Anne Munnion who later married Dr. Charles Downes. She was succeeded as Assistant Matron in 1950 by Miss Kay Young. Appointed in 1949 to be responsible for the surgical patients was Miss Jean Clemenson, known everywhere as 'Clem'. She was later chosen to assist in the nursing of His Majesty the King when he was operated on at Buckingham Palace in 1951. Other members of the nursing staff who will be fondly remembered by patients and staff of their time were Sister Brophy and Sister Ivy Church.

The appointment of Mr. Briant Poulter as Consulting Architect was confirmed at the end of the war, and Mr. A. P. Patey, who had been 'adviser on engineering matters to the Sanatorium' in the First World War was by now the 'Consulting Engineer'. In 1945, Captain Arnold, who had been Secretary to the Council since 1932, asked to be relieved of the routine and clerical work he had been doing and to continue as Secretary in an honorary capacity. Mr. J. A. Boulton was then appointed Assistant Secretary and

Fig. 9 Dr. West, from
The Edwardian, 1947.

Fig. 10 Dr. Downes,
from *The Edwardian*,
1947.

assumed responsibility for routine administration within the Sanatorium, Captain Arnold meanwhile remaining as Honorary Secretary to the Council in London. Boulton's considerable administrative duties in the Sanatorium were officially recognised in 1948 when the Council agreed that the Superintendent should continue to delegate to him the day-to-day management of the steward's department and the accountant's and occupational therapy departments. When Captain Arnold died in 1950, Mr. Boulton was appointed Secretary to the Council.

In February 1947 the Reverend J. H. Layton was obliged to resign his post of Chaplain to the Sanatorium owing to ill health, and the Reverend M. V. Mandeville was appointed. Unfortunately he was able to remain at Midhurst for a few months only and Canon Jacomb-Hood was asked to take on the post as visiting chaplain until a successor could be found. It was not until 1950 that the Reverend R. Scruby was appointed, and he was to stay at Midhurst until 1953.

Amongst the resident medical staff there were many changes as the Medical Superintendent gathered around him a team of young and capable doctors who were attracted by the spirit of the Institution and the excellence of the work it was doing. In 1946, Dr. P. W. Morse, the Deputy Superintendent since Dr. Herington's retirement on health grounds in 1944, returned to Canada. His successor as Deputy was Dr. Douglas Teare who had trained at Cambridge and St George's Hospital and who was only 30 years old on appointment in May 1946. Next to arrive was an Australian doctor who had already spent some years as assistant medical officer at Midhurst and had been responsible for the tomographic unit in the X-Ray Department – Dr. Len West who had just been released from the R.A.M.C. after five years' war service with Airborne Forces. He was to stay at Midhurst for another year only, but his presence added balance to a young and comparatively inexperienced team. Then came Dr. M. R. J. Snelling who was appointed from the R.A.F. in June 1946 in place of Dr. George Little who had had to resign owing to ill health.

These three – Doug Teare, Len West and Mac Snelling – together with Charlie Downes, who had been Pathologist with clinical responsibilities since 1944, helped the Medical Superintendent add to the growing reputation of Midhurst as a centre of excellence. When West left in 1947 to go to Sully as Deputy Superintendent, Downes was promoted first assistant in his place. Dr. J. P. Sharp then joined the staff from the R.A.M.C., and the vacancy of pathologist was filled in 1948 by Dr. J. A. U. Morgan.

In November 1949 there arrived at Midhurst another Australian doctor, Ian Gordon, who had recently come to this country with a view to widening his medical experience. He had entertained hopes of one day becoming a thoracic surgeon, but there were not many training vacancies in Britain at that time and when he was given the chance of working at Midhurst he accepted it willingly. He was placed in charge of three floors and the X-Ray department. He found the Midhurst experience greatly to his liking (although he received no salary for four months!) and, when he was asked to supervise the laboratory under the guidance of Dr. Gloyne during Morgan's illness, he accepted that too. He is still serving at Midhurst, 37 years later, as 'a full-time Consultant Pathologist, one of the last of the traditional clinical pathologists. He must be one of the only people still working at Midhurst who can remember what medical life at the Sanatorium was like in the late 1940s – an era when few but the Consultants owned cars and the Medical Superintendent was still plain 'Doctor' Geoffrey Todd!

In the days immediately after the 1939-1945 War, the Hospital recruited a number of displaced persons, in particular, Latvians. These remarkable people, penniless and Stateless, the flotsam of war, were offered work and security at Midhurst in return for which they have provided the Hospital with some of their most loyal and willing servants. The women worked as domestics, the men as stokers, fitters, cooks and gardeners. Several of them are still at Midhurst: Freddie Peka, who joined the Hospital in 1948, now works in the Engineering Department; Wally Dzenis, an electrician, joined in 1949; Charlie Strazdins, a stoker, in 1951. Charlie Lejasmeiers started work in the X-ray Department in the 1950s and then moved on to the Operating Theatres, where he was followed in the 1970s by his son, Victor, and where both still work. Johnnie Tetins and Adam Bukbardis were others.

Another appointment made after the war was that of Mr. Victor Howell, who joined the Sanatorium staff as Chef in 1948 despite the fact that Miss Fraser had held the post since before the war. Mr. Howell had previously been 'Chef de Sauce' at the Trocadero and was recommended for the appointment at Midhurst by Mr. Salmon, a prominent member of the Sanatorium Council and a Director of Lyons. It was an embarrassing situation for Mr. Howell and indeed for Miss Fraser who had held the position of food supervisor since 1935. However, the position was accepted: Mr. Howell became 'Chef' and Miss Fraser remained 'Food Supervisor' until her retirement in the early 1960s.

Chapter VIII

Years of Achievement: 1951-1964

A New Era

In the early 1950s, the following notice, framed in black, appeared on the first page of the Sanatorium's Annual Report:

> The Council and Members of the Institution with humble duty desire to place on record their profound sorrow at the death of their beloved President, King George VI. King George VI was the fourth reigning Sovereign to be President of the Sanatorium, and the close personal interest taken by His Late Majesty will ever be remembered with pride and gratitude.

The King had died in February 1952. The new Queen was graciously pleased to become the President of the Sanatorium in succession to His Late Majesty. She was the fifth successive reigning Monarch to confer this honour on the Institution which bore her great-grandfather's name. As President she was to see the Sanatorium reach the height of its fame and to preside over changes undreamed of by her royal predecessors.

On 1 August 1956, the Sanatorium was visited by Her Majesty the Queen. She was met at the entrance by the Chairman, Lord Portal, and the Medical Superintendent, Sir Geoffrey Todd. Inside the building, members of the Council and Consulting Staff and other members of the staff were presented. The Queen then walked round the Sanatorium and talked to many of the patients and nurses. Before leaving, the Queen went out on the front lawn, in spite of the heavy rain, and waved to all the bed patients who were on their balconies to see her. The visit was especially appreciated because it was made in the Sanatorium's Jubilee Year. Fifty years previously, almost to the day, 'The King's Sanatorium' had been opened by King Edward VII. Considerable though the changes had been since then, more were yet to come.

In the early 1950s only a few patients suffering from non-tuberculous chest conditions were treated at Midhurst; the Institution was still essentially a Sanatorium intended for the management of patients with pulmonary tuberculosis. True, the Annual Report for 1950 had emphasized the point that the Sanatorium possessed facilities for the management of all kinds of chest disease, but tuberculosis was still one of the most widespread forms of serious chest illness and it is hardly surprising that the great majority of patients being admitted to Midhurst were suffering from it. In 1951 there were no fewer than 100 names on the waiting list for admission, and all available beds, of which there were 170, soon to be raised to 180, were full: only 12 of these were allocated for non-tuberculous patients. A total of 540 patients were admitted in the year ending 30 June 1951. Of these 240 were 'long term' patients with pulmonary tuberculosis and all stayed at the Sanatorium until their treatment had been completed, an average period of more than 200 days. The other 300 patients, many of whom were from the Services, were referred specifically for diagnosis, investigation and short term treatment, usually surgery, after which they were returned to the Hospital from whence they had come. Most of these patients too had pulmonary tuberculosis.

The advent of the new drugs – Streptomycin, Isoniazid and PAS – changed the picture out of all recognition. As time went on it became clear that patients could be cured of tuberculosis; furthermore they could be cured without having to undergo long periods of bed rest in hospital, sometimes even without having to go into hospital at all. It became apparent also that the drugs would make it possible for surgeons to operate in cases which were previously thought to have been beyond surgery, and they could sterilise persistent cavities which the operation of thoracoplasty might have failed to close. It was then found that under cover of drugs, surgeons could actually resect (remove by operation) areas of diseased lung, an operation which had never previously been possible in tuberculosis owing to the danger of spreading the infection into healthy parts of the lung. The portions of diseased lung thus removed were subjected to bacteriological examination and it was discovered (at Midhurst as well as at other centres) that if the drugs had been correctly given, and for a sufficient length of time before operation, the resected portions of lung were sterile. They were, therefore, unlikely to cause further trouble and might just as well be left where they were. This discovery led eventually to the abandonment of resectional surgery altogether in cases of tuberculosis, apart from exceptional cases, since the drugs were able to bring about cure by themselves. But all this lay in the future. In the 1950s and early 1960s, whilst the battle against tuberculosis was being fought and won, Midhurst was gradually extending the scope of its work to include the diagnosis and treatment of chest diseases generally. Surgery was being used increasingly frequently in the treatment of lung cancer, non-malignant tumours and bronchiectasis. The surgeons at Midhurst, Mr. Clement (soon to become Sir Clement) Price Thomas, Mr. Norman Barrett and Mr. V. T. Powell (Vince Powell) together with their anaesthetists, Dr. R. Machray, Dr. B. G. B. Lucas and Mrs. R. Mansfield, found themselves operating on most days of the week and, by 1960, the majority of their cases were non-tuberculous. The resident medical staff and the nursing staff became skilled in the pre- and post-operative management of chest conditions and, when King George VI was advised to undergo major chest surgery in 1951, Mr. Clement Price Thomas was entrusted with the operation. He was assisted by Mr. Charles Drew, Dr. Machray was the anaesthetist, and Sister Clemenson from Midhurst was selected to be responsible for His Majesty's post-operative nursing care.

These were exciting times for everyone concerned with treating diseases of the chest, and Midhurst's place as a leading centre became recognised throughout the world. The list of Consultants glistened with illustrious names. All were men of international renown who had played notable parts in the development and understanding of every aspect of thoracic disease. They came regularly to Midhurst to see patients and to discuss their treatment with the resident medical staff. In this way the standard of work at the Sanatorium was kept very high.

The Medical Superintendent, Sir Geoffrey Todd, was now at the very peak of his career. He was on the governing bodies of all the organisations in Britain dealing with tuberculosis and diseases of the chest. He knew all the Midhurst consultants intimately and was acquainted with the leading figures in chest medicine throughout the world. As a physician his opinion was widely sought and respected. As Superintendent he reigned supreme. By his patients he was both feared and respected, even loved. Feared, because he was sometimes sarcastic and his manner could be forbidding. Loved, because he was essentially understanding and kind. He could read his patients' minds like a book and knew exactly with whom to be gentle and with whom to be tough. His ability to inspire confidence was outstanding. His patients were quietly certain that in his hands all would turn out for the best.

He was in great demand as a guest lecturer on many aspects of tuberculosis and had published, alone or in collaboration with his Midhurst staff, several important scientific papers in the *Lancet* and other journals. He had been the first Waksman lecturer in the U.S.A. and had delivered the Marc Daniels and Tudor Edwards lectures at the Royal College of Physicians, London. Appointed a Knight Commander of the Royal Victorian Order in 1951, he became Civilian Consultant in Diseases of the Chest to the R.A.F. and Honorary Consultant in Pulmonary Tuberculosis to the Army at Home. If any one person could be said to have made Midhurst pre-eminent, it was he.

After the war he gathered around him a team of doctors and nurses, all intensely loyal to Midhurst and its traditions, who became fired with his enthusiasm and eagerness to put Midhurst on the map, and keep it there. If proof were needed of Midhurst's growing reputation it could be seen in the number of doctors from all over the world, and especially from Australia,* who visited the Sanatorium to find out what was going on in the field of tuberculosis and to learn how things should be done. Newcomers to the staff were always made welcome, but they were subtly made aware of their place; they had to prove themselves before they were accepted. For Midhurst was now one of the élite, and like élitist organisations everywhere it had developed a well merited opinion of its own worth.

X-ray viewing sessions became an important feature of medical life at the Sanatorium. These had been started before the war, but they were developed to a new pitch after the war had ended. All the resident medical staff as well as ward sisters, radiographers and any students under training were expected to attend. Service doctors would often be present and so might consultants from abroad, from London, from Chichester or from Aldingbourne (then a chest hospital in West Sussex). Sir Geoffrey would sit before the viewing boxes, pointer in hand, in the middle of the front row, flanked by members of his own staff and by the visiting consultants, one of whom might be invited to sit beside him. In the second and subsequent rows sat the radiographer, ward sisters and less exalted visitors. The doctor responsible for the case would stand by the viewing panels, display the X-ray plates (no easy matter when there were many of them) and relate the history and findings. A general discussion would follow at which formality was abandoned and comment was frank. Sir Geoffrey conducted the proceedings himself, but he let everyone have his say, indeed he expected them to do so. He was always ready to listen to other opinions but his was usually the last word. Everyone who went to these meetings enjoyed them and no one left without feeling he had learned something.

Midhurst had sufficiently established its reputation by the mid 1960s to feel able to mount a three-day conference at the Sanatorium in 1962 on the subject of the treatment of tuberculosis. This conference was a resounding success. All the leading figures of the day, many of them from overseas, were invited to attend and the proceedings were published in book form. Two years later a similar conference was organised entitled 'The Nature of Asthma' and in 1966 a symposium was held on the subject of 'Carcinoma of the Bronchus and other malignant conditions of the Lung'. The proceedings of these meetings also were published.

Sir Geoffrey's team of doctors in the early 1950s consisted of Dr. Douglas Teare, who had been his deputy since his appointment in 1946; Dr. M. R. J. (Mac) Snelling, Dr. John Wilkinson (who succeeded Dr. Carruthers in 1952), and Dr. Ian Gordon who had by now assumed responsibility for the laboratory as well as continuing to look after patients. In that year the Consulting Staff decided that, for purposes of pay and seniority the Deputy Superintendent (Teare) should rank as a consultant, the 1st assistant (Snelling) as a senior hospital medical officer, the 2nd assistant (Wilkinson) as a middle grade registrar and 3rd assistant (if there was one) as a senior house officer. In 1955 Dr. Snelling left to take up the appointment of Physician Superintendent at the recently opened Lady Templer Hospital at Kuala Lumpur, Malaya. Dr. Rhys Jones took his place and, when Wilkinson went to Lincoln in 1957 as chest physician, two new doctors were appointed who were to remain familiar figures at Midhurst for many years – Dr. K. M. Hume, who stayed for 20 years, and Dr. P. J. Doyle who did not retire until 1983. Mike Hume was appointed 2nd assistant medical officer and later took charge of the new respiratory physiology laboratory which was regarded as an essential component of any up to date chest unit. Paddy Doyle had been invalided from the Royal Navy as a Lieutenant Commander after the war and

Fig. 11 Dr. Teare, from *The Edwardian*, 1947.

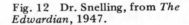

Fig. 12 Dr. Snelling, from *The Edwardian*, 1947.

had then taken up medicine as a second career. No sooner had he qualified in medicine than he had to undergo an operation at the Sanatorium in 1955. He knew all about Midhurst from the patient's point of view so his appointment as 3rd assistant medical officer in 1957 was singularly fitting.

There were no house officers or registrars at Midhurst in the 1950s and early 1960s. The assistant medical officers, even those of considerable experience, were responsible for every aspect of their patients' care and management. They would take the history in detail, examine their patients and counsel them, keep the notes up to date, take blood for the laboratory, accompany their patients to theatre and assist the surgeon at operations, deal with any post-operative complication, put up transfusions and drips – and all this in addition to their 'medical' tasks of aspirating pleural effusions, inducing artificial pneumothoraces, inserting chest drains and performing bronchograms, taking X-rays and even processing the films themselves. They were in every sense complete doctors who learned from hard experience that at Midhurst medicine and surgery were one and indivisible.

Laboratory, X-ray and Physiotherapy

The Department of Pathology occupied five rooms at the end of the surgical rooms on the ground floor. Dr. Ian Gordon was the resident pathologist. He had by this time given up responsibility for the X-ray department, but, in addition to the laboratory, he remained in charge of a considerable number of patients on the floors. Although he had not been a pathologist by inclination, he learned his subject the hard way, by actually practising it. As he went along he received guidance from the Consulting Pathologist to the Sanatorium, Dr. Roodhouse Gloyne, and later from Gloyne's successor as Consultant, Dr. Hinson, with whom he was always on good terms and from whom he learned much. His staff consisted of Mr. Rumsby, and Mr. and Mrs. Lunt. Geoff Rumsby, formerly a school teacher with a university training in science, but with no specialised medical knowledge, had come to Midhurst before the war and was trained for laboratory work by Dr. Hinson who was at that time the resident doctor in charge of the laboratory. Bill Lunt came to Midhurst after the war as a porter! He too received his laboratory training locally. Margaret had been an R.A.F. nurse who had been seconded to the Sanatorium for nurse training. She and Bill Lunt met at Midhurst and were married in the early 1950s. She gave up nursing, learned her laboratory work at Midhurst and soon became part of the laboratory team. The Lunts did not finally retire until 1980, almost at the same time as Geoff Rumsby.

Although the laboratory had been capable in 1951 of carrying out all the investigations that were then needed, their methods were continually being improved. Because blood transfusions were being given more frequently, the laboratory became increasingly involved in the techniques of cross matching and blood grouping. With the increase in surgery, prothrombin times had to be carried out. As more anti-tuberculosis drugs became available, sensitivity testing brought about a vast increase in their work. By 1965, there were four sections within the laboratory: bacteriology, where sputum was examined and sensitivity tests performed; bio-chemistry, which carried out blood chemistry and liver function tests; histology, where specimens were examined for cancer; and haemotology where blood disorders were investigated and transfusion techniques monitored.

A new department, the respiratory physiology laboratory, was formed in 1956. It was situated on the ground floor in a room used today as an office. Dr. K. M. Hume, a specialist in the physiology of breathing, was placed in charge. The laboratory was equipped with apparatus required for the investigation of various aspects of lung function and later with blood gas analysers and positive pressure respirators. Work started with tests of lung function on patients about to undergo thoracic surgery, and was later extended to include ventilatory tests on patients with asthma and emphysema. The Sanatorium began to admit such patients in 1957 and Dr. Hume was given a ward of his own in which to look after them.

In charge of the X-ray department, which was then situated on the ground floor where the present physiotherapy department is now sited, was the redoubtable Miss Watt. In her own sphere she ruled supreme and took advice from no one except the Medical Superintendent, and not always from him. Peter Bellingham and then Charlie Lejasmeiers (who later went to the operating theatres) helped out with the more ordinary tasks, otherwise Miss Watt did everything, including writing the patients' particulars in white ink on every single X-ray film. Miss Watt came to Midhurst in 1953 from the Westminster Hospital. When she retired in 1964 she was succeeded by Miss Margaret Easton who remained in the post until her retirement in 1986. So independent was Miss Watt, that when handing over to Miss Easton she told her nothing whatever about the work she was expected to do. Miss Easton's questions were met with an implacable 'Its not your responsibility'. The department had functioned efficiently under her regime nevertheless.

For several years after 1964, Miss Easton managed the department on her own with only Charlie Lejasmeiers to help her. When the amount of work became too much for the two of them, a succession of radiographers were taken on 'part-time' who maintained the high standard of work done by the department. One of these was Miss Patricia Holmes. She started work at Midhurst 'part-time', but later converted to 'full-time' and thus became Miss Easton's first 'full-time' assistant. She continued working in the department for over 10 years and did not retire until 1984.

The Consulting Radiologist to the Sanatorium was Dr.Peter Kerley who had been appointed in 1947. His contribution to the department was incalculable. He had been Consultant in charge when Midhurst was still a Sanatorium. He was there before and during the time when Miss Watt was the sole radiographer. He was Consultant in charge when Miss Easton replaced Miss Watt in 1964 and when Midhurst shed its sanatorium rôle and became a hospital. He did not retire until 1969 and he was knighted in 1972. What changes had occurred since he first came to Midhurst in 1947! When he left the active ranks of the consulting staff to become emeritus in 1969, radiography had become as diversified as the Hospital. The number of specialised X-ray examinations performed had increased many times over– barium meals, intra-venous pyelograms and cholecystograms, more orthopaedic X-rays, even television fluoroscopy. Throughout this period of change, Dr. Kerley was a constant inspiration and ensured that the department under Miss Easton never lacked for staff and equipment.

The physiotherapy department in the 1950s and 1960s was situated in rooms, which are today occupied by the School of Nursing. The senior physiotherapist at the time was Miss Mary Brachie and it was she who was largely responsible for developing the department into the highly specialised unit which contributed so much to the

Sanatorium's success as a thoracic hospital. In the 1950s the department dealt exclusively with chest conditions. The treatment of post-operative thoracic cases and of bronchiectasis, then a common condition, took up much of their time. Only later were their activities extended to include general medical and surgical conditions.

The Nursing Scene

There was an acute shortage of nurses after the war and Miss Schofield had difficulty in recruiting all she needed. Midhurst's isolated situation did not help matters, and means had to be devised of persuading nurses to forsake the city lights and come out to the country. One attraction was the opportunity for recreation and sport offered by Midhurst, another the excellent living conditions in the new nurses' home. But the best selling point of all was to offer nurses the opportunity of further training in specialised nursing.

Training courses for the Certificate of the British Tuberculosis Association (B.T.A.) were therefore introduced and, as long as tuberculosis remained the Sanatorium's main stock in trade, these attracted many nurses to Midhurst from the Services and from overseas, especially from Australia and New Zealand. (For nurses visiting this country and wishing to expand their nursing experience, an attachment at Midhurst was very much 'the thing to do'.) Another attraction was the introduction in 1955 of a King Edward VII Sanatorium Certificate which was awarded to those nurses who had spent at least 18 months in post graduate training at Midhurst and who had already succeeded in passing the B.T.A. Certificate.

As the incidence of tuberculosis declined, the British Tuberculosis Association revised their syllabus and offered a general Thoracic Nursing Certificate to replace the specialised Tuberculosis Certificate. The new syllabus was introduced at Midhurst, but it was only partially successful in attracting nurses in the numbers needed. Even with the support of 10 student nurses and a number of nursing officers seconded for training from the Queen Alexandra's Royal Army Nursing Corps and the Princess Mary's Royal Air Force Nursing Service, the total nursing strength was proving inadequate.

Eventually recourse had to be made, albeit with some reluctance, to employing nurses on short terms of engagement through agencies. There were disadvantages in this arrangement – it was expensive and the nurses never really settled down – so it was decided to try another tack and to discuss with the Royal College of Nursing the possibility of establishing a Pupil Nurse Training School at the Sanatorium. The hope was that some girls, after gaining their certificates, might decide to stay on for a year or two at Midhurst as State Enrolled Nurses. There was a risk that the numbers doing so might be insufficient to justify the expense involved, but after discussion with the Royal College of Nursing and the General Nursing Council it was decided to go ahead. Class rooms were equipped, tutors engaged, a syllabus prepared. Under the supervision of Mrs. Childs, who had planned the entire project with Miss Schofield, the first course started in 1964 and was attended by 10 pupils. Other courses followed annually and since then there have always been twenty to thirty nurses under training at one time, and many of them after qualifying have stayed on to work at Midhurst. Many of the early entrants were Malaysian girls – mostly from the Ipoh High School for girls. The arrangement owed much to Dr. Snelling who had left Midhurst for Kuala Lumpur in

1955. A few Gurkha nurses from Nepal were also attached for a time by arrangement with the Army Medical Department, Ministry of Defence.

Midhurst was not alone, of course, in finding it difficult to recruit young nurses; most other sanatoria were similarly affected. Where Midhurst was unique was that it never had difficulty in attracting and retaining the services of experienced nurses of high calibre who were made sisters and put in charge of wards. This was because Midhurst offered senior nurses security and a way of life which appealed to them. When Miss Schofield was appointed Matron in 1946, the Secretary of her old hospital said to her before she left, 'There is something about Midhurst. I am glad you are going there'. There certainly was, and indeed there still is, 'something about Midhurst' and there are many sisters and others at Midhurst today who would re-echo Miss Schofield's words, spoken some months after she had arrived, 'I'm glad I came'.

Amongst those who came to Midhurst during these 'years of achievement' and stayed there for many years were Sisters McGregor, Sharp (née Newport), Drane, Norton, Behr and Lee(née Bowles). Staff Nurse E. McGregor actually arrived in August 1949 and was promoted to Sister in June 1950, but she did not retire until July 1982. Always known affectionately as 'Mac', she was at various times during her long career at Midhurst, Sister in Charge of Floor 3 (now Norfolk Ward), Floor 2 (Barbara Agar Ward) and Floor 6 (Cassel Ward).

Denny Newport arrived in 1953 to take her B.T.A. Certificate and stayed on as Charge Nurse (or 'Red-Belt' as they were then called) to Sister Clemenson. She later took over a surgical floor (Floor 7) as Sister in Charge, married and became Denny Sharp in 1970, and remained on the surgical floors until 1982. She spent her last three years at Midhurst in charge of the admissions office – a change from nursing perhaps, but a great boon for the Hospital because the time needed for admitting patients was immediately cut by half! Today she is working in the library as a part-time volunteer.

Pam Drane and Wendy Norton arrived together as staff nurses in January 1959 to do their B.T.A. training and both are working still as senior sisters at Midhurst. After passing her B.T.A., Pam Drane stayed on the medical wards and has been Sister in Charge of Floor 4 (Cowdray) for many years. Wendy Norton worked on the surgical wards under Sister Clemenson and then obtained a surgical floor (Floor 8) of her own as a Sister. When Professor John Charnley began hip surgery at Midhurst in December 1969, she was given responsibility for his patients, and when King Khaled of Saudi Arabia was operated on by Charnley at the Wellington Hospital, she was a member of the team selected by Charnley to be responsible for the King's nursing care.

Sister Lee has been associated with Midhurst since 1957 when (as Nurse Bowles) she was detached from Chichester to do her training in chest work at the Sanatorium. After she had married Jack Lee, who is now assistant in the supplies department but was then working for Dr. Gordon in the laboratory, she joined the staff at Midhurst. She became a sister on Surgical Ward 1 in 1972 and later moved to Floor 5 (Todd Ward) in charge of post-operative thoracic cases. She is still working as a sister at Midhurst on Portal Ward. Sister C. Behr joined the staff as night sister in 1962. She remained night sister until 1968, being succeeded by Sister E. Churchill. Sister Behr retired in 1980 and Sister Churchill in 1979.

The Service Connection

For many years there had been a close relationship between Midhurst and the Armed Services,* and during the war the Sanatorium had been full of Service patients, but it was with the Royal Air Force that a very special link had been forged. Before the war, Wing Commander Rooke, a senior R.A.F. Consultant, and Dr. Geoffrey Todd had arranged that R.A.F. officers with tuberculosis might be sent to Midhurst for treatment. During the war, the Service link was strengthened. Squadron Leader Powell came to Midhurst in 1942 – and stayed there until 1979! Dr. Todd was appointed Civilian Consultant to the R.A.F. and Consultant to the Army at Home. Consultants from all three Services used to visit regularly. After the war, young service doctors wishing to specialise in chest diseases were seconded to Midhurst for training. The R.A.F. and Army Chest Units used to visit Midhurst fortnightly to present cases for discussion. Nursing officers from the three Services were seconded to Midhurst for specialised training – often for as long as 18 months. Male nursing orderlies from the Connaught Hospital at Hindhead (the Army Chest Centre) were attached to Midhurst for work in the wards.

In 1964 there occurred an event which was the happy culmination of Midhurst's close association with the Royal Air Force over 25 years – the opening of a new R.A.F. Chest Unit to replace that which had been recently closed at the R.A.F Hospital Wroughton. The new unit at Midhurst was accommodated on the top floor of the main building, today's Norfolk Ward, and it operated under the direction of an R.A.F. Consultant, Group Captain I. W. H. R. Cran, assisted by a Sergeant clerk. The nursing support and maintenance needs were provided by the Sanatorium. This R.A.F Unit, now situated on the ground floor in Portal Ward, is still active at Midhurst and the arrangement has brought nothing but benefit both to the R.A.F. and to the Hospital. Royal Air Force chest cases for diagnosis and treatment have been sent to the unit at Midhurst from all over the world, and a frequent event has been the arrival on the cricket field of an R.A.F. helicopter bearing a serviceman in need of urgent attention and specialised care.

Group Captain Ian Cran, who was later promoted to Air Commodore, was first and foremost an officer of the Royal Air Force, but during his long period of secondment to Midhurst he became so integrated with the Hospital, and so much involved in its affairs, that he was looked on by every one as a normal member of the Hospital staff, taking part in duty rosters and wearing a white coat over his uniform. He was still serving in the R.A.F. at the time of his untimely death at his home near Midhurst in 1978 at the early age of 63. At his memorial service at Easebourne, there were as many civilians as servicemen in the congregation, ample testimony to the esteem in which he was held by the local community. A service was held in the Hospital Chapel in May 1980 attended by the Director General, R.A.F. Medical Services, and other senior officers, when a plaque in his memory was unveiled and dedicated. The inscription said everything: 'Air Commodore Ian Cran, C.B.E., Q.H.S., Officer Commanding RAF Chest Unit. A beloved physician and friend'.

Buildings and Chapel

At a casual glance King Edward VII Hospital did not look very different in the 1950s and early '60s from the Sanatorium as it had been when it was opened in 1906, because exceptional care had always been taken to use matching bricks and materials whenever a building alteration or addition was made. But in fact there had been many

31. Dr. R. R. Trail.

32. Sir Geoffrey Todd.

33. Dr. Douglas Teare.

34. Mr. Tudor Edwards.

35. Sir Clement Price Thomas.

36. Sir John Charnley.

37. Sir Geoffrey Marshall.

38. Sir Kenneth Robson.

39. Air Commodore Cran.

Superintendents, Surgeons and Physicians

40. (*above*) After opening the Midhurst Medical Research Institute on 2 November 1973, the Queen signs the visitors' book watched by Mr. Derek Wilde, Sir Geoffrey Todd, Professor Cumming and Mrs. Sears-Black, with Dr. Gabe in the white coat behind.

41. (*below*) The Queen, accompanied by the Duke of Norfolk, meets Dr. Teare, Miss Beech and Mr. Boulton.

42. (*above*) Presentation of badges and certificates, 1974. Her Grace, Lavinia, Duchess of Norfolk, with Miss Allen, Mrs. Brook and Sister Scott, and pupils from Set 19 and Set 20.

43. (*below*) Representatives from the Private Patients Plan hand a cheque to the Matron, Miss Allen, in August 1979. Also shown in the picture are Dr. Large (left), Mr. Bradford (right), and Mr. Boulton.

44. (*above*) After opening the Mountbatten Unit on 31 July 1980, the Prince of Wales talks to Mrs. Lettley, Miss Richardson and Miss Slocock, with Mrs. Cock in the background.

45. (*left*) The Prince of Wales and Ted Rogers, 31 July 1980.

46. (*above*) Dr. White explains the technicalities of the Linear Accelerator to the Prince, while Dr. Irene Cade looks on.

47. (*below*) Signing the Macmillan Services contract, 10 September 1985. From left to right: Dr. McKenna; Her Grace, Lavinia, Duchess of Norfolk; Mr. Morgan-Grenville; The Countess of Westmorland (President of the National Society for Cancer Relief); Sir Geoffrey Hardy-Roberts; Major H. C. L. Garnett.

48. Matron and nursing sisters, May 1985. Back row, left to right: Sister Glasgow, Charge Nurse Garner, Sister Redmond, Mrs. O'Conor, Sister Sullivan, Sister L. Graham, Sister Hall, Mrs. Brook, Sister Porteous, Sister Porter, Sister Hancock, Mrs. Alexander, Miss Percy, Sister Jay, Sister Boxall, Sister Lindsey, Sister Jones. Middle row, Seated, left to right: Sister Houlston, Sister O'Rourke, Sister Daniel, Mrs. Wright, Miss Allen, Miss Peattie, Mrs. Shahab, Sister Norton, Sister Drane, Sister Watson. Front row, left to right: Sister Hay, Sister Norris, Sister Taylor, Sister Barns, Sister Lee, Sister Hitchcock, Sister Davis, Sister Peasey, Sister M. Graham, Sister Banks.

Personalities Past and Present

49. Dr. Geoffrey Todd, about 1937.

50. Mac Snelling, about 1954.

51. Miss Watt, 1960.

52. Ian Gordon, 1986.

53. Margaret Easton and Colin Bennell, 1986.

changes. An extension to the nurses' home had been completed. All the patients' bedrooms had been repainted and now had their own hand basins with running hot and cold water. Two small wards were planned for building on the north side of the patients' block – now the Brodie and Hansard Wards. (The money for one came from the sale of the Brodie's former home, Bottingdean, which had been left to the Sanatorium for homeless staff and patients, but which later had to be sold.*) The Nissen huts were demolished in 1962 and the physiotherapy and occupational therapy departments, the shop and the library (at that time run by the Red Cross) had been grouped together in a specially built annex erected in 1964. The dispensary remained on the ground floor near where the shop is situated today. The connecting corridor between the administration and patients' blocks became known as the Blue Lounge in deference to Lord Courtauld-Thomson's passion for blue paint and furnishings, and above it a new patients' lounge was constructed in 1961. A staff recreation hall for indoor games and dances was opened by Lord Courtauld-Thomson in 1952 as a memorial to the late Secretary to the Council, Captain Arnold. A new lecture hall for the doctors and nurses, with its own viewing boxes and projectors, was built in 1955 in memory of the late Chairman of Council, Lord Courtauld-Thomson, who died in 1954. (These two halls are today occupied by the supplies officer and his staff.)

Several new bungalows for resident staff had been built in the grounds (two of these, for retired members of staff with long service, were paid for out of the proceeds of the Bottingdean sale); the nurses' home was extended to provide 27 additional rooms; an open air swimming pool had been constructed (in 1961), a new main lift in the Hospital was provided and, in 1958, modern oil-fired boilers had been installed in place of the original coal-fired Lancashire boilers which had been in place since the Sanatorium was built. The electric circuits throughout the Hospital had been renewed, the rough ground to the south of the building, the site of the old 'mashie' golf course, had been cleared and levelled (with the assistance of Army sappers) and a cricket field prepared. The gardens were restored to their pre-war splendour and were opened to the public on special occasions. The vegetable garden continued in production for some years, and so did the pig and poultry farms, but they could never meet all the Hospital's needs and proved to be increasingly uneconomic to run. The vegetable garden and the poultry farm were discontinued in the early 1960s: the pigs were kept on for a few more years – they consumed all the Hospital's waste food! – but even they were finally given up in the early 1980s.

In March 1957 work was completed to fill in the open sides of the Chapel with glass partitions, and services could now be held indoors for the first time since the Chapel was consecrated. This work had been made possible by the Right Reverend Bishop Bell, Bishop of Chichester, who obtained a large contribution toward the cost from an anonymous donor. The open sides were filled by glass partitions designed by the Consulting Architect, Mr. Briant Poulter. Two stained glass panels were incorporated depicting the coats of arms of Canterbury and Chichester, and the completed work was dedicated by Bishop Bell whose interest had made the work possible. The closure not only made worship more comfortable for clergy and congregation: it made it feasible to purchase a new blowing unit for the organ to replace the old one which had rotted as a result of exposure. But it did little for the chapel acoustics which had been excellent before the closure but indifferent, to say the least, after it!

At about this time, agreement was reached that one nave of the chapel should be used by Roman Catholics, the other by Anglicans. This brought to an end years of indecision on the matter. Until then Roman Catholics had held their services in the 'Ladies Recreation Room', now the Cassel Lounge, and before that in a room in the basement. Several attempts had been made previously to let them use part of the chapel, but they had come to naught. Now, through the efforts of Her Grace, the Duchess of Norfolk, and Bishop Cashman of Arundel, the Chapel at Midhurst became one of only a few bi-denominational churches in England.

The Patients' Viewpoint

How did patients with tuberculosis respond to the Midhurst regime of the 1950s? Pulmonary tuberculosis, though not the 'killer' it once had been, was not to be trifled with. The chances of patients with persisting lung cavities surviving more than a few years were still poor. Even with the advent of the new drugs, long periods of bed rest and isolation in hospital away from home and work were still necessary. Nevertheless, the new drugs offered hope of recovery to the majority of patients, hope that had been denied patients before them, and this changed attitudes in a subtle way. There was not the same need for them to have faith in the Sanatorium system to make them well. Faith was still needed, and it was Todd's strength that he could inspire it, but it was faith of a more informed and understanding kind.*

The routine management of patients with tuberculosis at Midhurst was much the same as it had always been. There was still the same need for complete rest in bed while the disease was active, followed by visits to the lavatory, then to the bathroom, then downstairs to meals. Then followed the carefully controlled return to full activity through a series of graded exercise tests – half a mile a day for 10 days, a mile a day for the next 10 days – and so on until the stage was reached when a patient was permitted to walk three miles a day, and might even be granted a short pass to visit Midhurst. Life for the patient was disciplined. Everything he did was planned. There was a reason for every rule – and woe betide anyone, patient, nurse or doctor, who broke one. A transgressor might think he had been unobserved, but the news always reached the great man's ears and retribution was swift.

On the first day after a patient's arrival, he (or she) was seen by the Medical Superintendent and told exactly what was wrong with him and what he must do to get well. A sense of mutual trust was thereby created which lasted throughout the whole of his stay at Midhurst. On the day before his discharge the patient had a final interview with the Medical Superintendent and was told how to look after himself after leaving the protective atmosphere of the 'San' to enter the cold world outside. Meanwhile there had been numerous other talks with the sanatorium staff, often with Todd himself, to keep him informed of progress and of how he could assist in his own recovery.

In the 1950s, patients still had their meals in the main dining room. The doctors now used another room a little apart from the patients but within sight of them. In the 1950s the doctors did not have beer with their meals. This had been a privilege they had enjoyed before the war when beer was thought to have a 'protective' quality. The ban on alcohol for patients was supposedly still in force, but it was not taken very seriously. Sherry or wine before meals was certainly enjoyed by many patients and the staff knew all about it. The smuggling in of spirits, however, might still incur a wigging for the culprit were he to be caught.

The library continued to be much used and patients could buy confectionery, stationery, toilet articles and similar goods from the shop where they could also, if they wished, hand in any clothing in need of cleaning or repair. Trolleys from the shop visited the floors regularly to meet the needs of patients not allowed to leave the ward.

Newspapers and magazines were delivered daily to the Sanatorium by Messrs. Clark Brothers of Midhurst. Fruit, flowers and eggs could be bought from local nurserymen who delivered to the Sanatorium on Fridays (Messrs. Goldrings) and Saturdays (Messrs. Terry). A selection of clothing for sale was displayed in the billiard room on alternate Thursdays by Messrs. Bradley's Ltd., Gentlemen's Outfitters of West Street, Midhurst. A hair dressing service was (and still is) provided by Mr. P. Battensby.

The sub post office at the Sanatorium was still in being in the 1950s and 1960s to deal with parcels, registered letters, stamps and postal orders. Telegrams were sent off by the switch board operator. Letters from bed patients were collected by an up-patient in time for the regular collection from the box. Cheques could be cashed (as long as they did not exceed £10 in value) through the treasurer of the Patients' General Purposes Committee.

The General Purposes Committee had a chairman, secretary and treasurer elected from amongst the patients, and the committee was made up of representatives from each of the floors. There were secretaries for entertainment, television, gramophone and linguaphone, and a church warden. The president (ex-officio) was the Medical Superintendent. The duties of the committee were to put the views of the patients before the Sanatorium authorities and to provide and organise amenities and entertainments. Bridge, billiards and garden games were organised, and most patients had television sets in their rooms, which were hired from Messrs. Hamilton Cole Ltd. of Worthing and Messrs. Willmers of Pulborough. Cinema shows were held at least once a week and concerts and recitals were arranged frequently. 'Discs with Don' was a favourite. (Don was a patient who played records on request over the Sanatorium's broadcast system.) Occupational therapy was popular and the men could be seen making moccasins or using knitting machines whilst the women did embroidery or learned to type. A handicraft instructor visited patients regularly, and Mr. Adrian Hill continued to advise and assist patients who wished to study painting and sketching.

Patients always enjoyed Christmas at the Sanatorium. The floors were lavishly and ingeniously decorated; the doctors and nurses took round presents and joined in the fun. A special dinner was held, attended by staff and patients. Everyone was formally dressed; speeches were made and the alcohol ban was suspended. Just before Christmas the staff entertained the patients to a pantomime. This took many weeks to prepare but the audience seemed to enjoy it. (So did the staff, though pretending not to!) The Superintendent himself always played a major part in these shows. As Sheikh O Bey Todd in *The Desert Wrong* (1954), Sir Geoffrey's vocal rendition of 'I was born beneath the wattle: reared on grog from a medicine bottle' earned him enormous applause – and the admiration and respect of his entire staff. Of course with the Superintendent so closely involved, no doctor or sister could possibly escape: everyone was expected to participate in some way or another. A service doctor who played one of the 'wicked sisters' was invited to remove his moustache for the occasion, but this was one order from a superior officer he refused to carry out.

On the whole, morale amongst the patients was high. Despite the restrictions and regulations, perhaps because of them, patients enjoyed themselves. Everyone at the 'San' seemed anxious to be helpful. The atmosphere was relaxed and carefree. Protected from the hustle and bustle of the outside world, patients learned to take their time and to live within their limits. It was no accident that so few of them coughed, that so many looked extraordinary well. And when the time came for them to leave, they were physically and mentally well attuned to face up to the rigours of life outside.

Council, Consultants and Staff

The Sanatorium suffered a severe loss in November 1954 when the Chairman of Council, Lord Courtauld-Thomson, died. The Institution owed him much. He had been a member of Council since 1920 and its Chairman from 1922, a longer period in office than anyone before or since. He was succeeded by Marshal of the Royal Air Force, the Viscount Portal of Hungerford, who remained Chairman until 1969. Sir Felix Cassel, who had been a member of Council since 1932, died in 1952, and was succeeded by Lord Knollys, and in that year Mrs. Brodie was appointed Lady Visitor to the Sanatorium.

The Council in 1955 was composed of Brigadier, The Lord Tryon (Vice President), Lord Portal (Chairman) and the following members: Mr. Salmon, Lord Cowdray, Lord Knollys, Lady Mountbatten, Sir Robert Young and Sir Geoffrey Marshall. Mrs. Herbert Agar was appointed a member of Council in succession to Sir Robert Young in 1956, and the Council remained unchanged thereafter until the sudden death of the Countess Mountbatten of Burma in Borneo whilst on a tour of the Far East in 1960.

There were changes also amongst the Consulting Staff. Dr. Todd, Mr. Clement Price Thomas and Dr. R. A. Young received knighthoods in 1951, and in that year Mr. E. P. Brockman (Consulting Orthopaedic Surgeon) and Mr. Frank Cook (Consulting Gynaecologist) were appointed to the staff.

In 1956 Dr. Hope Gosse died and was succeeded the following year by Dr. Lloyd Rusby. In 1959 Sir Robert Young died. He had been a member of the Consulting Staff since 1925 and its Chairman for 13 years. As a member of Council he had served since 1949. His death was an irreparable loss and was felt keenly by everyone at the Sanatorium, for he had been a much loved figure. Another giant in the world of thoracic medicine, Sir Geoffrey Marshall, succeeded him as Chairman. Appointed to the panel of Consultants in place of Mr. Cook and Mr. Brockman (who resigned in 1959) were Mr. Ian Jackson (Consulting Gynaecologist) and Mr. H. E. Harding (Consulting Orthopaedic Surgeon). Dr. Brian Taylor, who had been one of the resident assistant medical officers at Midhurst before the war, was also appointed a member of the Consulting Staff in the same year. Lord Evans died in 1963, Dr. Neville Oswald succeeding him. In the following year Sir Ronald Bodley-Scott and Dr. (later Sir) Kenneth Robson were appointed. At the time of transition from Sanatorium to Hospital in 1964, the Consulting Staff consisted of Sir Geoffrey Marshall (Chairman), Mr. Barrett, Sir Ronald Bodley-Scott, Dr. Coope, Mr. Harding, Dr. Hinson, Dr. Hoyle, Dr. Hudson, Mr. Ian Jackson, Dr. Kerley, Mr. J. C. Hogg (who had succeeded Mr. Frank Ormerod as Consulting Laryngologist), Dr. Neville Oswald, Sir Clement Price Thomas, Dr. Robson, Dr. Rusby, Dr. Taylor and Mr. Williamson-Noble.

Mr. V. T. Powell was listed in the Annual Report for 1964 as 'Visiting Thoracic

Surgeon'. With Sir Clement Price Thomas and Mr. Barrett, he had been continuously active at Midhurst since demobilisation from the R.A.F. in 1946. The anaesthetists were Dr. R. Machray, Mrs. Mansfield and Dr. B. G. B. Lucas and the dental surgeons Messrs. G. D. Fleetwood, R. O. Murray and F. J. Summers.

Throughout this period Mr. Briant Poulter continued to act as Consulting Architect to the Sanatorium and the Honorary Legal Advisers remained the firm of Lewis & Lewis & Gisborne who had been appointed in 1942 after the death of Sir Reginald Poole, the Honorary Solicitor. In 1964 the firm became Messrs. Penningtons and Lewis & Lewis. Mr. C. J. Maby, who had been senior partner, became senior partner of the amalgamated firms.

The Consulting Engineer, Mr. A. P. Patey, resigned in 1959 after an association with the Sanatorium in an advisory capacity of more than 50 years. He was succeeded by Mr. T. A. L. Paton, senior partner of Sir Alexander Gibb and Partners. The Auditor was Sir Harry Peat until his death in 1959 when Mr. Henry Peat succeeded him.

The Reverend R. Scruby, curate at Rogate and later Archdeacon at Portsmouth, had been appointed Chaplain to the Sanatorium in 1950 and he was succeeded in 1954 by the Reverend Philip Pasterfield (later Bishop of Crediton), who continued as Chaplain until 1960 when he was succeeded by the Reverend John Wansey. Father O'Connell, the Roman Catholic Chaplain, resigned in 1953 and Father Waller, who continued at Midhurst for 27 years, came in his stead.

The administrative structure within the Sanatorium, and the staff itself, remained almost unchanged between 1951 and 1964. As Medical Superintendent, Sir Geoffrey Todd exercised total authority, and was responsible to the Council for everything that went on at the Sanatorium, but he delegated the routine administration to Mr. Boulton who in turn had working under him a team of departmental heads. The Steward was Mr. Brian Speed (ex-Royal Navy) who had been appointed in 1949 in place of Mr. E. J. Sudbury, a Lyons nominee, who had succeeded Jack Williams in 1946. Brian Speed remained at Midhurst for over 30 years, not retiring until 1981. In the stores department he was assisted by Jack Lee who had come first to Midhurst in 1952 as an R.A.M.C. nursing orderly on detachment from the Connaught Hospital (Army Chest Centre), Hindhead. In 1960 Jack Lee married a Nurse Bowles who was on secondment from Chichester and both he and Sister Lee are today still working at Midhurst.

The accounts were in the hands of Mr. Cairns who had been appointed in 1953 after Mr. Clarenbone's retirement. The resident engineer was Mr. J. Taylor who had previously been a fitter and then assistant to Mr. Hampton, taking over as the resident engineer on Mr. Ashburner's retirement in 1949. Jack Taylor was resident engineer until his death in 1963 when Mr. R. J. Harvey was appointed. Alan Bradley, still working at Midhurst, and one of the mainstays on the engineering side, was first appointed to the Midhurst staff in 1961.

The head gardener was still Mr. P. J. Allen. He did not finally retire until 1980, but Ian Scott, who started as a junior at Midhurst in 1964, took over as garden superintendent in 1983.

Catering was the joint responsibility of Mr. Victor Howell, the Chef, assisted after 1966 by Mr. Ron Luckhurst (who succeeded Howell as Chef on his retirement in 1983) and of Miss Ina Fraser, 'Food Supervisor', until her retirement in the early 1960s.

The Supplemental Charter

In 1964 the King Edward VII Sanatorium became known as the King Edward VII Hospital. The changed title was authorised under a Supplemental Charter granted by

Her Majesty the Queen. Under its new name, the Institution's primary function was still to provide treatment for patients with tuberculosis, but it was now authorised to treat other thoracic diseases and, in addition, to admit patients suffering from other conditions in order to fill any beds which might remain unoccupied. The reasons for this alteration in title and rôle lay in the past. The incidence of tuberculosis throughout the world had been falling and in Britain there were more tuberculosis beds than there were patients to fill them. Sir Geoffrey Todd had recognised the problem as early as 1957. He proposed that patients with asthma and bronchitis should be admitted to fill the vacant beds. He also warned the Consulting Staff and Council that the time might be coming when the Regional Hospital Board, who were having difficulty in filling their own tuberculosis beds, might find it necessary to withdraw their maintenance grants. This would have had serious implications for Midhurst which depended on the Board for funding about 90 N.H.S. patients at the Sanatorium.

The trend continued. Not only did the number of tuberculosis admissions fall but the duration of their stay in the Sanatorium was reduced by effective chemotherapy. So far did the pendulum swing away from tuberculosis that in 1961 under eight per cent of the beds in the Sanatorium were occupied by tuberculous patients. The position was eventually reached in 1962 when it was no longer possible to fill the beds to an economic level with patients of the type envisaged by the original Charter; and the danger that the Regional Board might have to withdraw their support remained, although they had been very loyal to Midhurst in the past. The Council asked the medical Consulting Staff for their suggestions as to what might be done to make full use of Midhurst yet maintain the primary object, the treatment of pulmonary tuberculosis.

The Consultants considered all the possibilities (including one that the Sanatorium might be used as a home for elderly patients), and they decided finally to recommend to Council that all types of thoracic disease must be accepted and, if beds were still available, that patients with other medical and surgical conditions should also be admitted. These recommendations were accepted and formed the basis for a petition by the Council to the Privy Council for an alteration to the Royal Charter. Consent was given, and the Supplemental Charter authorising the Sanatorium's new rôle and title as a Hospital became operative in 1964. From Sanatorium to Hospital, the metamorphosis was now complete.

Chapter IX

The Changing Scene: 1965-1971

The change from Sanatorium to Hospital was by no means easy. The size of the staff had to be increased. The tempo of work had to accelerate and some of the staff found this hard to accept. Public attitudes also were changing. Patients were becoming more demanding and insisting on even higher standards of care and attention, food and other facilities. In days gone by, patients had had to queue for admission. Now private hospitals everywhere were clamouring for customers. Midhurst had to face this challenge, and did so with notable success.

In the years following the grant of the Supplemental Charter there was a short-lived improvement in the admission rates due to the admittance of a few non-thoracic conditions from local areas, but it was proving as hard as ever to maintain full bed occupancy, or anything approaching full occupancy. The reason was that, although the numbers admitted with non-tuberculous thoracic conditions continued to rise, they were never kept in hospital for long enough to compensate for the decline in numbers of the 'long term' tuberculous patients. The economic aspect of the matter also gave rise to anxiety. The Army had opened their own chest unit at the Cambridge Hospital, Aldershot, and had, on that account, to decline an offer of beds at Midhurst. The Royal Air Force continued to pay the full costs of their Unit at Midhurst, but the number of private patients in residence was disappointingly small, about twenty on average. The Ministry of Pensions paid for a few ex-Service patients, but it was still the Regional Hospital Board who paid for most of the patients at Midhurst, and they could not be expected to do so indefinitely. In March 1967 the Medical Superintendent repeated his warning that as soon as the Regional Hospital Board had a sufficient number of beds in their own Hospitals they would be bound to reduce their support for Midhurst. The Council were so concerned about rising costs and declining bed occupancy that in March 1968 they invited the Medical Committee (the name now adopted for formal meetings of the Consulting Staff) to consider the long-term prospects of the Hospital and to make recommendations about future policy. In October 1968 Sir Geoffrey Marshall, Chairman of the Medical Committee, signed a Report to Council which was to be the basis of policy for the next 10 years. The Consultants felt that the Hospital should remain a National Institution. They pointed out the many advantages it already possessed and said there was really only one cause for anxiety, namely that an insufficient number of patients were being admitted to keep it full. They felt that good might come from advertising its advantages and that both national and local aspects should be emphasized.

Significantly, they saw the need for the Hospital to move away from its purely chest rôle and to develop instead a capability for dealing with all kinds of medical and surgical cases, at the same time retaining its traditional interest in thoracic disease. They recommended that in order to attract more patients all members of the Consulting Staff should be in active hospital practice: all consultants over the age of 65 should become 'emeritus'. They further recommended that 12 new consultants should be invited to join the Medical Committee, most of them from London, but some from local district hospitals. It was hoped that this might increase the input of local patients.

Sir Geoffrey Marshall's report was accepted by the Council in January 1969 and acted upon forthwith. The following consultants were invited to accept appointment to the Consulting Staff – Dr. J. C. Batten, Mr. M. G. Cox, Mr. N. Cridland, Dr. P. A. Emerson, Mr. W. F .P. Gammie, Dr. P. J. D. Heaf, Dr. I. H. Kerr, Dr. Howard Nicholson, Mr. V. T. Powell, Dr. F. H. Scadding and Dr. E. W. Thompson-Evans. These appointments to the Consulting Staff included several from hospitals in the vicinity (Mr. Cox, Mr. Cridland, Mr. Gammie and Dr. Thompson-Evans), the hope being that the number of admissions of patients from local areas would increase and that there would be greater diversification of work done. It was hoped, in particular, that the appointment of local consultants in various aspects of surgery would result in an increase of general surgical work performed at Midhurst.

In this way the local aims mentioned in the Marshall Report were satisfied. But how best to enhance the national identity of the Hospital? The possibility of undertaking cardiac surgery was considered, but nothing came of the idea. What other courses were there? By a happy chance Professor John Charnley, M.Sc., F.R.C.S., a pioneer in Hip Joint Replacement Surgery, became interested in the possibility of performing hip joint replacement operations at Midhurst. Through Sir Norman Joseph, a member of Council, he had met the Duke of Norfolk, who had recently become Chairman of the Council in succession to Lord Portal. Sir Geoffrey Todd and Dr. Teare then visited his hospital at Wrightington for three days in early 1969 and Mr. Charnley in turn had come down to Midhurst, and reported favourably on the Hospital and the services it could offer. He recommended that a special clean air enclosure be provided in one of the theatres and that rooms on Floor 8 (now Miles Reid Ward) be modified. He also offered facilities at Wrightington for training the Midhurst staff who were to be responsible for the after care of his patients. Preparations went ahead and in December 1969 Mr. Charnley carried out the first of the many low friction arthroplasties he was to perform at Midhurst. Charnley was a surgeon of international repute and patients were sent to him from all parts of the world. He visited Midhurst regularly once a fortnight, travelling by train from Wrightington and being met at Euston station by the Hospital car driven by Mr. 'Alfie' Purdew. He would conduct an outpatient clinic, see the patients he had operated on during his previous visit, and perform six of the low friction arthroplasty operations which he had devised and perfected himself. Between visits his patients were looked after by Dr. Doyle and a nursing team led by Sister Norton. Years later Charnley once confided to Todd that before starting at Midhurst he had been worried about the after care his patients might receive there. But once he had started work, and had met Dr. Doyle, Sister Norton and Mrs. Cock (the Superintendent Physiotherapist), he knew his patients would be in good hands. His results from Midhurst prove the point. Hundreds of satisfied patients and only two fatalities out of over 1,300 operations performed – a remarkable achievement.

The Marshall Report in 1968 had pointed out that, of the 130 patients who were normally under treatment at Midhurst, only 25 were private patients, the others being from the Royal Air Force, the Ministry of Pensions and from the Regional Hospital Board. But the numbers paid for by the Board had fallen from 120 to 85 and would undoubtedly fall still further. Sir Geoffrey Todd had pointed this out before and his solution, made to the Consulting Staff in 1967, was to attract more private patients. The 1968 Marshall Report had the same solution in mind when it recommended the appointment of local consultants to the staff, and the arrival on the scene of Mr. John Charnley, all of whose patients were private, pushed private bed occupancy higher.

Whilst these interesting medical developments were taking place, changes were occurring in the composition of the Council and amongst the members of the Consulting Staff. Mr. B. A. Salmon, who had been a member of the Council for 29 years died in May 1965. In his business life he had been a Director and Chairman of J. Lyons and Co., and his experience of the business and catering world was profound. He spent a great deal of time at Midhurst, and before the war had been responsible for introducing modern catering methods to replace the out of date system which had been in use since the Sanatorium had started. He was succeeded on the Council by a fellow director of Lyons, Sir Norman Joseph.

The next appointment to the Council was made in 1966 when Lieutenant Colonel Miles Reid, M.C., J.P., was invited to join the Council and at the same time to become the first Chairman of the Association of Friends of the Hospital. This organisation was formed following discussions between Mrs. Agar, Lady Todd and Colonel Miles Reid. Its purpose was to appeal for funds to assist the Hospital, to provide equipment, and to increase the amenities for patients and staff. The proposals to form the Committee were approved by the Council and the 'Friends' got off to a flying start with a generous donation of £20,000 from Mr. L. Carr-Jones, who had been a grateful patient of Dr. Hume's at Midhurst. A constitution for the new Association of Friends was drawn up, booklets were printed and issued to the public and to former patients with appeals for support, and a cricket match and fête was held on 22 May 1966 to launch the enterprise. The 'Friends' have continued ever since to function as the Hospital's main fund raising body.

Further changes in Council and Consulting Staff came about in 1967 and 1968. After the death of Lord Knollys, in 1966, Lady Pamela Hicks became a member of Council and, when Sir Clement Price Thomas retired from the Consulting Staff in 1967, he was succeeded on the Consulting Staff by Mr. Charles Drew.

In March 1968 the Council set up a finance sub-committee of two members to consider and advise on the administration of the Hospital's financial affairs. Colonel Miles Reid was one member; Mr. Frank Bradford, a recently retired bank manager, the other. The decision to form a finance sub-committee in a watchdog rôle was timely. Over the previous few years there had been a misappropriation of funds by the accountant which, though suspected and reported by the Hospital Secretary, had gone undetected for some time. The affair was played down as far as possible, but in 1966 the accountant concerned was required to resign. The accounts were then taken over temporarily by Mr. W. H. Mitchell who had recently joined the staff as administrative assistant to Mr. Boulton. Mr. Edward Melbert was appointed hospital accountant in July 1967 and Wally Mitchell, who is today Secretary to the Hospital, was able to return to his normal duties as administrative assistant, a post which he held until 1968 when he was appointed Assistant Secretary.

Further important changes in the composition of the Council were made in May 1968. It had been agreed in the previous year that His Grace the Duke of Norfolk should be invited to join the Council and that he should in due course succeed Lord Portal as Chairman. It was thought opportune in May 1968 to institute these arrangements. Accordingly, later in 1968, Lord Portal retired and the Duke became Chairman. In 1969 Brigadier G. T. Hardy-Roberts (later Sir Geoffrey Hardy-Roberts) was invited to become a member of the Council. Brigadier Hardy-Roberts had for many years been associated with hospitals and had been a popular and effective House Governor, or Secretary-Superintendent, at the Middlesex Hospital. After leaving that appointment, he held the post of Master of the Royal Household at Buckingham Palace for several years before taking up his appointment as a member of the Council. When the Vice-President, Brigadier, The Lord Tryon, resigned in 1972, His Grace the Duke of Norfolk succeeded him as Vice President of the Institution whilst continuing to serve as Chairman of the Council. Brigadier Hardy-Roberts was then invited to become Vice Chairman of the Council, a position he occupied until his retirement from the Council in 1982.

In 1965 Mr. Edward Sieff, through the generosity of Marks & Spencer (of which Company he was Deputy Chairman) and the Agnes Spencer Charitable Trust, gave the Hospital £50,000 to be spent on medical equipment and the fabric of the Hospital. This donation, together with money accumulating from Lord Portal's earlier Appeal for Funds, and with support from the 'Friends', enabled the Hospital in the late 1960s to embark on an extensive programme of building and modernisation. After consultation with the Consulting Radiologist, Dr. Peter Kerley, much modern equipment was installed in the X-ray department: a new Siemens tomography unit and automatic processing plant, an image intensifier, a new portable X-ray apparatus and many smaller items, the total cost being about £20,000. The laboratory was also modernised and modern equipment installed including a blood refrigerator, a freezing microtome and a new sterilising oven.

The operating theatre was remodelled by taking in the adjoining corridor and the rooms previously occupied by offices and the doctors' library.* A new autoclave and air-conditioning plant were installed and, later, the clean air enclosure which had been recommended by Mr. Charnley. In all the surgical rooms, and many of the medical rooms, piped oxygen and suction was provided. New oil-fired ovens were installed in the kitchen and a new system of feeding was introduced so that food could be taken by heated trolley to patients on the wards. The patients' library and shop, together with the occupational therapy and physiotherapy departments, had been grouped together since 1964 in a new wing extending from the west wing of the Hospital. In 1965 the occupational and art therapy departments were moved to make way for the new pupil nurses training school. Later the shop and physiotherapy department were moved to the positions they occupy today, thus providing room for the pharmacy.

The remodelling of the operating theatre suite required major works in the main building. A new passage was built to replace that which had been incorporated in the theatre. Rooms on the first floor were built for the Matron, the Secretary and administrative staff. A new doctors' dining room was provided and further staff bedrooms and offices on the first and second floors. The old patients dining room was converted for staff use and the patients had their meals in their own rooms or in day rooms.

In 1966 the Hospital played a small but vital part in an incident which made headline news at the time. On a stormy evening in November an Iberian Airways airliner crashed on Blackdown Hill, only a few miles from the Hospital, with the loss of all on board. Mr. Boulton went to the scene immediately to find the rescue services faced with the gruesome task of clearing up the remains. There was nothing to be done that night, but next day Midhurst's offer to help was accepted and the Hospital found itself used by the authorities as their headquarters from which all subsequent arrangements were made. The mortuary and post-mortem room were put at their disposal and a specialist pathologist and dental officer from the Royal Air Force lived in the Hospital for several weeks.

In 1969 a magnificent gift of £5 million was made by Sir Halford Reddish, Chairman of Rugby Portland Cement, for the express purpose of founding a medical research centre in the precincts of the Hospital to promote research into various aspects of cardio-respiratory disease. (Sir Halford had been a patient of Sir Geoffrey Marshall's who referred him to Sir Geoffrey Todd at Midhurst in the 1960s. He had been so impressed with the Hospital that he had already given considerable sums of money for various improvements , one of which was the construction of the Geoffrey Marshall Hall.)

It was decided that the new Institute should be administered independently of the Hospital but that there should be close liaison between Hospital and Institute personnel and a pooling of resources. Trustees to administer the fund were appointed and a Board of Governors was set up comprising representatives of the Hospital Council, of the Royal College of Physicians, of the Universities of London and Southampton, and two of the benefactors' own choosing. Sir Geoffrey Todd was closely involved in planning the new Institute and after he had retired from his Hospital post as Medical Superintendent he became the Institute's first Chief Administrator.

When the gift was made in 1969, Sir Halford expressed no disagreement to his name being associated with it, but 10 days before the press announcement was made from St James's Palace he declared his wish that his name should not be revealed. This put Sir Geoffrey Todd in a corner. He was due to be interviewed on the following day by Southern Television and he knew he would be asked the donor's name. Eventually he agreed to being interviewed 'live' outside the Hospital,but only on condition that he was asked no questions about the donor's identity.*

The end of the decade brought the retirement of Miss Margaret Schofield who had held the post of Matron for 24 years, longer than anyone before her. Her devotion, skill and dedication had contributed much to the success of the Hospital and to the welfare of her staff. She had seen the Hospital through the difficult years of transition and had been in large measure responsible for the introduction of the Pupil Nurses Training School which by the time of her retirement was passing out twenty or thirty new nurses each year. She retired on 31 December 1969, but happily she was not lost to Midhurst. She settled down in the town and has continued to take an active interest in Hospital affairs. She was succeeded as Matron by Miss Joan Beech.

Exactly one year later, on 31 December 1970, the Hospital's Medical Superintendent, Sir Geoffrey Todd, handed over the reins of office to the man who had for so long acted as his deputy, Dr. Douglas Teare. It was the end of an epoch. Sir Geoffrey had first arrived at Midhurst 37 years before. When he took over as Medical Superintendent he was just 33 years of age and the Sanatorium had been open for fewer than 28 years. On his retirement aged 70, Midhurst had been active for nearly 65 years and its rôle, if not its character and style, had been transformed. Todd had seen the Institution through the vicissitudes of peace, war, and peace again. He had guided, cajoled, coaxed, bullied, argued and, by sheer will power, forced it through the awkward periods of change and diversification. He had seen it emerge fully fledged as a Hospital of the highest standing capable of dealing with any and every patient sent to it. For 37 years Midhurst *was* Todd and Todd *was* Midhurst. He was indeed a giant of his time.

Chapter X

Development and Expansion: 1971-1978

When Dr. Douglas Teare assumed office as Physician Superintendent in January 1971, the Council had already accepted Brigadier Hardy-Roberts' proposals made the previous year that the administrative structure of the Hospital should be modified to conform with standard practice in other hospitals. A tripartite system of management was therefore introduced which entailed each of the three Principal Officers (the Superintendent, the Matron and the Secretary) having their responsibilities clearly defined and each having direct access to the Chairman and the Council. It was intended that there should be frequent discussion between the Principal Officers and it was thought unlikely that there would be many occasions when they failed to reach agreement and had to refer to the Council for a ruling. The new system was a distinct break with the traditional practice under which the Superintendent's authority had been absolute, but the principle was accepted by the three officers concerned and in practice it was to work well. Dr. Teare, who was heavily engaged in clinical work, was content to shed part of his administrative load. In order to emphasize the mainly clinical content of his duties, he was henceforth to be known as the Physician Superintendent. The other two principal officers (Mr. Boulton and Miss Beech) welcomed the opportunity to share the responsibilities of management.

The other changes in the administrative structure related to the various committees concerned in policy making. A Finance Committee was formed to replace the two-man body which had exercised financial control hitherto. A Nursing Committee was set up to deal with nursing problems and advise the Council accordingly. A House Committee was envisaged (but it was not a success and met once only) and the Medical Committee was re-fashioned. The old Medical Committee which had served the Council so faithfully for the previous 65 years was unique in being composed of consultants who lived and practised at a considerable distance from the Hospital. For geographical reasons they were unable to maintain as close contact with the Hospital as was now felt to be desirable. In the recent past several consultants had been appointed to the staff who lived and worked within easy reach of the Hospital and who might on that account be better able to advise on day to day matters. It was decided therefore that a sub-committee of the Medical Committee should be formed, composed of consultants practising locally, which would meet as often as necessary to advise the Council on day to day medical matters.* The main Medical Committee, as already constituted, would meet twice a year, one meeting to be at Midhurst, the other in London, and continue to advise the Council on major matters of medical policy, including the recommendation of names for appointment to the Consulting Staff.

With its administrative system thus revised, the Hospital entered a period of intense activity, putting into effect the policy decisions made by the Council in 1970. These had been to encourage the admission of as many private patients as possible and at the same time to broaden the range of disorders which could be admitted to Midhurst – a process to become known as 'diversification'. In furtherance of these aims, the panel of consultants was enlarged further to include more consultants from local areas and in specialties not previously represented at Midhurst. In March 1970, a further three locally based consultants were appointed, Dr. J Mickerson, Dr. J. D. Whiteside and Dr. J. L. Price, and in October 1970 four from further afield – Dr. A. J. Robertson and Dr. C. M. Ogilvie from Liverpool, Dr. Lawson McDonald from London and Dr. M. R. Geake from Preston. In March 1971 the Consulting Staff was enlarged still further by the appointments of Dr. Ray Bettley (a consulting dermatologist), Air Commodore I. W. H. R. Cran (who was already in charge of the R.A.F. Unit at Midhurst), Dr. James Dow, Dr. William Gooddy and Dr. C. F. G. Prideaux.

In the years that followed, more appointments were made, mainly of consultants from Guildford, Chichester and Portsmouth. Some of the new appointments were to supplement or replace members of the existing Hospital Consulting Staff. These had to receive Her Majesty's approval as had always been the practice since the Sanatorium had been incorporated by Royal Charter in 1912. Others were appointed Consultants to the Hospital on the recommendation of the Medical Committee and subsequent approval by the Council. By 1985 the full panel consisted of over 80 active consultants and 19 who were emeritus. Not all were appointed to the Medical Committees, but their names all appeared in the Hospital prospectus and Annual Reports. (See Appendix 5.)

The interest of local practitioners in the expanding Hospital was awakened by inviting them to social and medical meetings and, in March 1971, the Chairman of the Council, His Grace the Duke of Norfolk, wrote to every local consultant and family practitioner to point out how the Hospital's rôle had changed and how admirably it was suited for the care of private patients in their own rooms.

Nor was the Hospital's principal rôle as a Chest Unit for National Health Service patients forgotten. Soon after the closure of Aldingbourne Chest Hospital, Midhurst was recognised as one of the only two Regional Sub-Centres for Thoracic Surgery and, on Mr. Powell's retirement from the National Health Service in 1971, Mr. Richard Rowlandson succeeded him as Consultant Thoracic Surgeon for National Health Service patients. He in turn was succeeded by Mr. Meredith Brown in 1978. In 1979 Mr. R. E. Sayer, another thoracic surgeon, joined the staff as Consultant.

These measures resulted in the Hospital becoming ever busier in terms of numbers of patients admitted and operations performed, but, encouraging though this was, there were still too many empty beds and it soon became apparent that close collaboration between the Hospital and the nascent Institute must be the key to the future success of both bodies. A joint Hospital/Institute Liaison Committee was therefore set up early in 1971 comprising representatives of the Hospital (Brigadier Hardy-Roberts, Lt. Col. Miles Reid, Mr. Frank Bradford, Dr. H. D. Teare, Mr. J. A. Boulton and Miss Joan Beech) and the Board of Governors of the Institute (Mr. J. W. Landon, Mr. Donald Scott and Sir Geoffrey Todd, who was by this time the Institute's Chief Administrator). The purpose of this liaison committee was to consider and advise on matters of common interest to the two organisations such as the joint provision of heating, lighting, water and other services, the siting of new buildings and the planning of extensions. Much of the Committee's early work was concerned with the choice of site for the new building, the acquisition of land and the extent to which existing Hospital accommodation might be utilised by the Institute, but it was soon recognised that there would be a continuing requirement for a liaison committee, not only during the period of building but also when the Institute was in full operation. The long term aspects of collaboration between the two units were thus kept constantly under review. At an early stage it was decided that the Hospital should eventually provide a number of beds for use by Institute physicians (Barbara Agar Ward was later allocated for this) and it was hoped that the Hospital and the Institute could establish common accountancy arrangements and the Institute be enabled to participate in contracts under which the Hospital purchased its equipment.

In January 1971, Dr. Gordon Cumming, from Birmingham University, was appointed Director 'Designate' of the Research Institute. Having been co-opted as a member of the liaison committee, and written an appreciation of the Institute's likely development and future role, he was formally appointed as its Director in November 1971. Meanwhile, a scientific sub-committee had been formed, composed of a group of clinicians and scientists, to direct research and to determine what equipment would be needed. Building of the new Institute started in April 1972. The work was contracted to Sir Robert McAlpine and Son. The architectural design was by Messrs. Philip Bennett and Son. Sir Alexander Gibb and Partners, as Consulting Engineers to the Hospital, played a co-ordinating rôle. The work advanced rapidly and medical and scientific staff started to move in towards the end of 1972. The building was taken over in April 1973 and a commissioning period followed during which equipment was installed and additional staff engaged.

The completed building, handsomely styled in brick with a tiled mansard roof, and lavishly staffed and equipped, was opened by Her Majesty the Queen on 2 November 1973. It was an auspicious occasion. The Queen was met by the Duke of Norfolk in his capacity of Lord Lieutenant. Before the opening ceremony, which was essentially an 'Institute' occasion, the Queen attended a reception in the Geoffrey Marshall Hall. Members of the Hospital staff were presented and later Her Majesty lunched with members of the Hospital Council, members of the Institute's Board of Governors and senior members of the staffs of the Hospital and the Medical Research Institute.*

After the Institute had been opened, the programme of clinical investigation began. There were about sixty scientific officers on the staff and the scope of their work was wide. Dr. Cumming and the five senior clinical consultants (Dr. Michael Thomas, Dr. Ivor Gabe, Dr. Mark Noble, Dr. Keith Horsfield and Dr. W. M. Thurlbeck) looked after their own patients in the Barbara Agar Ward and offered specialised out-patient sessions to which practitioners and other consultants could refer patients. These sessions were in cardiology, cardio-vascular disease, cardio-pulmonary medicine and general medicine. The Institute physicians, who were all appointed Honorary Consultants to the Hospital (Dr. Cumming being appointed also to the Hospital Medical Committee), took part in the training of nursing and ambulance staff and they helped in the investigation of hospital cases, notably in cardiac catheterisation, angiography, pulmonary function tests and radio-isotope studies. They also attended scientific meetings and gave lectures in many parts of the world, thus ensuring that the name of Midhurst became known in most European medical centres. In 1974 one of the Institute's medical research officers was appointed an honorary medical registrar to the Hospital and an advisory technical service from the Institute was also established which provided maintenance and repair facilities for Hospital equipment.

Until February 1975, the joint Hospital/Institute Liaison Committee continued to meet regularly to discuss matters of joint concern and to advise their parent governing bodies. One of their functions was to promote harmonious working relations between the staffs of the two Institutions. Owing to initial misunderstandings this proved less easy to achieve than had been expected, but with goodwill on both sides early difficulties were overcome and a sound working relationship was established.

Meanwhile much was being done to bring the Hospital completely up to date and capable of dealing with the large variety of cases now coming to it. In 1974 a seven bed Special Care Ward under the care of Dr. Michael Thomas was opened for the treatment of acute cardiac and respiratory emergencies. The new unit, fully instrumented and monitored, was installed adjacent to the Barbara Agar Ward and was connected by a first floor link corridor with the Institute where an angiography, cardiac catheterisation and radiography unit was establised.

The increase in the amount of general surgery performed at Midhurst during the 1970s necessitated the construction of additional theatres, the modernising of the existing theatre suite and the extension of piped oxygen and suction to many of the patients' rooms in Norfolk and Portal Wards as well as on both surgical floors. A fully air-conditioned complex of two new theatres was opened in 1976 and the original theatres up-graded to provide a total of four modern units (one of which was already fitted with a clean air enclosure for hip joint replacement surgery). At the same time a Central Sterile Supply Department, with equipment of the latest design, was completed, and a connecting corridor was built from the theatres suite to a new lift giving access to all floors in the main building. The funds for many of these projects were provided most generously by Sir Halford Reddish.

Professor John Charnley, who was knighted in 1977, increased the amount of operating he did at Midhurst to six cases a fortnight. Patients were sent to him for hip joint replacement surgery from all over the world. In 1977 he was requested by the Foreign Office to go to Riyadh, in a professional capacity, to visit King Khaled Bin Abdul Azziz of Saudi Arabia. Hip joint replacement was advised. Professor Charnley agreed to perform the operation and insisted that he should carry it out at Midhurst. In the event it was found impossible to provide accommodation locally for the King's entourage and Charnley agreed, with some reluctance, to carry out the operation at the Wellington Hospital in London. However, he selected a team from Midhurst to assist him and be responsible for the King's post-operative care.*

A new X-ray Department, situated between the Hospital and the Research Institute, was completed in 1975. Equipped with a rotational tomography unit and much other modern apparatus, the department's work continued to increase. A mammography and breast screening service was established and facilities made available for fibre optic endoscopies. The scope of the Department was further enhanced in 1977 by the installation of an EMI Whole Body Scanner, made possible by the generosity of Sir Halford Reddish who had already given so much to the Hospital. The radiological consulting staff during this period consisted of Dr. Ian Kerr, Dr. J. L. Price and Dr. C. E. Corney. Dr. W. F. White and Dr. I. M. S. Cade were the Consultants in Radiotherapy. Miss Margaret Easton was still the Superintendent Radiographer, assisted by Miss Holmes, and Mr. Colin Bennell joined the Staff in 1977 as Technical Officer in charge of the new scanner.

The work of the Department of Pathology had increased in the 1970s to the point at which more and more laboratory space and more staff were urgently needed. As soon as the Institute had opened, therefore, rooms were set aside in the new building for the use of Dr. Gordon and his staff which then consisted of Geoff Rumsby, the Lunts, and (from 1973) the Strudwicks – Jim and Ann. Haematology was now provided for, and Dr. C. J. T. Bateman, a consultant from Chichester, was appointed to supervise. The space vacated by the laboratory on the ground floor of the surgical wing was then converted into additional surgical rooms. These were adapted for the close observation of post-operative cases and were used exclusively for Professor Charnley's patients.

The Department of Physiotherapy, previously situated in the wing now used by the School of Nursing, moved in 1975 to the site of the old X-ray Department which it still occupies today. The Senior Physiotherapist from 1967 to 1974 was Mrs. Monica Wilson who was succeeded in 1974 as Superintendent by Mrs. Rosamunde Cock who still occupies the post. They were ably assisted by a succession of full-time and part-time trained physiotherapists (who included Mrs. I. A. Laband, Mrs. Hilary Craig and Mrs. Kathleen Watson). Whereas the Department in the 1950s and early 1960s had been concerned solely with chest work, there was a considerable broadening of interest in the late 1960s with increasing departmental involvement in the management of non-thoracic conditions, many of them surgical. The specialised management of hip cases after surgery, however – today a principal feature of departmental work at Midhurst – was not undertaken until December 1969 when Professor Charnley started work at the Hospital. The high reputation enjoyed today by the department has been due in no small measure to the skill and devotion of its present Superintendent, Mrs. Rosamunde Cock.

A further extension of the Hospital's work, again in collaboration with the Institute, was the inauguration in 1976 of a service for the care of patients with malignant disease for whom no further active curative treatment was possible. Set up in conjunction with the National Society for Cancer Relief, the Douglas Macmillan Continuing Care Service provided domiciliary care for these patients and operated from the Hospital, where a trial unit of five (later increased to nine) beds was established for short term admissions. The Service was initially managed by Dr. Lesley Wills and later by Dr. Elizabeth Smout under the supervision of Dr. Cumming and Dr. Horsfield.

In the 1970s additional bungalows for the staff were built and much of the existing staff accommodation renovated. The shop was transferred to the site it still occupies in the entrance hall, its previous site being used to accommodate a larger pharmacy which remains there today, and in 1970 a fine new recreational hall named after Sir Geoffrey Marshall was completed. In 1972, the Council decided to discontinue the practice of numbering the wards and instead to give them the names of persons who had rendered valuable service to the Hospital. Floor 1 became Portal Ward; Floor 2, Barbara Agar; Floor 3, Norfolk; Floor 4, Cowdray; Floor 5, Todd; and Floor 6, Cassel. The Surgical 'Floors' 7 and 8 became Surgical Wards 1 and 2. In 1981 they were re-named the

Hardy-Roberts and Miles Reid Wards after two men whose devotion to the Hospital had been almost without equal. After Sir John Charnley's death in 1982, the suite of rooms used exclusively by his patients became known as the Sir John Charnley Unit.

1974 saw the formation by Lady Barclay of a group of ladies to undertake voluntary service at the Hospital. There were about twenty of these public spirited ladies in the first group to volunteer, but their numbers increased as the the venture prospered: today there are over a hundred. They were organised by roster to act as receptionists in the entrance hall and to carry out other essential services in the Hospital. The 'Voluntary Ladies', as they have become known, have since then remained a distinctive feature of the Midhurst scene. Their work has expanded to cover clerical and patient services on the wards and in the library, in addition to the main hall reception duties which were their original 'raison d'être'. In 1981 Lady Barclay relinquished her position and was succeeded as co-ordinator by Lady Newson-Smith.

The structure and composition of the Council and the Institution underwent several important changes during Dr. Teare's term of office as Physician Superintendent. When Teare took over from Sir Geoffrey Todd in January 1971, Lord Tryon was still Vice President of the Institution, but he had already signified his wish to resign and his resignation was accepted early in 1971. The Chairman of the Council since 1969, His Grace the Duke of Norfolk, announced that the Queen had agreed that Brigadier Hardy-Roberts should hold the appointment of Deputy Chairman to the Council and take Lord Tryon's place as Her Majesty's representative at meetings of Council. The appointment of Vice President was then allowed to lapse but it was revived in 1972 when the Duke of Norfolk became Vice President of the Institution and Chairman of the Council. This was at a time when, as Earl Marshal, he had acquired nation-wide acclaim for his management of important state occasions. It added greatly to the Hospital's prestige that a man of his status and distinction should have assumed responsibility for so small a hospital and to have taken such a close and personal interest in it.

Meanwhile the composition of Council was changing and membership of the Institution expanding. In May 1971, Lady Pamela Hicks and Mrs. Herbert Agar relinquished their places on the Council and were appointed members of the Institution. They were followed in 1972 by Lord Cowdray and Sir Norman Joseph who were likewise appointed to the Institution, their places on the Council being taken by the Hon. Mrs. J. Lakin and the Hon. Lady Barttelot. Mr. Donald Scott in 1971, and Mr. T. Coghlan in the following year, were invited to serve as members of the Council which, by 1973, was composed of the following members in addition to His Grace the Duke of Norfolk and Brigadier Sir Geoffrey Hardy-Roberts who were Chairman and Deputy Chairman respectively: Lt. Colonel Miles Reid, Mr. Frank Bradford, the Hon. Lady Barttelot, the Hon. Mrs. Lakin, Sir Kenneth Robson (who, as Chairman of the Medical Committee, had been invited to join the Council in succession to Sir Geoffrey Marshall), Mr. Donald Scott and Mr. T. Coghlan. Mr. Gammie, Chairman of the Medical sub-Committee, and Dr. Cumming, Director of the Midhurst Medical Research Institute, attended all Council meetings.

The members of the Institution in 1973 included all members of the Council and eight additional members, all of them distinguished figures, who had been on the Council or had rendered notable service to the Hospital in other ways.

His Grace the Duke of Norfolk died in January 1975 after a long illness during which he continued to concern himself closely with the needs of the Hospital. Even when no longer well enough to attend meetings, he insisted on being kept informed of all that was going on. The Hospital has always been well served by its Chairman of Council, but by none better than the Duke of Norfolk. He saw the Hospital through many difficulties arising from shortage of patients, 'diversification', and a change of Superintendent, but it was the part he played in the creation of the Research Institute which was perhaps his most notable contribution. It was largely due to him that the Halford Reddish benefaction to link a research department with the Hospital was not rejected on the grounds that Midhurst was not a suitable place for research to be carried out. In his opinion the Hospital's prestige would gain from this development, as indeed it did.

After the Duke's death, Sir Geoffrey Hardy-Roberts, as Deputy, took the Chair for a few months until Her Grace, Lavinia, Duchess of Norfolk, succeeded her late husband as Vice-President of the Institution and Chairman of Council, a position which, with grace and distinction, she continues to occupy today. She was quick to see the need to achieve cohesion against the background of a diversified Hospital and a much enlarged staff. By her regular visits to wards and departments and her generous entertainment of members of the staff at her home, she stimulated the growth of Midhurst esprit de corps which today stands at an unprecedentedly high level. There is more to leadership than making administrative decisions. Staff have to be seen at work and to know that their efforts are appreciated: the present Chairman is a constant inspiration to everyone at Midhurst to give of their best.

Other changes in the composition of the Council were linked with changes in the chairmanship of the Medical Committee. Sir Kenneth Robson, a Council member and Chairman of the Medical Committee since 1969 after Sir Geoffrey Marshall's retirement, had rendered notable service to both bodies. Much of the wise advice on medical matters given to the Council during the period of 'diversification' stemmed from Sir Kenneth's shrewd estimation of people and events. He imbued everyone with the concept of public service, with the idea that to hold an appointment at Midhurst was an honour and a privilege. In particular he was responsible for insisting that membership of the Medical Committee should be broadened to include consultants from outside London.

On Sir Kenneth Robson's retirement in 1974, he was succeeded by Dr. Neville Oswald who was followed two years later, both on the Council and as Chairman of the Medical Committee, by Mr. Charles Drew. In 1977, Lieutenant General Sir James Baird, lately Director General of the Army Medical Services, was appointed a member of Council in succession to Lieutenant Colonel Miles Reid who had resigned after 10 years' valuable work for the Hospital during which he had endeared himself to everyone with whom he had come into contact.

Mr. H. Peat, who had succeeded Sir Harry Peat in 1959 as the Hospital's official Auditor, held the position until 1980, and the firm of which he was senior partner, Messrs. Peat, Marwick, Mitchell and Company, continues to do so today. The position of Honorary Legal Advisor to the Hospital was occupied by Mr. C. J. Maby of Messrs. Pennington and Lewis & Lewis until 1976. Since then Mr. D. T. Davies, senior partner of the same firm, has been the Legal Advisor although the traditional title of Honorary Legal Advisor was discontinued in 1977.

After the retirement in 1968 of Mr. Briant Poulter, Mr. W. J. Biggs held the appointment of Consulting Architect to the Hospital for one year. On his retirement in 1969 the firm of Messrs. T. P. Bennett and Son were designated Consulting Architects to the Hospital; but after 1976 the services of private consultants, notably Mr. George Denny, were called on as required.

The traditional office of Consulting Engineer to the Hospital, for so many years filled by Mr. A. P. Patey, was accepted by Mr. T. A. L. Paton, senior partner of Sir Alexander Gibb and Partners, and in due course the firm became designated Consulting Engineers to the Hospital and their name appeared in the Annual Reports until 1977.

The Church of England chaplain throughout much of this period was the Reverend John Wansey who had been appointed in 1960. He retired in 1977 and was succeeded by the Reverend David Evans who was then Rector of Lynch but who soon moved to the parish of Easebourne. The Roman Catholic chaplain was Father C. Waller who had held the position since 1953 and who continued to do so until his retirement in 1980 when he was succeeded by the Very Reverend Canon D. Fogarty.

The Hospital medical staff under Dr. Teare consisted of Dr. Paddy Doyle, Dr. Mike Hume and Dr. Ian Gordon. Professor Gordon Cumming, Dr. Keith Horsfield, Dr. Ivor Gabe, Dr. Mark Noble and Dr. Michael Thomas, all on the strength of the Midhurst Medical Research Institute, looked after patients in the Barbara Agar Ward and elsewhere in the Hospital. These consultants were backed up by a number of senior house officers – only one in 1971, but three were in post by 1975 – and by a surgical registrar on rotation from St Richard's Hospital, Chichester, and a medical registrar detached from the Midhurst Medical Research Institute.

The principal nursing staff consisted of Miss Joan Beech (Matron), Miss J. Clemenson (Assistant Matron) and a number of sisters, many of whom are still in charge of wards and departments at Midhurst, or have only recently retired after long service: Sisters E. McGregor, Pam Drane, Cynthia Gozzi, Helen Houlston, Evelyn Jones, Denny Sharp, Maureen Lee and Wendy Norton. Sister E. Behr and Sister E. Churchill were Night Sisters, and Mrs. E. Hunt, Theatre Sister. Miss Clemenson retired in November 1971 after 22 years' service at the Hospital and was succeeded as Assistant Matron by Miss M. I. Allen. When Miss Joan Beech resigned in December 1974, Miss Allen became Matron and Mrs. J. Wright became the new Assistant Matron. Sister Helen Pring (later Mrs. Green) became Senior Theatre Sister in 1974 and on her retirement in 1981 Sister J. H. Daniel was appointed. Miss Sally Jay (later Mrs. Cave) was in charge of the R.A.F. patients on Portal Ward from 1974 until her retirement in 1981. Her work for the R.A.F. at Midhurst was marked by the award of a Commander in Chief's commendation in 1981. Sister J. Davis was in charge of the patients on the Coronary Care Unit and Miss L. Graham was appointed to the Recovery Unit in 1978 when that unit opened, soon afterwards becoming Sister in charge. At the same time Sister Aileen Hay was appointed Sister in charge of Barbara Agar Ward.

The nursing establishment was modified in the 1970s to provide for two sisters on each ward, thus reducing the need for staff nurses, a grade which has never been easy to recruit. Internal recruiting from nurses qualifying from pupil nurse training at Midhurst was maintained at a satisfactory level and the Nursing School, under the direction of the Tutor, Mrs. M. Brook, and the Clinical Tutor, Mrs. G. Scott, continued to attract a large number of entrants, many of them from Malaya. In 1977 alone, 145 applications were received by the School of Nursing including 54 from overseas.

Amongst the administrative staff during the period, Mr. Boulton, the Secretary, and Mr. Mitchell, the Assistant Secretary, provided continuity at the top, but there had been several changes in the Accounts Department. Mr. Edward Melbert, who had been appointed in 1967 in place of Mr. A. Cairns, proved to be an effective and respected Accounts Officer, but he had never been physically strong and his health broke down in 1974. He was obliged to resign in July and he died a few months later. Mr. Eric Taylor, from the National Health Service, was appointed Accounts Officer in May 1974 in succession to Mr. Melbert, but unfortunately he died suddenly only three years later. His assistant, Mr. Fleming, who had once been the Sergeant attached to the R.A.F. Unit in Portal Ward, took over the accounts temporarily pending the appointment of a permanent Accounts Officer, but he too died suddenly some weeks before the arrival in July 1977 of Mr. M. J. Seagrove who had already been interviewed and selected for the post. Happily Martin Seagrove is still Officer in Charge of the Accounts Department, with Dennis Pearce as his deputy.

On the secretarial staff, Miss Jeni Slocock came to Midhurst in 1957 and became Sir Geoffrey Todd's secretary in 1961 when Miss Beryl Walters left. On Sir Geoffrey's retirement she became secretary to Dr. Teare and continued in this capacity until Dr. Teare retired. She then became secretary to Dr. S. E. Large after he had been appointed Director of Medical Services. For many years, Miss Slocock was responsible for arranging appointments for all Sir John Charnley's patients, an onerous task indeed because his patients came to Midhurst from all over the world. Today, she fulfils a similar rôle for Sir John's successor, Mr. John Older, as well as assisting Mr. Stewart Clarke with his medical administrative duties and acting as co-ordinator of the Hospital's medical secretarial services.

From 1974 the Records Office was in the hands of Miss Joan Fenning who was succeeded on her retirement in 1981 by Mrs. Patricia Chorley who had until then been the senior medical secretary. She in her turn was succeeded by Miss Felicity Pilditch.

Miss Pat Chalk joined the Hospital in 1967 as typist in the steward's office, before it was retitled the supplies department. She went on to become assistant to the supplies officer, Mr. Brian Speed, and, when Mr. Tony Kelly was appointed supplies officer in succession to Mr. Speed, Miss Chalk was made assistant supplies officer, the post she holds today.

Another long-serving member of the secretarial staff is Mrs. Marian Bradley, wife of the Hospital's deputy engineer. The Bradleys came to Midhurst in 1961 when Alan joined the Hospital after service in the R.A.F. In 1973 Mrs. Bradley became secretary to Mr. Mitchell and in addition provided the secretarial services for the 'Friends' of the Hospital, and she continues in both rôles to the present day.

Others of the secretarial staff who came to Midhurst in the 1970s and who are still working there are Miss Sue Richardson, who was appointed as secretary to Mr. Boulton in 1976, Mrs. Sue Gale, Mrs. Teresa Fleet and Mrs. Maxine Gravett.

Hall porters and telephonists are important figures in hospital life and Midhurst has been lucky in those who have served them. When Mr. Rogers first joined the staff in 1971, the head porter was Mr. Barrow. He retired in 1974 and Ted Rogers took his place. Barrow had been the first 'head' porter. Before his day all porters had been designated 'hall' porters and all came under Mr. Speed, the Steward. But with Barrow, and then Ted Rogers (whose wife has for long worked in the Hospital as supervisor in the dining room), the hall porters have assumed a status of their own. Amongst those who have reflected so admirably the Hospital's image have been Mr. Aston, Len Bentley, John Jeffries, Hughie Hopkins (the night porter), Peter Hardy, Albert Henry and, more recently, Messrs. Whitehead, West and Thorp-Hincks in the front hall, and Janet Bow and Mary Minter in the telephone exchange.

During this period there were many long serving members of staff still in post. Mr. Victor Howell, appointed in 1948, was still head chef. He was supported by Mr. Ron Luckhurst who was to succeed him as head chef in 1983 when he retired.

Mr. Robert Harvey who had been resident engineer since 1949 retired in 1978 and Mr. P. Bullock took his place. Of the Latvians who had joined the engineering staff after the War, only three remained – Freddy Peka, Wally Dzenis and Charlie Strazdins. All three are still serving at Midhurst today.

Others active on the Midhurst scene were Mrs. Reed, Miss Thair and Miss Murrell. Mrs. Gladys Reed took over as laundry manageress on the departure of Mr. Jackman in 1955. For 30 years, until her retirement at the end of 1985, Mrs. Reed worked wonders. Her cheerful countenance, her ability to get the most out of her staff (and the machinery!) and her unfailing loyalty were outstanding. Displaying similar characteristics are the domestic services manageress, Miss Joy Thair, who was appointed to the Hospital in 1977, and Miss D. Murrell who has been in charge of the Hospital shop and post office since 1972.

Early in 1976 Dr. Douglas Teare announced that he wished to retire on 30 June 1977. He had suffered from indifferent health for some time and would in any case reach the normal retiring age of 60 by the middle of 1977. He had made a substantial contribution to the success of the Hospital during a particularly difficult period of its history and was deservedly one of its most popular Superintendents, especially with his patients who readily responded to his cheerful manner and breezy optimism. During his last 18 months at Midhurst he was occupied in the consideration of a number of important new ventures to improve services at the Hospital, but these were not to materialise until after he had retired – a new out-patient department, radiotherapy facilities, a postoperative intensive care unit and the introduction to Midhurst of open heart surgery. But it was during his period in office that the ideas germinated and he was responsible for much of the early planning.

The matter of his succession raised many questions. Should he be another clinically orientated 'Physician Superintendent' or should he be first and foremost an administrator? The advent of the Research Unit and the introduction in 1971 of a tripartite system of management had between them eroded much of the Superintendent's authority. Yet to appoint an administrator pure and simple was flying in the face of all Midhurst tradition. Mr. Geoffrey Godber, who had been invited by the Council in 1976 to review the administrative structure at the Hospital, recommended that the new Physician Superintendent (the title was to be retained) should be the effective Chief of the Hospital and head of the Management Team. Others held the view that a clinically orientated doctor should be appointed who need not necessarily possess the qualities or the inclination to be seen as head of the Hospital. The problem was eventually solved, after advice had been sought from the Medical Committee, by dropping the traditional title of 'Superintendent' and appointing two new officers to replace Teare when he left – a full time clinician with some administrative tasks who would be Senior Physician, and a medical administrator with some clinical responsibilities who would be Director of Medical Services. At the same time a 'quadripartite' system of management would be introduced, with authority vested in four principal officers – The Senior Physician (or Director of Clinical Services), the Director of Medical Services, the Hospital Secretary (now to be called Director of Administrative Services) and the Matron (to be called Director of Nursing Services).

During the six months which elapsed between Dr. Teare's retirement and the establishment of the new administrative system, Dr. K. M. Hume left to take up a new post in Saudi Arabia and Dr. Whiteside, who had been on the Hospital's Consulting Staff since 1970, acted as Superintendent in locum tenens.

In January 1978 the two new principal officers arrived: Dr. M. R. Geake, a Consultant from Preston, who had been one of the Hospital's consultants since 1970, and Dr. S. E. Large, a recently retired Major General from the Army Medical Services. Dr. Geake was to be the Senior Physician, Dr. Large, Director of Medical Services. They joined the Management Team alongside Mr. Boulton, Secretary and Director of Administrative Services and Miss Allen, Matron and Director of Nursing Services. The new quadripartite system of management was now in being.

Chapter XI

Midhurst Today: 1978-1985

At the beginning of 1978 the Chairman of the Council was still Her Grace, Lavinia, Duchess of Norfolk. Brigadier Sir Geoffrey Hardy-Roberts was Vice Chairman (as well as being Chairman of several Hospital Committees) and the remaining seven members of Council were: Mr. Frank Bradford (who was Chairman of the Finance Committee), the Hon. Lady Barttelot, Lt. General Sir James Baird, Mr. T. Coghlan, the Hon. Mrs. Lakin, Mr. Donald Scott and Mr. Charles Drew (who was also Chairman of the Medical Committee). In attendance at all meetings of the Council were the four Principal Officers of the Hospital (Dr. Geake, Dr. Large, Mr. Boulton and Miss Allen), the Director of the Midhurst Medical Research Institute (Professor Gordon Cumming), the Chairman of the 'local' Medical Committee (Mr. W. F. P. Gammie) and Mr. J. R. B. Morgan-Grenville who had recently become a member of the Institution and was later to be appointed a full member of the Council.

Morale at Midhurst in 1978 was as high as it had ever been, but so much had happened in the previous few years that the Hospital was unrecognisable from the Sanatorium of the 1950s and early 1960s when most of the patients suffered from tuberculosis and Sir Geoffrey Todd reigned supreme as Superintendent.

The progression of the Hospital from its former status as a Sanatorium was by now proceeding apace and the process of diversification was continuing. The Research Institute had been in operation since 1973 and effective collaboration with the Hospital had been achieved. Sir John Charnley continued to visit Midhurst regularly. The Hospital was keeping its place as one of the leading Thoracic Centres in the country, but more and more general medical and surgical cases were now being treated. The Douglas Macmillan Continuing Care Unit continued its domiciliary work using seven beds in Todd Ward as its hospital base. The Mammography and Breast Screening Clinic organised by Dr. John Price and Dr. Barbara Thomas continued to provide a useful service for the community. The R.A.F. Chest Unit of 20 beds was still accommodated in the Portal Ward.

After Air Commodore Cran's death in September 1978, the unit was supervised by Hospital consultants until a permanent replacement from the Royal Air Force, Squadron Leader J. A. C. Hopkirk, could be made available. In the summer of 1978 a Post-Operative Recovery Ward was opened adjacent to the Theatres, and in July 1978 Mr. (later Sir) Keith Ross carried out the first open-heart operation at Midhurst. This was the first of a series of such operations carried out by Sir Keith Ross and Mr. James Monro at the Hospital.

On Sir Halford Reddish's death in 1978 the Hospital lost its greatest benefactor since its foundation. His flow of generosity continued until his death, for it was in 1978 that a sum of money was promised which would pay for a new Out-patients Department of four consulting suites and an up-to-date Oncology Unit to incorporate a linear accelerator and a complete range of ancillary radiotherapeutic equipment. Dr. W. F. White was the consultant responsible for much of the planning and for selecting and calibrating the equipment, and he and Dr. Irene Cade were appointed Directors of the new department. The new building was opened by H.R.H. the Prince of Wales on 31 July 1980 and named 'The Mountbatten Wing', thus commemorating a family connection which had persisted since Sir Ernest Cassel had financed the foundation of the Sanatorium in the early years of the century.

The recent surge in activity at Midhurst was part of the Council's strategy designed to bring more patients to the Hospital and to maintain a high proportion of bed occupancy. How successful was it proving? In terms of numbers of patients admitted, very successful; but in maintaining a high proportion of occupied beds, less so. Indeed, it was becoming apparent that, since the heady days of the 1960s when full bed occupancy had been the norm, there had been a steady decline in the average number of beds occupied. The reason was simple – patients were being kept in hospital for much less time than had been customary in the past. The matter of declining bed occupancy was serious because hospital charges were based on the number of beds occupied and bed occupancy was, and still is, one of the principal factors determining hospital income. The target of high bed occupancy and how best to attain it was to exercise the minds of Council and the Hospital Management Team for many days to come.

In the hope of attracting more patients, the Council authorised Sir Geoffrey Hardy-Roberts in 1978 to discuss with a leading firm of Advertising Consultants measures which might achieve greater usage of the Hospital's resources. An agreement was reached with them and a series of meetings was held with the Management Team with a view to publishing a brochure which would be used to promote our interests in this country and abroad. Unfortunately, the Company had never before undertaken hospital promotional work of this kind, and their best efforts on our behalf never achieved any degree of success, but in other ways the Hospital's name and reputation continued to be made known to the medical profession and to the public at large. Clinical meetings were held to which local general practitioners and hospital consultants were invited; there were visits to the Hospital by Health Authorities and Community Health Councils and reciprocal visits were made by the Hospital's Principal Officers. Yet the average number of beds occupied during the late 1970s continued to fall some way short of the target of 145 which was the figure Sir Geoffrey Hardy-Roberts had suggested was necessary to ensure financial stability. The Council therefore asked Mr. Morgan-Grenville to be Chairman of a working party to study the question of bed occupancy and to make recommendations. The other members of the working party were Miss Allen, Mr. Boulton and Dr. Large. Dr. Geake, Professor Cumming and Dr. Doyle were consulted as necessary. The working group met frequently during 1979 and their report was received by Council early in 1980.

The Report emphasized that, owing to the restriction on numbers of patients paid for by the Area Health Authorities, higher patient levels would have to be sought primarily from the private sector. Its principal recommendation was that the Hospital 'marketing effort' might well be improved and that it should be developed through the agency of existing Hospital staff rather than through the introduction of a Marketing Executive. Changes in the admissions system were advocated, and the importance of maintaining a high degree of customer satisfaction was stressed. Other recommendations were that a ward improvement programme should be initiated with private bathrooms being provided wherever possible, catering should be improved, and television and telephones should be available in every room. In regard to the development of 'new business', it was accepted that money should be channelled into 'people' rather than 'equipment'. New consultants were to be encouraged to work at the Hospital, and local general practitioners were to be made more completely aware of the facilities offered by the Hospital, especially in the recently introduced fields of oncology and radiology, continuing care, and control of pain.

The public sector was not neglected. The committee made several recommendations for enhancing the Hospital's relationship with the Area Health Authorities, and raised the possibility of the Hospital carrying out (under contract for the National Health Service) specialised operations in fields where the waiting lists were long.

The question of bed occupancy and rising costs remained to the fore throughout 1980. Sir Geoffrey Hardy-Roberts analysed the problem in two memoranda which were discussed by the Council on 19 January 1981. He argued that as expenditure could not be reduced without lowering the standards of patient care, and as patient charges could not be raised more than were warranted by national inflation, a concerted effort must be made to put into effect the principal recommendations of the Morgan-Grenville Report, as modified in the light of subsequent discussion amongst the various bodies to which it had been circulated. But before a plan could be made and the recommendations implemented, he felt that the Council should review its own composition and constitution. Since this would necessarily have been an invidious task for the Council as then constituted, he recommended that a Commission of five be appointed to study these and related problems and to make suggestions for dealing with them.

The following were therefore invited by Council on 19 January 1981 to consider what changes should be made in the composition of the Council and of the Institution in order that the recommendations of the Morgan-Grenville Study Group might be effectively implemented: Lt. General Sir James Baird (who was later elected Chairman), Mr. W. F. P. Gammie, the Hon. Mrs. Lakin, Dr. J. N. Mickerson and Mr. J. R. B. Morgan-Grenville. Mr. J. A. Boulton was nominated to be Secretary, in attendance. The members met on many occasions during the course of 1981 and in August published a preliminary report which was circulated for comment to the Council and both Medical Committees.

The Commission's recommendations were far reaching. They advocated limited terms of office for the majority (eight) of Council members and a return to the original concept of 'The Institution' as an 'Upper House' which would nominate eight members of Council (other than the President and Vice-President) and whose authority over Council would be paramount. Membership of the Institution would include all the members of the Council with some ten non-council members in addition so that the Institution would always outnumber the Council. This was in accordance with the terms of the original Charter of Incorporation and the arrangement would provide the opportunity to invite distinguished people from within and without the local area to become Members of the Institution.

Other important recommendations by the Commission were that the Council should delegate execution of policy to a new Executive and Finance Committee and that a Hospital Director should be appointed who would effectively be the Head of the Hospital with authority over a Chief Medical Officer, a Matron, an Administrative Secretary and a Finance Officer. Changes in the medical staff were recommended (to coincide with the impending retirement of several principal officers) and the committee structure was to be changed by the establishment of a single locally based Medical Advisory Committee to replace the two medical committees already in existence. It was the clause in the report relating to the appointment of a Hospital 'Director' which aroused concern. A diagram in the report showing the proposed new Director standing alone at the top of the administrative tree was singled out for criticism as it was felt that the introduction of a 'supremo', were he to be medically qualified or not, would be resented by senior medical staff in post and might affect adversely the quality of candidates applying for the top medical jobs in future.

Representations were made by senior members of the staff as a result of which the Commission agreed that the title of the new appointment should be 'Chief Executive' and that the diagram in question should be replaced by a sentence to indicate that the Chief Executive should be Chairman and co-ordinator of the Management Team.

The other bone of contention was the Commission's proposal that there should be only one Medical Advisory Committee, answerable to the Executive and Finance Committee, to replace the two medical committees currently in existence. Although the proposed new medical committee was to include a number of London consultants, it was to be locally based, and its introduction would in effect spell the end of the existing Committee, usually referred to as the 'London' Medical Committee. The issue was delicate because the London Committee was the lineal descendant of the panel of London Consultants, which had been set up with the King's approval at the time the Sanatorium was opened in 1906 to give advice to the Executive Committee, the forerunner of the Council, on all matters relating to the care and treatment of the patients. For years this body of distinguished medical men had been giving their time freely to Midhurst affairs. Their advice had always been impartial and motivated only by what was in the best interests of the Sanatorium. The suggestion that they should now become absorbed into a locally based body, however well attuned the new Committee might be to deal with local problems, was resented as showing lack of appreciation of their true worth.

These views were considered by the Council in March 1982 and it was decided that for the time being both medical committees should continue in being. The former 'Local' Medical Committee would be renamed 'The Medical Committee' and would continue, as proposed by the Commission, as a locally based body answering to the Executive and Finance Committee, and be responsible for offering advice on all day-to-day medical matters. It would no longer be a sub-committee. The 'London' Medical Committee would be renamed 'The Medical Advisory Committee' and would be asked to continue in being for a further period. It would be responsible to the Executive and Finance Committee for advice on higher medical appointments and on the broader aspects of medical policy. There would be an automatic right for the Chairmen of both bodies to report in person to the Executive and Finance Committee, but no automatic right for either to become a member of the Council. Council's decision was accepted and both medical committees continued in being, with Mr. Gammie as Chairman of the Medical Committee, which was to meet every month at Midhurst, and Dr. Robertson (who succeeded Mr. Drew in 1981) as Chairman of the Medical Advisory Committee, meeting twice a year, once in London at the Royal College of Physicians and once at Midhurst.

Meanwhile, the main body of the Commission's Report had been approved at an Extraordinary Meeting of the Institution on 28 September 1981, and its principal recommendations were put into effect. The composition of the Council and the Institution was changed. Sir Geoffrey Hardy-Roberts, who had been a member of the Council since 1969 and its Deputy Chairman since 1970, retired from the Council, but continued to serve as a member of the Institution. His contribution to the Hospital had been immense. With his organisational flair, his unparallelled experience and his understanding of people, he had done much to enhance the image of the Hospital and keep it in the forefront of affairs. Mr. Frank Bradford, the Hon. Lady Barttelot and Mr. T. B. L. Coghlan also resigned as members of Council, but continued as members of the Institution where their knowledge and experience could continue to be drawn on. Mr. Bradford's association with the Hospital dated from 1968 when he joined the Committee of Friends of the Hospital. He became its Chairman in 1977 and during his Chairmanship more than £250,000 was raised for the benefit of the Hospital. He had been appointed a member of the Finance Committee in 1971 and became its Chairman in 1977 in which capacity his great experience as a banker was utilised to full effect. In their place as members of the Council, the Queen approved the following: Mr. J. R. B. Morgan-Grenville, who had been in attendance at all meetings since 1978, Mr. C. J. Lucas and Mr. L. O'Connor.

One of the cardinal features of the Commission's report was that the Council should meet quarterly and should be primarily concerned with decisions of strategic long-term planning and general guidance of policy. The detailed management of the Hospital was to be delegated to a subordinate committee to be known as the Executive and Finance Committee which would supersede the existing Finance Committee and have responsibility to the Council. The Executive and Finance Committee was to be composed of three members of the Council – Mr. Morgan-Grenville (Chairman), the Hon. Mrs. Daphne Lakin and Mr. Leslie O'Connor were the first to be appointed – and the four Hospital Principal Officers who at the time were Doctors Geake and Large, Mr. Boulton and Miss Allen.

The Committee's brief was to monitor the Hospital's work standards, allocate resources, deal with the recruitment and welfare of staff (other than the Principal Officers) and to negotiate contracts with private bodies and with the Area Health Authorities. They were to review Hospital staffing establishments, set Hospital charges for treatment, approve staff salaries, and deal with complaints from patients. Also they were to keep the bed occupancy levels under review and explore new areas of treatment. Most importantly, they were to be responsible for monitoring the Hospital's spending and income, and for making recommendations to the Council. This was a tall order and it is not surprising that when the newly constituted Committee met for the first time on 11 November 1981, the meeting lasted eight hours with only a short break for lunch! But much ground was covered and the rules of procedure were laid down. Since then the Committee has met regularly at monthly intervals, leaving the Council free to consider the broader issues at their quarterly meetings and the Hospital Management Team to concentrate on the day to day running of the Hospital. The emergence of the Executive and Finance Committee can now be seen as one of the major administrative advances at Midhurst in recent times.

One of the first matters to be considered was the formulation in April 1982 of a Hospital Strategic Plan, an important document which outlined the measures which should be taken to ensure the Hospital's continuing viability as a 'general' hospital with a bias to cardiac and thoracic treatment and with a high proportion of its patients in the acute category.

One of the most important elements of the Strategic Plan was the development of bed occupancy. The target recommended was an average occupancy of 140 beds, compared with the 120 bed average which had been recently achieved. It was considered that the target figure could be attained by better communications with local consultants and general practitioners and by an improved presentation of the Hospital to the community. More importantly, it was considered that bed occupancy could be enhanced by developing new areas of treatment, by defending existing areas of treatment, and by maintaining the highest standards of medical and nursing care. The appointment of a new Chief Executive to the Hospital and the replacement of Doctors Geake and Doyle in 1983 by new consultants were important factors. Economies were to be made, an extensive ward improvement programme embarked on, and the changes in the administrative structure recommended by the Commission were to be brought into effect.

The year 1982 saw a start made on implementing The Strategic Plan. The appointment of Chief Executive was advertised and 120 replies were received. Three candidates were interviewed and a selection made, but an offer to the successful candidate had to be withdrawn on medical grounds and the post had to be re-advertised. Interviews were held on 26 November 1982 and Mr. John Goldsworthy, then the District Administrator of the Worthing Health Authority, was selected for the appointment which was to become effective on the retirement of Mr. Boulton on 1 April 1983.

The senior Hospital medical posts were reviewed in 1982 in the light of the changing scene at Midhurst and the impending retirements in 1983 of Doctors Large, Geake and Doyle. Dr. I. T. Gabe had already become a member of the Hospital's Consultant Staff in June 1982. He was appointed Senior Physician and a member of the Management Team in April 1983 after Dr. Geake had retired. Dr. M. I. M. Noble was appointed Consultant in General and Thoracic Medicine in November 1983, and Mr. S. D. Clarke Consultant Surgeon to the Hospital in May 1983, Mr. Clarke being the first surgeon to be appointed to a full-time consultant post at Midhurst. Dr. Large, who retired in August 1983, was not replaced as Director of Medical Services. His responsibilities were taken over in part by the Chief Executive, in part by the Senior Physician and in part by Mr. Clarke. To complete the senior Hospital team of Consultants, Dr. Michael Thomas was, in April 1985, appointed Consultant Cardiologist. The Macmillan Service remained under the Directorship of Dr. Miriam McKenna, assisted by her husband, Dr. R. H. Freeman. The R.A.F. Chest Unit continued to operate in the charge of Squadron Leader (later Wing Commander) J. A. C. Hopkirk, who had taken over in 1980.

The number of Hospital pre-registration house officers was increased in August 1983 to six, three house physicians and three house surgeons. With a surgical registrar and three senior house officers in medicine, and frequently with an additional R.A.F. officer on attachment, this represented a solid base from which to provide 24-hour on-the-spot medical and surgical cover.

After the appointment in 1983 of Mr. John Goldsworthy as Chief Executive, the administrative system within the Hospital was modified. Two new Administration Teams were formed, a Management Team (Mr. Goldsworthy, Dr. Gabe, Mr. Clarke, Miss Allen, Mr. Mitchell and Mr. Seagrove) responsible to the Executive and Finance Committee and a Medical Management Team (Dr. Gabe, Dr. Gordon, Dr. Noble, Mr. Clarke, Wing Commander Hopkirk and, soon afterwards, Dr. Thomas) to advise the Management Team on medical matters. With the Executive and Finance Committee meeting once a month under the Chairmanship of Mr. Morgan-Grenville, the day to day management of the Hospital was again on a sound footing after a period of some uncertainty whilst the changes were being made. The two Medical Committees and the Nursing Advisory Committee under the Chairmanship of the Hon. Mrs. Lakin continued to meet regularly. The Council met quarterly, still under the Chairmanship of Her Grace, Lavinia, Duchess of Norfolk. The Institution, presided over by Her Majesty the Queen, remained at the summit of the management structure, meeting once a year with the Vice-President, Her Grace, Lavinia, Duchess of Norfolk, taking the Chair.

The affairs of the Midhurst Medical Research Institute were meanwhile causing some concern. Although relations between the Hospital and Institute had become close in the late 1970s, the Institute always found it difficult to find a sufficient number of patients to take part in their research activities. Financial problems were also arising. The Institute had been founded by a donation of £5 million, £1 million of which had been used to provide the building and the equipment. The balance had been invested by the Board of Trustees to provide an income. This had proved more than adequate to meet expenditure during the 1970s, but in 1980 expenditure exceeded income by a considerable sum. For the future the recession made it difficult to increase revenue and a reduction in expenditure could only be achieved by cutting staff and reducing the volume and content of research activities being carried out. An alternative solution was to arrange a merger with another organisation, and during 1980 and 1981 several possibilities were considered. One was that the Hospital and Institute might themselves merge, but financial difficulties precluded this. Others were that the Institute might become associated with the University of Southampton, or with St George's Hospital, or with the University of Surrey. The course finally taken was to approach the Cardio-Thoracic Institute at the Brompton Hospital with a view to arranging an amalgamation with them. The prospect of the union was welcomed by the Governors of both organisations, and negotiations to effect a merger were begun late in 1981. The Hospital took no direct part in these, but in March 1982 Mr. Morgan-Grenville discussed with the Chairman of the Board of Governors of the Institute how the Hospital might best contribute to a successful outcome of the talks. It was decided that the Hospital could assist financially to some extent by relieving the Institute of the greater part of the salaries of two senior Consultants and by paying a rental for those parts of the Institute which were used for Hospital purposes, in particular the Laboratory.

The Hospital Council were initially entirely enthusiastic in their support for the proposed merger, believing that an association with the Brompton Hospital through the Cardio- Thoracic Institute would enhance the Hospital's reputation, but doubts arose as the negotiations proceeded and the terms of the merger became apparent. Their main concern was that if in the future the Cardio-Thoracic Institute were to withdraw altogether from the Midhurst site, and there were well justified fears that they might do so, there were no safeguards built into the agreement against their sub-letting the building to some other organisation whose proximity to the Hospital might be unwelcome. There were financial implications too. The Hospital Laboratory would have to be found alternative accommodation for which the capital expenditure would be considerable. By August 1983, the Council's objections to the agreement on the terms then proposed were so strong that a special meeting of the Council was held on 24 August 1983 to consider how to proceed. What imparted a note of urgency to this meeting was that although the Cardio-Thoracic Institute had previously offered a Letter of Intent giving the Hospital first refusal on the leasehold should they vacate the Midhurst premises, no such letter had yet been received. Moreover, the proposed merger was shortly to come before the University of London for ratification. After submissions had been made to the Council by those in attendance at the meeting (Sir Geoffrey Todd, Sir Geoffrey Hardy-Roberts, Dr. Mickerson, Dr. Gabe, Dr. Gordon and Mr. Goldsworthy), the Council agreed unanimously that the terms of the merger were unacceptable and not in line with the wishes of the donor, the late Sir Halford Reddish, and that every effort should be made to stop the merger going forward, particularly any decision by the Academic Council of the University of London to whom a letter pointing out Council's objections was to be sent. If matters had already gone too far, an approach was to be made to the Charity Commissioners.

The next stage in the matter was that a Hospital Negotiating Team met the Board of Governors of the Midhurst Medical Research Institute on 12 September 1983 and put forward a proposal regarding the purchase of the leasehold of the Midhurst Medical Research Institute building at an agreed cost. This was accepted by the Midhurst Medical Research Institute and by the Cardio-Thoracic Institute in principle and this agreement was included in the papers forwarded to the University of London, in consideration of which the Hospital's letter of objection was withdrawn.

From that point matters progressed slowly but surely. In May 1984 the Court of the University of London agreed to the proposed merger, but the affair was not yet quite settled since the act could not be concluded until the agreement of the original Trustees had been obtained and the Charity Commissioners had signified their approval. Once this was done, there was no further delay and in October 1984 the merger was confirmed by Mr. Wilde (on behalf of the Midhurst Medical Research Institute) and Professor Turner-Warwick (Dean of the Cardio-Thoracic Institute). The Midhurst Medical Research Institute was then dissolved and its resources formally transferred to the Cardio-Thoracic Institute on 30 November 1984.

During the 1980s, activity in the Hospital continued to increase, particularly attendances in the Out-patients Department. In 1985 there were 7,250 attendances compared with 5,600 in 1981. The number of admissions also increased. In 1981 it was 3,580; in 1985 it had risen to 4,500. More operations were carried out (2,435 in 1985) and the daily bed occupancy showed a small but welcome rise. Private patients accounted for about 40 per cent of the admissions, R.A.F. and Macmillan Service patients about 15 per cent and the remainder were National Health Service patients admitted under contractual arrangements with the local District Health Authorities. It was considered to be in keeping with the charitable status of the Hospital to allow a few patients from the local community to be treated even though no payment was being made to the Hospital. In addition, special arrangements were made with Worthing, Portsmouth, Bath and Brighton Health Authorities which enabled nearly 100 patients from the National Health Service to have hip joint replacement operations done at Midhurst.

The Hospital departments continued to be as busy as ever and the range of activities provided by the Hospital Out-patients Department was extended to include gastroenterology, rheumatology, E.N.T., general and vascular surgery, male sterilisation, varicose vein injection, urology, psychiatry and neurology.

The Laboratory, with Dr. Ian Gordon in charge, retained its accommodation in the Institute building. The staff underwent several changes after the retirement of the Lunts and Geoff Rumsby in 1980. The Strudwicks are still there, as are Sally Waters and Hilary Masters, but others have moved on. Sadly Aida Paris Hart developed a fatal illness, and Mike Haydon who joined the Staff from the R.A.M.C. in 1980 moved to another appointment. The Respiratory Laboratory continues in being and has acquired much new equipment. Mrs. Letley retired in 1981 and the department is now in the hands of Miss Sue Parker.

The Oncology Department under the Directorship of Dr. W. F. White and Miss I. Cade, and with Dr. Svoboda attending once a week, increased its work load and took on extra patients whilst new equipment was being installed at Portsmouth. Mrs. Sue White has been Superintendent of the department since its opening in 1980. The recently established Pain Clinic continued to use the facilities of the Oncology Department, clinics being held by Doctors Hughes, Fozard and Ker. The Pharmacy under Miss S. Roper increased the number of items it supplied, particularly to out patients. The X-ray Department (Miss Margaret Easton and Mr. Colin Bennell) acquired an ultrasound scanner in 1984 and a new whole body scanner in 1985. Daily radiological consultant cover became possible in 1984. The Physiotherapy Department (Mrs. A. R. Cock) continued to treat a wide range of conditions, both for inpatients and a number of outpatients.

The Macmillan Service, under Dr. M. A. McKenna and her husband, Dr. R. H. Freeman, expanded its services, and now possesses a professional team which includes two Consultants, four Home Care Sisters, a Principal Social Worker and a Voluntary Services organiser. Help and support continue to be given to patients at home or in hospital, but emphasis is on the Home Care Service which is conducted by Miss Canterford, Mrs. Morgan, Miss Vince and Mrs. Fowler. The Unit at Midhurst is believed to be the only unit of its kind which is established in a general hospital and supported financially by the National Society for Cancer Relief.

The School of Nursing under Mrs. Brook assisted by three Clinical Teachers (Mrs. C. Jones, Mrs. O'Conor and Miss Percy) remains one of Midhurst's greatest assets, passing out some thirty State Enrolled Nurses annually, and the Dental Department (Mr. Bevan Thomas and Mr. John S. Lee) continues its valuable work for staff and patients.

The Library maintains a consistently high standard under Mrs. L. Lane, the Librarian, her deputy Mrs. Laband, and, recently, Mrs. M. Turner. The voluntary bookbinders, Mrs. Knox and Mrs. Thomson, have given valuable support. It has not only been the patients who have enjoyed using the library; the staff also have benefited immeasurably.

The·'Friends', under the leadership of Mr. John Boulton, continue to be the main fund raising body for the Hospital. Their financial contributions have made it possible to purchase many items of expensive equipment for the Hospital and to renovate many of the staff quarters. Donations made under deed of covenant have always been the main source of income for the 'Friends', but the biennial Fêtes and Christmas Bazaars (organised by Lady Morrison-Scott) have raised large sums of money. Other fund raising activities arranged by the Committee of Friends during the '80s have been a dress show in conjunction with Marks and Spencer at the Chichester Festival Theatre, a concert at the Hospital by the entertainers 'Instant Sunshine', piano recitals, and a display and sale of pictures by local artists organised by Mr. Royd Robinson.

Since 1980 there have been considerable changes in the fabric, equipment and installations of the Hospital. Television sets have been provided for every patient's room. A new ambulance entrance, a gift from the 'Friends', was finished in 1980. Above it, improved accommodation for the medical staff has been built. An extensive programme of ward improvements has been embarked on. The Hardy-Roberts and Miles Reid Wards were re-decorated and up-graded to provide a number of rooms with better furniture and lighting, new carpets and curtains, and their own bathrooms and lavatories. In 1984, an operating theatre extension was completed which provided two more anaesthetic rooms and an endoscopy room. The improvements continue: today the Macmillan Unit is being enlarged, fire precautions are being extended, work is proceeding on various energy saving programmes and a computer is being installed which will run a complete management service.

Such is the Midhurst of today. The year 1986 will see the 80th anniversary of the opening of the Hospital, or King's Sanatorium as it then was, by its founder, His Majesty King Edward VII. Great though the changes have been since that far-off day in June 1906 when the King declared his Sanatorium open, Midhurst remains as ever a happy place, a place where patients feel they are in good hands, a place where management and staff give of their best and know their efforts are appreciated.

In the very early days, whilst the Sanatorium was still being built, King Edward VII expressed the hope that the work, when finished would be 'a model of its kind'. If he could see his 'Sanatorium' as it is today he would, I venture to suggest, be well satisfied.

Appendix One

Extracts from the *Sussex Daily News* of 14 June 1906

Opening of the Sanatorium

Not Midhurst only, but all the neighbouring towns and villages united yesterday in welcoming their Majesties the King and Queen to Sussex on the occasion of the opening of the palatial King's Sanatorium, built on the heights three miles north of Midhurst, and dedicated now to the campaign against consumption which his Majesty has for years past fostered by every means in his power. There was no mistaking Midhurst's special interest in a ceremony of great national importance. The quaint old town, with its illustrious historical associations, had transformed itself. Much of the singular beauty of its picturesque architecture, that which is so admired, and treasured so jealously and proudly, was for the few fleeting hours of a day lost to view— hidden by shrouds of every hue, banners of every shape. There was a blaze of waving colour to welcome the King and Queen— a truly admirable assortment floating from every staff, window, turret, tower and tree. A King and his Queen do not give honour to a town every day, and Midhurst, where ancient things die slowly, where there is the survival of a romantic glamour, sprung out of its quiet and fascinating old-worldliness into radiant vivacity, and gave unmistakable expression to its loyalty.

Much has already been written of the very fine Sanatorium of which so much is expected, but visitors to it during the construction have been comparatively few, and, among the distinguished guests invited to yesterday's opening ceremony, there was the keenest desire to investigate its appointments and make themselves familiar with all the arrangements for dealing with the hundred patients it is proposed to accept, and whom it is hoped to send away cured every four months, to be replaced by others requiring treatment.

Arrival at Midhurst

During the morning the town was alive with visitors, and each train which ran into the station brought crowds of people from all directions. Among the early arrivals were very strong forces of police, Yeomanry, Volunteers, and Church Lads Brigades. The townspeople were up with the lark, busy as bees, and great improvements were made in the decorations. The excitement grew as the day advanced, and the crowds from the surrounding villages gradually took up positions of vantage along the route. During the bright afternoon the streets were thronged with people from a wide district, but as the hour of four approached it was at the London and Brighton Railway Station that the crowd found its magnet, and though only the local committee and officials were

117

allowed within the square approach, there was brisk competition along the Chichester road for every exalted position. At the station, besides a true representation of Sussex nobility, were figures of every branch of Midhurst society, and all of the old town's institution had adequate delegations. Outside the station sections of the 2nd V.B. Royal Sussex Regiment under the command of Major B. T. Hodgson, V.D., were drawn up. There were the 'E' Company (Horsham), Sergeant Leamy and 30 men; 'F' Company (Arundel), Sergeant Matthews and 20 men; and 'G' Company (Chichester), Sergeant Turner and 20 men. The regimental band was also present. When the roar of the Royal train was heard the crowd of heads began to sway and all eyes were eagerly turned in one direction. It was evident that everyone was longing to seize the first opportunity of giving vent to long pent up feelings. The Royal train which had travelled via Dorking, Horsham and Pulborough, reached Midhurst punctually at four o'clock.

While the Volunteer Band was playing the National Anthem, Enid, the pretty little six year old daughter of Mr. John Taylor, of North Street (formerly of Pheasant Court, Petworth), who was attended by Master R. Casstell Knight a son of a well-known and popular townsman, Mr. George Knight, presented to her Majesty a beautiful bouquet of orchids and lilies of the valley, which was graciously accepted.

For the next few minutes there was a splendid demonstration of patriotism, and as lusty a tribute of fealty to their Majesties as could anywhere have been paid. For Midhurst it was indeed a remarkable sight, and the vividly conveyed impressions of that June afternoon will not fade quickly from the eager memories of those who were present. When their Majesties walked from the platform towards their carriage, a reverberating cheer burst from the long lines of spectators. The news that the Royal visitors had arrived spread with wonderful rapidity from point to point, and corner to corner along the Chichester road, and it was carried on from mouth to mouth down the processional route.

From Station to Town

All began to strain anxiously to catch a glimpse of the procession, which soon started from the shadows of the terminus, amid a hurricane of cheering. Members of the Sussex Imperial Yeomanry – fine, stalwart fellows, beautifully mounted – under the command of Lieutenant C. E. Crabbe, formed a splendid cavalcade. Quartermaster-Sergeant Harold Field was mounted on the horse which headed the Coronation procession with Major Ames, the tallest man in the Army at the time, and from whom the animal was recently purchased by the Sussex yeoman.

There were features which few found time to notice, all eyes were peering for the Royal carriage, for he who looked 'every inch a King', and she the worthiest of 'Queenliest Queens'. It is no wonder that King Edward is popular, admired, beloved; it is not surprising that wherever he goes among his own people and kindred there is a demonstration of affectionate fervour, deafening acclamations, and a frantic welcome. Looking at him yesterday, hundreds were impressed by his genial bearing and friendly smile. And the Queen! Her gracious acknowledgments only stimulated the ringing outburst and proofs of affection. Along the Chichester road, where there were gaily dressed groups of school children, past row after row of fluttering flags went the Royal carriage, drawn by handsomely caparisoned horses, greeted by roll after roll of shouts and the waving flags of every colour. While most of the members of the reception party were driven behind the Royal carriage, the Duke and Duchess of Norfolk were borne swiftly to the Sanatorium in a motor-car. The great crowds seemed to breathe one poignant sentiment; everywhere there were expressions of admiration and acts of devotion, but one cheery rusticated old soul, ruddy of countenance, struggling to wipe the shining beads of perspiration from her rosy cheeks, seemed to utter in a strident key, what all really felt: 'What a day! God bless 'em!' It was a sight such as Midhurst had never seen before.

Drive to the Sanatorium

As England's beloved Rulers made their progress through the square, round after round of welcoming cheers arose. The people had come out to do honour to their King and Queen, and right royal was the reception accorded them. The throng was a well-dressed one. Ladies were in their most tasteful summer attire, while their husbands and sweethearts were in cool becoming garb, fitting the month of June.

Passing through charming Easebourne village the roll of cheering was carried on. Dodsley Lane is one of the beauty spots of the county, and their Majesties must have been most pleasurably impressed by the scene. The Workhouse at the foot of the steep Fernhurst road was eventually reached and here the equipage was warmly greeted by the inmates who lined the grounds, and also by a large number of visitors.

At the Sanatorium

For fully two hours prior to the time at which their Majesties were due to arrive, the vicinity of the Sanatorium presented an animated scene. Soon after two o'clock the guests from London began to arrive in carriages from the Haslemere Station. At the main entrance to the building they were conducted to the dining hall, where the important ceremony was to take place. Meanwhile the children from the Midhurst, Easebourne, Fernhurst, West Lavington, and Woolbeding schools were stationed in a line under the great pine trees facing the entrance, Mr. George Singleton, head master of Easebourne School, being in charge. Presently the Guard of Honour arrived, a hundred men of the 2nd Vol. Battalion, Royal Sussex Regiment, under Captain Bennett, Lieutenants A. P. R. Godman and E. H. Staffurth and formed up into lines in the open space just outside the entrance door. The Chief Constable of West Sussex, Captain Drummond, M.V.O., who wore his uniform, was also early on the scene. By four o'clock all was in readiness, and the 250 or 300 guests had taken their seats in the dining hall.

It was almost half-past four when their Majesties arrived. As the escort approached, the school children sung ' God save the King', and when the Royal carriage came in sight the Guard saluted, their Majesties acknowledging the reception accorded them. In the entrance hall the King and Queen were received by His Majesty's Advisory Committee. Their Majesties were immediately conducted to a dais in the dining hall, where a couple of gilded chairs, upholstered in red, had been placed for their use. The Queen, who was quietly attired in a costume of black crepe de chine trimmed with black crepe, with insertions of lace, and a black Mary Stuart toque, was then presented with an exquisite bouquet of pink Malmaison carnations by Miss Katherine Broadbent.

His Majesty, still standing and facing the assembly, was next addressed by Sir William Broadbent, explaining the lines upon which the Sanatorium had been constructed. The most interesting passage ran :

The class for which special provision is to be made includes those belonging to the various professions who may fall victims of phthisis and are unable to afford the expense incident to treatment in private sanatoria, clergymen and other ministers of religion, medical men, members of the teaching profession, together with clerks and others employed in business offices or members of their families. By your Majesty's express desire the wealthy classes are not to be altogether excluded from the advantages of a sanatorium which, if it realises your Majesty's beneficent intention, is to be the best of its kind and 12 rooms are set apart for their reception.

His Majesty made the following gracious reply:

It gives the Queen and myself great pleasure to be here today to open this magnificently situated building. I thank the most generous donor through whose munificence I have been enabled to form this Sanatorium which bears my name, and I am well assured that it will be a great pleasure to him to know that the noble gift which he placed at my disposal has been so usefully bestowed, and that it will be the means of affording relief to those suffering from the devastating scourge of tuberculosis. I congratulate the members of the Advisory Committee upon the whole-hearted manner in which they have carried out the trust I repose in them, and I thank them for the inestimable value of their advice and experience, and for the expenditure of time and labour, which despite the many calls upon them, they have given to the work. It is my desire that this institution shall afford accommodation for that large class of persons of slender means, in professional and other employments, for which no provision for sickness of this kind at present exists. It is also my wish that those persons of larger means who can afford to pay for treatment here should not be entirely excluded from the advantages to be derived from this institution, and I have accordingly decided that a small number of beds shall be reserved for them.

It has ever been my endeavour and that of the Queen to do all within our power to mitigate suffering and to check the ravages of disease. The Queen has shown her deep interest in the fight against tuberculosis by becoming the Patron of the proposed Queen Alexandra Sanatorium at Davos, and by permitting that institution to be called by her name, and it is our earnest hope that the Sanatorium which is now opened, and its research laboratories, equipped with every resource of modern science, may assist to advance the physiological knowledge of pulmonary diseases, and that the institution may, by treating the disease in its early stages, be the means of prolonging the lives of those whose career of honourable usefulness has been interrupted by this terrible malady.

I pray that God's blessing may rest upon this building and upon all who work within it, and all who come to it for aid, and that it may be a means of alleviating suffering and saving life for this and many generations to come.

The Bishop of Chichester offered prayers, and the hymn 'O God, our Help in ages past', was sung, the Midhurst Church Choir in the gallery leading.

His Majesty then in a loud voice said 'I declare this building now open'. The King having consented, Sir William Broadbent presented to their Majesties Mr. H. Percy Adams, the architect, who handed the King an album of photographs of the building; Mr. Charles Longley the builder; Miss Jekyll, the horticulturist on whose design the grounds had been laid out; Dr. Noel Bardswell and Dr. Basil Adams, medical officers of the sanatorium; and Miss Blanch Trew, matron.

After the presentation, their Majesties then made a long tour of inspection, Sir W. Broadbent accompanying the Queen and Sir F. Treves pointing out to his Majesty the details of the building. The inspection over, their Majesties partook of tea in the recreation room.

Their Majesties left the Sanatorium at a quarter to six, having previously signed the visitors book and made a brief inspection of the Guard of Honour drawn up outside.

Prior to leaving the building the King expressed his pleasure at all he had seen, and hoped that Dr. Bardswell would be able to make the Sanatorium a great success.

Appendix Two

Extracts from Sanatorium 'house' journals

1. From the *King Edward VII Magazine*, November 1906.

The Lung Brigade

Half a league, half a league,
Half a league onward.
All through the pine wood walk
Go the one hundred.
'Forward the Lung Brigade
Straight for the moor!' he said:
There the microbes to baulk
Go the one hundred.

'Forward the Lung Brigade!'
Every man Jack obeyed,
Although it rained and blew
Lightened and thundered:
There's steak and kidney pie,
Wherewith your health to buy,
Their's but to stuff or die:
Up through the pine wood walk
Go the one hundred.

Fresh air to right of them,
Fresh air to left of them,
Fresh air in front of them
Breathe the one hundred;
And as their bodies swell,
Boldly they eat and well,
Sweets as they take their walk,
Striving the 'Mikes' to quell
Feed the one hundred.

Many of the sex so fair,
Some with dishevelled hair
Arms to the elbow bare,
Pacing the upland, while
All Midhurst wondered:
'My word this is no joke!
Walking without a cloak,
Great coat or paletôt;
Surely their health's not broke,
Someone has blundered.'
Thus thro' this life they go,
Noble one hundred.

The Busy T.B.

How doth the little gay T.B.
Delight to buzz and bite,
He changes rhonchi into râles
And crepitates all night.

He likes a trip upon the sea,
And when he is afloat
He digs away with all his might,
And laughs at Creosote.

Some send his victim to the links
To play the game of golf;
Poor chap, it makes him puff and blow,
The 'Tubbies' only scoff.

Emulsions, hypophosphites, oil,
He mops the lot and jeers;
Even iodide of arsenic
For him presents no fears.

At sprays and atomisers all
He chortles in his joy,
And chemists' elixirs of life
Upon his palate cloy.

But once inside King Edward's San,
That truculent little germ
Receives his first rude shock in life,
And does a little squirm.

He barks into the Stethoscope
And rattles all his toes,
But the Medical Super. knows him well,
His life draws to a close.

Milk, suet pudding, splendid air,
Are not the things he likes;
Rest hours, exercise, and care,
Play havoc with the 'mikes'.

He bars the omnivorous phagocyte,
Opsonins give him fits;
The struggle for existence
Distracts his failing wits.

At last all decadent he lies,
No more can he bear fruit,
His ragged corpse is bundled out:
Requiescat, little brute!

2. From the *Edwardian*, Spring 1949

The Best Friend

Now shall I walk
Or shall I ride?
'Walk', Pleasure said.
'Ride', Todd replied.

Now what shall I—
Stay home or roam?
'Roam', Pleasure said;
And Todd—'Stay home.'

Now shall I dance,
Or sit for dreams?
'Sit', answers Todd;
'Dance', Pleasure screams.

Which of ye two
Will kindest be?
Pleasure laughed sweet,
But Todd cured me.

Appendix Three

List of names approved by the King in 1912

Institution

Sir Frederick Treves, Bart., G.C.V.O., C.B. (Chairman)
Sir Francis Laking, Bart., G.C.V.O., K.C.B. (Vice Chairman)
The Lord Cowdray
Sir Walter Lawrence, Bart., G.C.I.E.
Rowland Bailey, Esq., C.B., M.V.O.
Colonel Lascelles, M.V.O.
P. Horton-Smith Hartley, Esq., M.V.O., M.D.
George Evelyn Pemberton Murray, Esq.

His Grace The Duke of Norfolk, K.G.
His Grace The Duke of Richmond and Gordon, K.G., G.C.V.O.
The Viscount Esher, G.C.B., G.C.V.O.
The Viscount Knollys, G.C.B., G.C.V.O., K.C.M.G.
The Lord Leconfield
General The Right Hon. Sir Dighton Probyn, V.C., G.C.B., G.C.S.I., G.C.V.O.
Sir John Broadbent, Bart., M.D.
Sir Richard Douglas Powell, Bart., K.C.V.O., M.D.
Sir George Lewis, Bart.
Sir Felix Semon, K.C.V.O., M.D.
Sir Hermann Weber, M.D.
Sir John Brickwood
Sir William Barclay Peat
His Honour Judge Lumley Smith, K.C.
Theodore Williams, Esq., M.V.O., M.D.
James Buchanan, Esq.

The Lady Gifford
Mrs. William James
Mrs. Bischoffsheim
Miss Gertrude Jekyll

Council

Sir Frederick Treves, Bart., G.C.V.O., C.B. (Chairman)
Sir Francis Laking, Bart, G.C.V.O., K.C.B. (Vice Chairman)

The Lord Cowdray
Sir Walter Lawrence, Bart., G.C.I.E.
Rowland Bailey, Esq., C.B., M.V.O.
Colonel Lascelles, M.V.O.
P. Horton-Smith Hartley, Esq., M.V.O., M.D.
George Evelyn Pemberton Murray, Esq.

Consulting Staff
C. Theodore Williams, Esq., M.V.O., M.D. (Chairman)
Sir William Osler, Bart., M.D., F.R.S.
Sir James Frederick Goodhart, Bart., M.D.
Sir Clifford Allbutt, K.C.B., M.D., F.R.S.
Sir J. Kingston Fowler, K.C.V.O., M.D.
Sir Bernard Dawson, K.C.V.O., M.D.
Sir Hermann Weber, M.D.
Sir St. Clair Thomson, M.D., F.R.C.S.
Theodore Dyke Acland, Esq., M.D.
John Mitchell Bruce, Esq., M.D.
William Bulloch, Esq., M.D.
Percy Kidd, Esq., M.D.

Lady Visitors: The Lady Gifford, Mrs. William James

Hon. Legal Adviser: Sir George Lewis, Bart.

Hon. Auditor: Sir William Barclay Peat

Appendix   Four

**A selection from the 30 Rules governing the appointment of
the Medical Superintendent, about 1934**

1.   He must be duly registered in England to practise in Medicine and Surgery, according to the Act of the 21st and 22nd Vic. Cap. 90, intituled 'An Act to regulate the qualification of Practitioners in Medicine and Surgery'.

2.   He shall be appointed for a period of one year, but shall be eligible for re-election at the expiration of this period. His appointment shall be subject to three months' notice on either side *at any time*.

3.   He shall reside in the House provided for him, but shall take at least one meal each day, such meal being either lunch or dinner, with the Patients in the Sanatorium.

4.   He shall have paramount authority in the Sanatorium, subject to that of the Council.

5.   Subject to such control, he shall have the general direction and management of all the Medical, Nursing, and General Staff, Officials and Servants.

6.   He shall have power to appoint, and if necessary, to discharge, the junior members of the Staff (but not the Assistant Medical Officers, Pathologist, Matron, Secretary-Steward, Chaplain, Head Engineer, Assistant Engineer, Head Porter, Gardener, Chauffeur, or Cook), such discharge to be submitted to the Council at their next Meeting for confirmation.

7.   He shall be responsible for, and have the direction of, all that concerns the Medical and Surgical treatment of the Patients; their moral management, exercise, amusements and employments, subject to the advice of the Council and of the Consulting Staff.

10. He shall personally visit, as often as practicable, the Patients in their bedrooms, and shall arrange for the daily visits of the Assistant Medical Officers. He shall also make an occasional night-round accompanied by the Sister or Nurse, and report to the Council any serious irregularities which may fall under his notice. In making this round (as in all nightwork) felt or indiarubber slippers shall be used.

30. The Medical Superintendent is appointed subject to the above regulations and to any further regulations which the Council may see fit to make.

Appendix Five

King Edward VII Hospital, Midhurst

President of the Institution
Her Majesty the Queen

Vice-President of the Institution and Chairman of the Council
Lavinia, Duchess of Norfolk, C.B.E.

Deputy Chairman of the Council and Member of the Institution
Donald D. Scott, Esq., D.L., J.P.

Members of the Council and of the Institution
C. E. Drew, Esq., L.V.O., V.R.D., F.R.C.S.
The Hon. Mrs. Lakin
J. R. B. Morgan-Grenville, Esq., F.C.A.
L. O'Connor, Esq., C.B.E., F.C.C.A., I.P.F.A.
A. John Robertson, Esq., M.D., F.R.C.P., M.F.O.M.
Professor Margaret Turner-Warwick, M.D., Ph.D., F.R.C.P., F.R.A.C.P., F.F.O.M.

Members of the Institution
Lt. General Sir James Baird, K.B.E., M.D., F.R.C.P.
The Hon. Lady Barttelot
Frank Bradford, Esq.
T. B. L. Coghlan, Esq.
Brigadier Sir Geoffrey Hardy-Roberts, K.C.V.O., C.B., C.B.E., D.L., J.P.
The Lady Pamela Hicks
C. J. Lucas, Esq., D.L., J.P.
The Hon. Lady MacDonald-Buchanan

Principal Officers
J. E. Goldsworthy, Esq., M.A., A.H.A. (Chief Executive)
Miss M. I. Allen, S.R.N., S.C.M. (Matron)
I. T. Gabe, Esq., M.D., F.R.C.P. (Senior Physician)

Legal Adviser: D. T. Davis, Esq., R.D.

Auditors: Messrs. Peat, Marwick, Mitchell & Co.

Consultant Staff, January 1986

Emeritus Consultant Staff

General Medicine:

Sir Richard Bayliss, K.C.V.O., M.D., F.R.C.P.
M. R. Geake, Esq., M.B., B.Chir., F.R.C.P.
E. H. Hudson, Esq., M.A., M.B., B.Chir., F.R.C.P.
H. Nicholson, Esq., M.D., F.R.C.P.
N. C. Oswald, Esq., T.D., M.D., F.R.C.P.
A. John Robertson, Esq., M.D., F.R.C.P., M.F.O.M.
N. L. Rusby, Esq., M.A., D.M., F.R.C.P.
F. H. Scadding, Esq., M.D., F.R.C.P.
H. D. Teare, Esq., C.V.O., M.B., B.Chir., M.R.C.S.,
L.R.C.P., M.H.K.
J. D. Whiteside, Esq., M.D., F.R.C.P., F.R.C.P.I.

Thoracic Medicine:

Sir Geoffrey Todd, K.C.V.O., O.B.E., D.L., C.St.J.,
M.B., Ch.M., F.R.C.P., F.R.A.C.P.

Thoracic Surgery:

L. L. Bromley, Esq., M.Chir., F.R.C.S.
C. E. Drew, Esq., L.V.O., V.R.D., F.R.C.S.
V. T. Powell, Esq., F.R.C.S.

Gynaecology and Obstetrics:

I. M. Jackson, Esq., F.R.C.S., F.R.C.O.G.

Neurology:

W. Gooddy, Esq., C.St.J., M.D., F.R.C.P.

Diseases of the Skin:

F. Ray Bettley, Esq., T.D., M.D., F.R.C.P.

Pathology:

K. F. W. Hinson, Esq., M.R.C.S., L.R.C.P.,
F.R.C.Path.

Dental Surgery:

F. J. Summers, Esq., L.D.S., R.C.S.

Consultant Staff

General Medicine:

*J. C. Batten, Esq., M.D., F.R.C.P.
*T. J. H. Clark, Esq., M.D., F.R.C.P.
*S. W. Clarke, Esq., M.D., F.R.C.P.
*Prof. Gordon Cumming, B.Sc., Ph.D., D.Sc., M.B.,
Ch.B., F.R.C.P., F.R.I.C.
*Peter A. Emerson, Esq., M.A., M.D., F.R.C.P.,
F.A.C.P.
*J. M. Hinton, Esq., M.A., B.M., B.Ch., F.R.C.P.
*Wing Commander J. A. C. Hopkirk, B.A., M.B.,
B.Chir., M.R.C.P., R.A.F.
K. Horsfield, Esq., D.Sc., Ph.D., M.D., F.R.C.P.
Major General S. E. Large, M.B.E., M.D., F.R.C.P.,
D.P.H.

*J. N. Mickerson, Esq., M.D., F.R.C.P.
I. M. Morrison, Esq., M.B., B.S., M.R.C.P.
M. I. M. Noble, Esq., D.Sc., Ph.D., M.D., F.R.C.P.
*C. M. Ogilvie, Esq., M.D., F.R.C.P.
R. D. Simpson, Esq., M.A., M.R.C.P.
M. G. M. Smith, Esq., M.A., F.R.C.P.

General Surgery:

E. C. Ashby, Esq., M.Chir., F.R.C.S.
S. D. Clarke, Esq., M.Ch., F.R.C.S.
*W. F. P. Gammie, Esq., M.A., B.M., B.Ch., F.R.C.S.
P. M. Perry, Esq., M.S., F.R.C.S.
R. A. P. Scott, Esq., M.Ch., F.R.C.S.
J. Stubbs, Esq., Ph.D., M.S., F.R.C.S.

Gynaecology and Obstetrics:

J. L. Beynon, Esq., F.R.C.S., M.R.C.O.G.
J. G. Francis, Esq., F.R.C.O.G.
J. R. M. Gibson, Esq., M.B.,B.S., F.R.C.O.G.
C. A. R. Lamont, Esq., M.B.,Ch.B., F.R.C.O.G.
*M. A. Pugh, Esq., F.R.C.S., F.R.C.O.G.

Cardiac Surgery:

J. L. Monro, Esq., M.B., B.S., F.R.C.S.
Sir Keith Ross, Bt., M.S., F.R.C.S.
D. F. Shore, Esq., M.B., Ch.B., F.R.C.S.

Cardiology:

N. Conway, Esq., M.B., F.R.C.P.
*I. T. Gabe Esq., M.D., F.R.C.P.
*D. G. Gibson, Esq., M.B., B.Chir., F.R.C.P.
*A. M. Johnson, Esq., M.D., F.R.C.P.
*E. Lawson McDonald, Esq., M.A., M.D., F.R.C.P.,
F.A.C.C.
Michael Thomas, Esq., M.A., M.D., F.R.C.P.

Ear, Nose & Throat Surgery:

M. G. Cox, Esq., M.A., M.B., B.Chir., F.R.C.S.,
D.L.O.
C. Ian Johnstone, Esq., M.B.,B.S., F.R.C.S.
J. A. Seymour-Jones, Esq., F.R.C.S., D.L.O.

Genito-Urinary Surgery:

G. Forbes Abercrombie, Esq, F.R.C.S.
F. A. W. Schweitzer, Esq., M.S., F.R.C.S.
*J. Vinnicombe, Esq., M.A., M.Chir., F.R.C.S.

Orthopaedic Surgery:

*A. Catterall, Esq., M.Chir., F.R.C.G.
Brian Elliott, Esq., M.B., B.S., F.R.C.S.
W. E. G. Griffiths, Esq., F.R.C.S., F.R.C.S.(Ed.)
John Older, Esq., M.B., B.S., B.D.S., F.R.C.S.
J. D. M. Stewart, Esq., M.A., M.B., B.Chir., F.R.C.S.

Thoracic Surgery:	*M. Meredith Brown, Esq., R.D., F.R.C.S. I. K. R. McMillan, Esq., F.R.C.S. *R. Rowlandson, Esq., M.A., M.B., B.Chir., F.R.C.S. R. E. Sayer, Esq., M.B., F.R.C.S.
Ophthalmic Surgery:	P. J. Fenton, Esq., M.B., B.S., F.R.C.S. A. Lytton, Esq., M.B., B.S., F.R.C.S., D.O.
Oral and Maxillo-Facial Surgery:	J. Townend, Esq., M.B., B.S., B.D.S., F.D.S., R.C.S. J. Ll. Williams, Esq., M.B., B.S., F.D.S., R.C.S.
Plastic Surgery:	P. J. Whitfield, Esq., F.R.C.S.
Dental Surgery:	D. Bevan-Thomas, Esq., B.D.S., L.D.S., R.C.S. J. S. Lee, Esq., B.D.S., L.D.S., R.C.S.
Rheumatology and Rehabilitation:	A. C. Boyle, Esq., M.D., M.R.C.P. B. D. Owen-Smith, Esq., M.A., M.B., B.Chir., F.R.C.P., D.Phys.Med.
Anaesthetics:	J. R. Bennett, Esq., B.A., M.B., B.Chir., F.F.A., R.C.S. A. B. Conyers, Esq., M.R.C.S., L.R.C.P., D.R.C.O.G., D.A., F.F.A., R.C.S. J. R. Fozard, Esq., M.B., B.S., M.R.C.S., L.R.C.P.,D.Obst.R.C.O.G., F.F.A.R.C.S. J. M. Manners, Esq., M.B., Ch.B., D.R.C.O.G., D.A., F.F.A., R.C.S. E. Mendus-Edwards, Esq., M.R.C.S., L.R.C.P., F.F.A., R.C.S., D.A. Dr. Janet C. Missen, M.A., B.M., B.Ch., F.F.A., R.C.S. M. R. Nott, Esq., M.B., B.S., D.A., F.F.A., R.C.S. *B. Philpott, Esq., M.B., B.S., M.R.C.S., L.R.C.P., D.A., F.F.A., R.C.S. J. R. Stoneham, Esq., M,B., B.S., M.R.C.S., L.R.C.P., F.F.A., R.C.S., D.A.
Diagnostic Radiology:	E. H. Burrows, Esq., M.Rad., F.R.C.R., D.M.R.D. C. E. Corney, Esq., M.B., B.S., F.R.C.R., D.M.R.D. *I. H. Kerr, Esq., F.R.C.P., F.R.C.R. B. J. Loveday, Esq., M.B., B.S., M.R.C.S., L.R.C.P., F.R.C.R., D.M.R.D. J. L. Price, Esq., R.D., M.B., B.S., F.R.C.R., D.M.R.D. Dr. L. J. Rockall, F.R.C.R.

Radiotherapy: Miss I. M. S. Cade, M.S., F.R.C.S., F.R.C.R.
                                V. H. J. Svoboda, Esq., M.U.Dr.(Prague), F.R.C.R.,
                                D.M.R.T.
                                W. F. White, Esq., M.B., B.S., F.R.C.R., D.M.R.T.

Pathology: *C. J. T. Bateman, Esq., M.A., F.R.C.Path.
                                 W. I.Gordon, Esq., M.B., B.S., F.R.C.Path.

Dermatology: Ashley V. Levantine, Esq., M.B., B.S., M.R.C.S.,
                                M.R.C.P.

Psychiatry: Timothy E. Sicks, Esq., A.B., M.B., M.Phil.,
                                M.R.C.Psych.

Hospital Medical Staff
Senior Physician: I. T. Gabe, Esq., M.D., F.R.C.P. (Consultant in Gen-
                                eral Medicine and Cardiology)

Consultants: S. D. Clarke, Esq., M.Ch., F.R.C.S. (Consultant
                                Surgeon)
                                W. I. Gordon, Esq., M.B., B.S., F.R.C.Path. (Consult-
                                ant Pathologist)
                                M. I. M. Noble, Esq., D.Sc., Ph.D., M.D., F.R.C.P.
                                (Consultant in General and Thoracic Medicine)
                                M. Thomas, Esq., M.A., M.D., F.R.C.P. (Consultant
                                Cardiologist)

Junior Medical Staff: One Surgical Registrar
                                Three Senior House Officers (Medicine)
                                Three House Physicians
                                Three House Surgeons

Royal Air Force: Wing Commander J. A. C. Hopkirk, B.A., M.B.,
                                B.Chir., M.R.C.P., R.A.F. (Adviser in Chest Medi-
                                cine)

Macmillan Service: Dr. Miriam A. McKenna, M.B., D.Obst.R.C.O.G.,
                                F.F.A., R.C.S. (Medical Director)
                                R. H. Freeman, Esq., C.B.E., M.B., F.R.C.S.

Standing Committees
Executive and Finance Com-   J. R. B. Morgan-Grenville, Esq. (Chairman)
mittee:

Medical Advisory Committee: Dr. C. M. Ogilvie (Chairman)

Medical Committee:	W. F. P. Gammie, Esq. (Chairman)
Nursing Advisory Committee:	The Hon. Mrs. Lakin (Chairman)
Management Team	J. E. Goldsworthy, Esq., M.A., A.H.A. (Chairman) Miss M. I. Allen, S.R.N., S.C.M. I. T. Gabe, Esq., M.D., F.R.C.P. S. D. Clarke, Esq., M.Ch., F.R.C.S. W. H.Mitchell, Esq., A.H.A. M. J. Seagrove, Esq.
Chief Executive:	Mr. J. E. Goldsworthy
Administrative Secretary:	Mr. W. H. Mitchell
Finance Officer:	Mr. M. J. Seagrove
Supplies Officer:	Mr. A. Kelly
Medical Records Officer:	Mrs. M. P. R. Chorley
Admissions Office Manager:	Mrs. R. Tarrant
Chief Medical Laboratory Scientific Officer:	Mr. P. Oakes
Pharmacist:	Miss S. Roper
Resident Engineer:	Mr. P. Bullock
Deputy Engineer:	Mr. A. F. Bradley
Head Chef:	Mr. R. Luckhurst
Domestic Services Manager:	Miss J. Thair
Laundry Superintendent:	Mrs. G. Reed
Garden Superintendent:	Mr. I. S. Scott
Chaplain (Church of England):	The Rev. D. B. Evans
Chaplain (Roman Catholic):	The Very Rev. Canon D. Fogarty
Superintendent Radiographers:	Miss M. Easton Mrs. S. J. White Mr. C. S. Bennell

Superintendent Physio- therapist:	Mrs. A. R. Cock
Physiology Technician:	Miss S. P. Parker
Dietitian:	Mrs. J. Rich
Clinical Teachers:	Mrs. P. O'Conor Mrs. C. Jones Miss T. Percy
Matron:	Miss M. I. Allen
Deputy Matron:	Mrs. J. R. Wright
Administrative Sisters:	Miss J. G. Peattie Mrs. S. Shahab
Tutor:	Mrs. C. M. Brook
Departmental and Ward Sisters:	Mrs. M. Lee, Miss S. Banks (Portal Ward); Miss A. L. R. Hay, Miss S. Peasey (Barbara Agar Ward); Miss H. Houlston, Miss D. Latham (Norfolk Ward); Miss P. M. Drane, Mrs. V. Hall (Cowdray Ward); Miss W. Norton, Miss A. Porter (Miles Reid Ward); Miss C. M. A. Porteous, Miss G. Barns (Hardy-Roberts Ward); Miss F. J. Davis, Mrs. R. A. Jay, Miss S. Hancock (Coronary Care Unit); Miss L. Graham, Mrs. S. K. Sullivan, Miss C. Hitchcock, Miss M. Graham (Recovery Unit); Mrs. J. H. Daniel, Mrs. P. Rice, Mrs. D. Chennell, Miss C. Norris, Mrs. M. Taylor, Mrs. C. Chandler, Mrs. D. M. Glasgow (Operating Theatres); Mr. G. Garner (Central Sterile Supply Department); Mrs. E. Jones, Mrs. G. Lindsay, Mrs. G. Scott (Out-patients); Mrs. T. O'Rourke, Mrs. M. O'Brien, Mrs. L. Watson (Night Sisters); Mrs. J. M. Boxall, Mrs. G. Etherington (Macmillan Unit Ward Sisters); Miss J. Canterford, Mrs. S. Morgan, Mrs. J. E. Vince, Mrs. F. Fowler (Home Care Sisters); Miss D. Peacop (Relief Sister)

* = Member of the Medical Advisory Committee

Source References and Notes

Chapter One

Page 2: Lee, Sir Sidney, *King Edward VII*, Vol II, page 400, Macmillan, 1927.

Page 2: Dr. Horton-Smith added the name Hartley in 1904 in accordance with the will of his father-in-law whose daughter he married in 1895.

Page 3: Although Mr. Percy Adams was appointed principal architect, he was assisted by the young Dr. Charles Holden, partner in the same firm. After Dr. Holden's death, the following notice appeared in *The Times* of 2 May 1960. 'Most of Holden's work was done as a member of Adams, Holden and Pearson . . . In such cases it is not easy to define the individual contribution, but it may be said that Holden was pre-eminently the designer of the firm and that the aesthetic quality of their work was mainly due to him'.

Page 3: The account of Besold's appointment, Aman's delaying tactics and Aman's reconciliation with the Advisory Committee came from 'The Story of Midhurst', an unpublished account by a former patient. 1962.

Page 4: Lee, p.402.

Page 6: This account of the building operations, and the story of the King's visit to the Sanatorium, are quoted from *Longleys of Crawley*, a pictorial history of James Longley and Co., with kind permission of the publishers.

Page 7: A contemporary newspaper noted how the architect provided the public with the following curious statistics: 6,680 tons of stone were quarried for the road constructed between the site and the Haslemere-Midhurst road. For the main building, 640 square yards of paper were covered with the architectural drawings; 4,500,000 bricks were used; 500,000 tiles; 5,000 tons of sand and 1,000 tons of cement.

Page 7: The Knighton's Well 'Road' was, in fact, a track leading past a cottage of that name on Lord Egmont's land. Workmen from Midhurst used it as a short cut on their daily walk to and from the site. Lord Egmont objected. The out of court settlement was to the effect that workmen on the site could use it, but future Sanatorium employees must not do so. For many years the contract signed by Sanatorium employees contained a clause denying them use of the track.

Page 9: As completed in 1906, the Sanatorium looked very much as it does today, but the main buildings as planned were dominated by a clock tower which, for reasons not now apparent, was never built.

Page 10: The story about the King and the absence of the lavatories has been told at Midhurst for years – often by those seeking to discredit the 'experts'. This version is quoted from Alan Dick, *Walking Miracle*, by kind permission of the publishers, Messrs. Allen and Unwin.

Page 10: It was said that funds did not run to the construction of a separate house for the Superintendent, but this may simply have been a ploy to persuade the 'difficult' Dr. Besold to leave. 'Uppershaw', the Superintendent's own house, was built a few years later.

Page 12: Ian Nairn and Nikolaus Pevsner, *The Buildings of England: Sussex*, Penguin Books, 1965. Reproduced by kind permission of Penguin Books Ltd.

Chapter Two

Page 14: Lee, Sir Sidney, *King Edward VII*, Vol II, page 403. Macmillan 1927.

Page 14: After the death of Dr. Theodore Williams a tablet was erected in his memory on the north wall of the Chapel.

Page 18: The winning Sanatorium design even provided accommodation for valets and ladies' maids.

Page 20: During the day patients carried their own aluminium flasks which were disinfected daily in the sputum room by a specially-trained porter. At night, ordinary sputum mugs were placed at the bed side.

Page 21: Anonymous writer in *The Young Man* (a contemporary magazine).

Page 21: *Morning Post*, 14 June 1906.

Chapter Three

Page 36: Dr. Cockill continued to take an interest in Sanatorium affairs until his death in 1930. He frequently stood in as *locum tenens* to cover absence of Sanatorium medical staff. After his death a sum of money was left in his memory to be used at the discretion of the Superintendent to assist patients in need.

Page 37: The men's hydropathic room, later converted into the X-Ray Department, was situated on the ground floor to the west of the main entrance from the gardens. Today, the room is an office.

Chapter Four

Page 47: The follow up of patients involved sending questionnaires annually to every patient who had been discharged. So greatly was tuberculosis feared by the public that the questionnaires were always sent in plain envelopes. Even so, some patients refused to co-operate in the follow up in case it should become known that they had had tuberculosis.

Chapter Five

Page 52: It was not only patients who found it cold. Mr. Battensby, who was engaged as the Sanatorium's hairdresser in 1954, was given a tiny room on the ground floor, bereft of heating and open to the elements. 'How are you getting on, old chap?', he remembers Todd asking him. 'Very well thank you, Sir, but I'm rather cold', he replied. Todd's rejoinder was 'Well no one dies of tuberculosis in this Sanatorium: they only die of pneumonia'.

Page 57: Mr. Stanley Hall had succeeded his father as Consulting Architect in 1923.

Page 59: Clarenbone took his duties seriously. Concern had been felt over the number of eggs being produced. Pilfering was suspected. He decided, therefore, that he should count the chickens regularly. Bowler hat on head, clipboard in hand, he would repair to the coops daily and count the birds as they were driven out. Any discrepancy meant an immediate recount.

Page 60: Moseley was a semi recluse who rarely went further afield than the *Duke of Cumberland* on a Saturday. His unrivalled personal knowledge of all the drains, pipes and cables in the building rescued the authorities from many an embarrassing situation when official records were lacking.

Chapter Six

Page 66: Todd's ability to cut the pompous down to size was illustrated in countless Midhurst stories. The example of the senior R.A.F. doctor here quoted, in modified form, is from Alan Dick's *Walking Miracle* and is reproduced by permission of Messrs. Allen and Unwin. Many stories told about Todd are apocryphal. The one related below is true. It happened in 1949, soon after Dr. Gordon's appointment to the Midhurst staff. After a busy night on duty, Ian decided one Sunday morning to 'lie-in'. At 9.00 a.m., Dr. Geoffrey Todd appeared round his bedroom door and said, 'What's the matter? Are you sick or something?' Ian replied that he was well, but had been up all night on duty. All Todd said was, 'Well get up – Australians don't lie in bed in the morning'.

Page 66: Later The Countess Mountbatten of Burma.

Chapter Eight

Page 76: Amongst the Australian doctors attached to Midhurst after the War were Alan King (an ex P.O.W.), Maurice Joseph, Ian McKay, Ken Fairley, Bob Gould, Geoff McManus, Bruce Geddes and Bob and Dorothy Elphick. Many had been recipients of Wunderly travelling scholarships, founded after the War by Sir Harry Wunderly, a distinguished Australian physician who was at that time the Commonwealth Tuberculosis Officer.

Page 81: Service specialists seconded to Midhurst in the early 1950s for training in chest diseases included: Wing Commander I. W. H. R. Cran, Lt. Colonel J. Mackay Dick, Major J. H. Biggart and the author, who was then a major in the R.A.M.C.

Page 82: Apart from the two 'Brodie' bungalows (paid for from the sale of Bottingdean), and five bungalows for senior nursing staff paid for by Sir Halford Reddish, six bungalows were 'built' by Hospital staff. These were pre-fabricated houses purchased, second hand, from a site at Brighton and re-assembled in the grounds on a concrete base with a four-and-a-half inch cavity brick wall around them. A pitched tiled roof covered the original flat roof. They are still in good repair and giving good service.

Page 84: Todd's patients had unbounded confidence in him. A war time patient, a test pilot, recalls Todd saying at a moment when his future in test flying looked bleak, 'Dont worry, old man, flying is only a sedentary occupation after all'. He never forgot that remark, even after his return to experimental flying at Farnborough. It seemed to bring everything into perspective and he knew he would come through. In the patient's own words 'that was the magic of Todd'.

Chapter Nine

Page 92: The 'remodelling' of the operating theatres was achieved in stages. The first, in 1945, was the conversion of three sitting rooms and three bedrooms in the medical staff quarters into five surgical patients rooms and a ward kitchen. This left the corridor outside the theatres for general use. The second stage was the conversion of this corridor for theatre use and the construction of an entirely new corridor for general traffic. The third move was the building of two additional theatres with ancillary rooms made possible by the Sir Halford Reddish donation. The doctors' Library disappeared in 1948 when the Surgical Wing was built, as did the Laboratory and the 'doctors' lawn' which lay between. Much of the work was done by Hospital staff.

Page 93: Sir Halford's reasons for wishing to remain anonymous were quite simple: he wished to avoid being pestered and he had a morbid fear of being kidnapped and held to ransom.

Chapter Ten

Page 96: The sub committee of the Medical Committee met for the first time under the Chairmanship of Mr. W. F. P. Gammie on 28 January 1971. The original members were Mr. W. F. P. Gammie, Dr. J. L. Price, Mr. M. G. Cox, Mr. V. T. Powell, Dr. J. D. Whiteside, Dr. C. F. G. Prideaux, Wing Commander

I. W. H. R. Cran, Dr. J. N. Mickerson and Dr. H. D. Teare (Secretary). The Committee met every two months and its numbers grew as the number of local consultants on the staff increased.

Page 97: On the occasion of the opening of the Institute, a muted demonstration was staged by an anti-vivisection group to protest against the presence in the Institute grounds of an animal house. After parading through the streets of Midhurst in the morning they agreed to a low-key afternoon session and stationed themselves at the main road junction for the Queen's departure. The threat of a demonstration led to intense precautions by the Police and Special Branch Officers during the visit and for several days and nights beforehand.

Page 98: The team from Midhurst which took part in one or both stages of King Khaled's operation included Dr. J. R. Bennett, Dr. Trevor Guthrie, Sister Norton, Sister Pring, Mrs. Cock, Elizabeth Taylor (an S.E.N. who assisted inside 'the tent'), Charlie Lejasmeiers and Nicholas Martin.

Glossary

Artificial pneumothorax (A.P.): The intentional introduction of air by means of a needle into the pleural space resulting in partial collapse of the lung. This allowed the lung to relax and encouraged cavities to close. The air from an A.P. was absorbed slowly by the body and, as long as the disease remained active, had to be replaced regularly. For this purpose patients attended *refill clinics* at which they would be examined behind an X-Ray screen and then given the requisite refill of air. The procedure was repeated until the underlying disease process was deemed to be healed, at which point the lung was allowed to re-expand to fill the thoracic cavity.

Anti-bacterial drugs, antibiotics: M & B 693 (May and Baker) – one of the earliest anti-bacterial drugs to be invented, in the late 1930s. Penicillin appeared later, towards the end of the War. Neither was effective against the tubercle bacillus.

Anti-tuberculosis drugs: The first to be invented, in the 1940s, was Streptomycin. Its main disadvantage was its tendency to produce streptomycin-resistant strains of organism. It could also affect balance and hearing. It was discovered later, after exhaustive trials in which Midhurst played a prominent part, that the emergence of drug resistant strains could be greatly reduced if Streptomycin was given at the same time as other anti-tuberculosis drugs, Para Amino Salicylic Acid (PAS) and Iso-nicotinic Acid Hydrozide (INAH).

Bronchiectasis: A condition of saccular dilatation of the terminal air passages which might follow a number of affections of the lung. Characterised by the production of large amounts of infected sputum.

Bronchogram: An X-Ray photograph of the bronchial tubes after an opaque medium has been injected into them.

Chaulmoogra Oil: An oil expressed from the seeds of a species of Burmese tree which was once used in the treatment of Leprosy, a disease caused by a bacillus having similar characteristics to the tubercle bacillus.

Diathermy: The therapeutic use of the heating effect produced by the passage of a high-frequency electric discharge. The term is applied to the high frequency current itself but more usually to the machine producing it.

Dreyers diaplyte vaccine: A vaccine, now obsolete, prepared from tubercle bacilli after treatment with formaldehyde and defatting with acetone.

Finsen Lamp: A source of ultra violet light radiation designed by a Copenhagen physician for the treatment of chronic ulcerating skin disease. Considered at one time to be of value in the treatment of tuberculosis.

Opsonic Index: A measurement of the body's immunising response to the injection of tuberculin.

Phrenic Avulsion: An operative procedure on the phrenic nerve at the root of the neck so that the diaphragm on that side was paralysed and thus raised, and there was partial collapse and relaxation of the corresponding lung.

Pneumoperitoneum: Air or gas within the peritoneal cavity. Performed deliberately through the abdominal wall, the procedure raised the diaphragm. This reduced the size of the thoracic cavity thus producing partial collapse and relaxation of the lung.

Resection: Surgical removal of part of the body, usually a major part, e.g. whole lung (pneumonectomy), lobe of lung (lobectomy), segment or segments of lobe (segmentectomy), pleura (pleurectomy).

Skiagram: X-Ray radiograph.

Thorocoplasty: An operation devised to secure permanent collapse of the lung in cases of chronic pulmonary tuberculosis. It consisted of the partial or complete resection (removal) of a number of ribs thus causing the thoracic wall to fall in and the underlying lung to collapse. The operation was very effective, especially when cavities remained open despite A.P. or other methods of treatment.

Tuberculin: A fraction or extract of the tubercle bacillus, formerly used in the treatment of tuberculous patients. Later used in the Mantoux test and similar tests for tuberculin sensitivity.

X-Ray terms

Fluoroscopy: To investigate radiologically with a fluorescent screen.

Radiograph: The recorded image of an object on an X-Ray plate or film.

Screen (fluorescent screen): The flat surface on which is projected the shadow of the patient being examined.

Tomograph: An X-Ray apparatus which makes a radiograph of a layer or section of the lung tissue at any required depth.

Index